HULK

WITHDRAWN

BANNER DOA

VOLUME 01

HULK VOL. 1: BANNER DOA. Contains material originally published in magazine form as HULK #1-4. First printing 2014. ISBN# 978-0-7851-9061-5. Published by MARVEL WORLDWIDE, INC., a subsidiary of MARVEL ENTERTAINMENT, LLC. OFFICE OF PUBLICATION: 135 West 50th Street, New York, NY 10020. Copyright © 2014 Marvel Characters, Inc. All rights reserved. All characters featured in this issue and the distinctive names and likenesses thereof, and all related indicia are trademarks of Marvel Characters, Inc. No similarity between any of the names, characters, persons, and/or institutions in this magazine with those of any living or dead person or institution is intended, and any such similarity which may exist is purely coincidental. **Printed in Canada.** ALAN FINE, EVP - Office of the President, Marvel Worldwide, Inc. and EVP & CMO Marvel Characters B.V.; DAN BUCKLEY, Publisher & President - Print, Animation & Digital Divisions; JOE QUESADA, Chief Creative Officer; TOM BREVOORT, SVP of Publishing; DAVID BOGART, SVP of Operations & Procurement, Publishing; C.B. CEBULSKI, SVP of Creator & Content Development; DAVID GABRIEL, SVP Print, Sales & Marketing; JIM O'KEEFE, VP of Operations & Logistics; DAN CARR, Executive Director of Publishing Technology; SUSAN CRESPI, Editorial Operations Manager; ALEX MORALES, Publishing Operations Manager; STAN LEE, Chairman Emeritus. For information regarding advertising in Marvel Comics or on Marvel.com, please contact Niza Disla, Director of Marvel Partnerships, at ndisla@marvel.com. For Marvel subscription inquiries, please call 800-217-9158. **Manufactured between 8/22/2014 and 9/29/2014 by SOLISCO PRINTERS, SCOTT, QC, CANADA.**

10 9 8 7 6 5 4 3 2 1

P9-DWZ-455

WRITER **MARK WAID**

PENCILER **MARK BAGLEY**

INKER **ANDREW HENNESSY**

COLORIST **JASON KEITH**

LETTERER **VC'S CORY PETIT**

COVER ART **JEROME OPEÑA** (#1-3) WITH **DEAN WHITE** (#1 & #3) &
JASON KEITH (#2); AND **MARK BAGLEY, ANDREW HENNESSY** &
JASON KEITH (#4)

ASSISTANT EDITOR **EMILY SHAW**

EDITOR **MARK PANICCIA**

COLLECTION EDITOR
SARAH BRUNSTAD
ASSOCIATE MANAGING EDITOR
ALEX STARBUCK
EDITORS, SPECIAL PROJECTS
**JENNIFER GRÜNWALD &
MARK D. BEAZLEY**

SENIOR EDITOR,
SPECIAL PROJECTS
JEFF YOUNGQUIST
SVP PRINT, SALES &
MARKETING
DAVID GABRIEL
BOOK DESIGN
NELSON RIBEIRO

EDITOR IN CHIEF
AXEL ALONSO
CHIEF CREATIVE OFFICER
JOE QUESADA
PUBLISHER
DAN BUCKLEY
EXECUTIVE PRODUCER
ALAN FINE

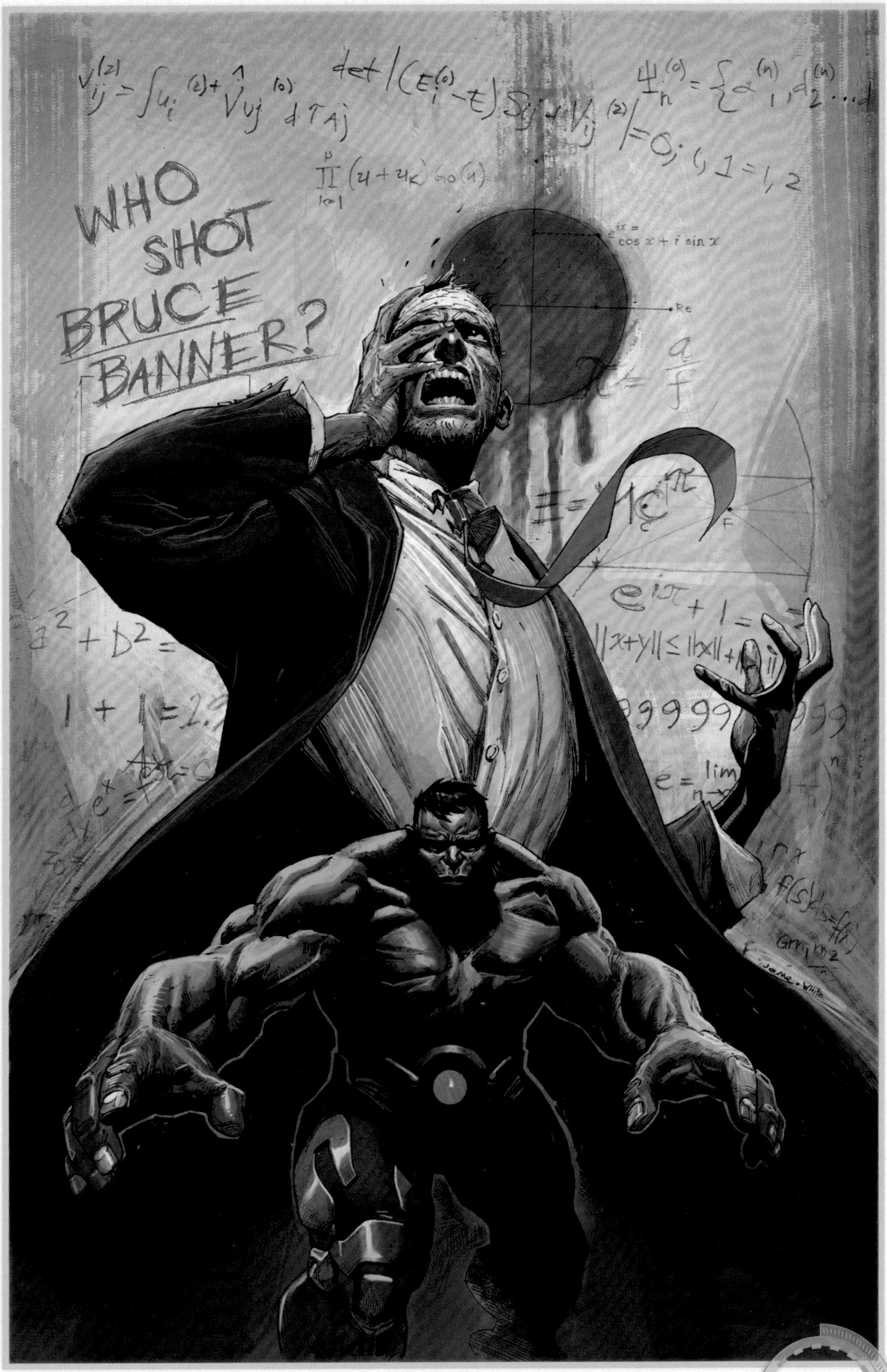
WHO
SHOT
BRUCE
BANNER?

ONE OF THE BIGGEST MYSTERIES IN HULK HISTORY BEGINS!

Dr. Bruce Banner is a super-genius. When he gets angry, he turns into the rampaging green monstrosity known as the Hulk. He's made a lot of enemies over the years.

Dr. Banner has managed to get his anger under control (for the most part.) Bruce and his green counterpart have been working for S.H.I.E.L.D., under the direction of Maria Hill.

Did we mention he's made a lot of enemies...?

WHO SHOT THE HULK #1

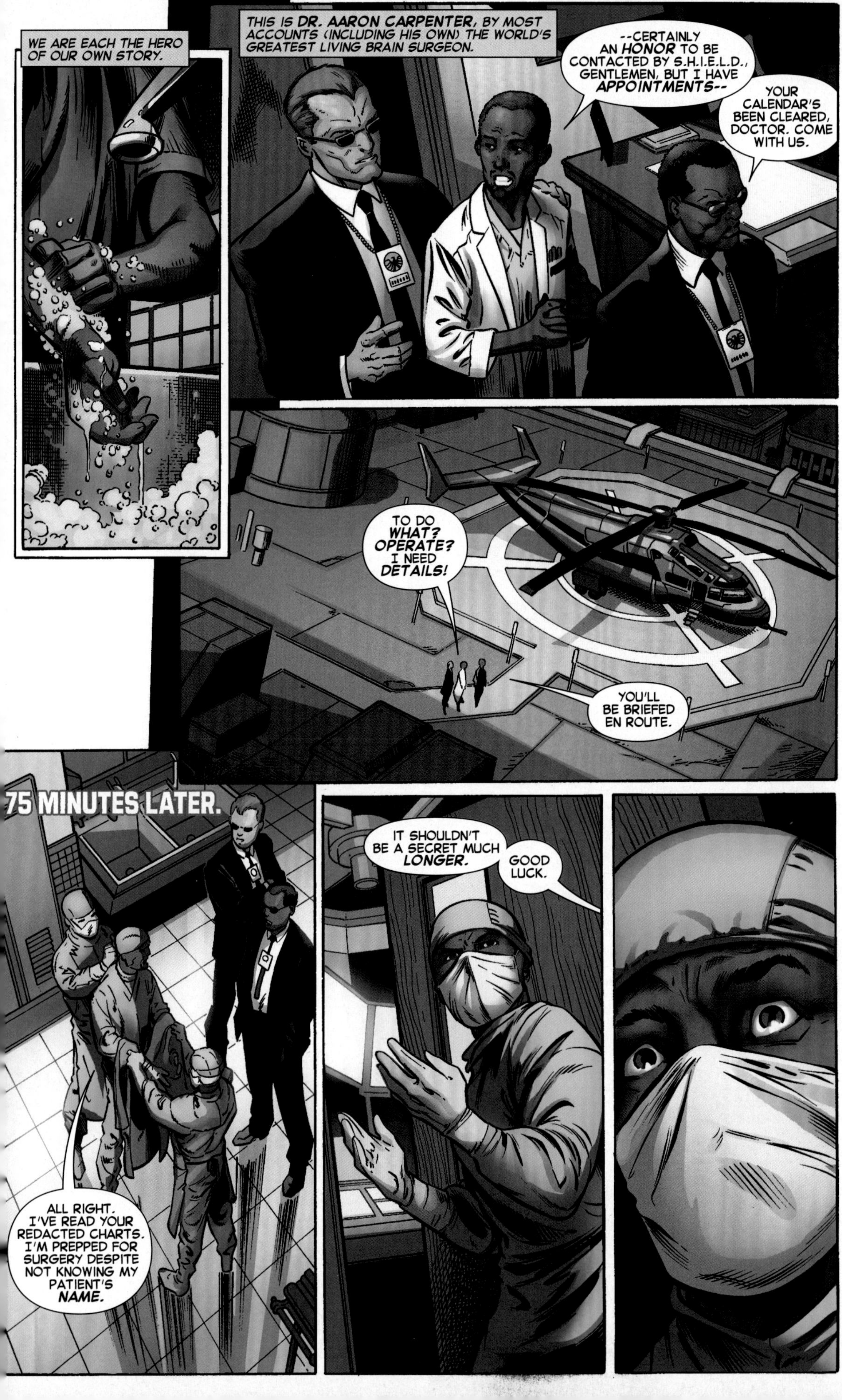
WE ARE EACH THE HERO OF OUR OWN STORY.
THIS IS DR. AARON CARPENTER, BY MOST ACCOUNTS (INCLUDING HIS OWN) THE WORLD'S GREATEST LIVING BRAIN SURGEON.
--CERTAINLY AN HONOR TO BE CONTACTED BY S.H.I.E.L.D., GENTLEMEN, BUT I HAVE APPOINTMENTS--
YOUR CALENDAR'S BEEN CLEARED, DOCTOR. COME WITH US.
TO DO WHAT? OPERATE? I NEED DETAILS!
YOU'LL BE BRIEFED EN ROUTE.
75 MINUTES LATER.
ALL RIGHT. I'VE READ YOUR REDACTED CHARTS. I'M PREPPED FOR SURGERY DESPITE NOT KNOWING MY PATIENT'S NAME.
IT SHOULDN'T BE A SECRET MUCH LONGER.
GOOD LUCK.

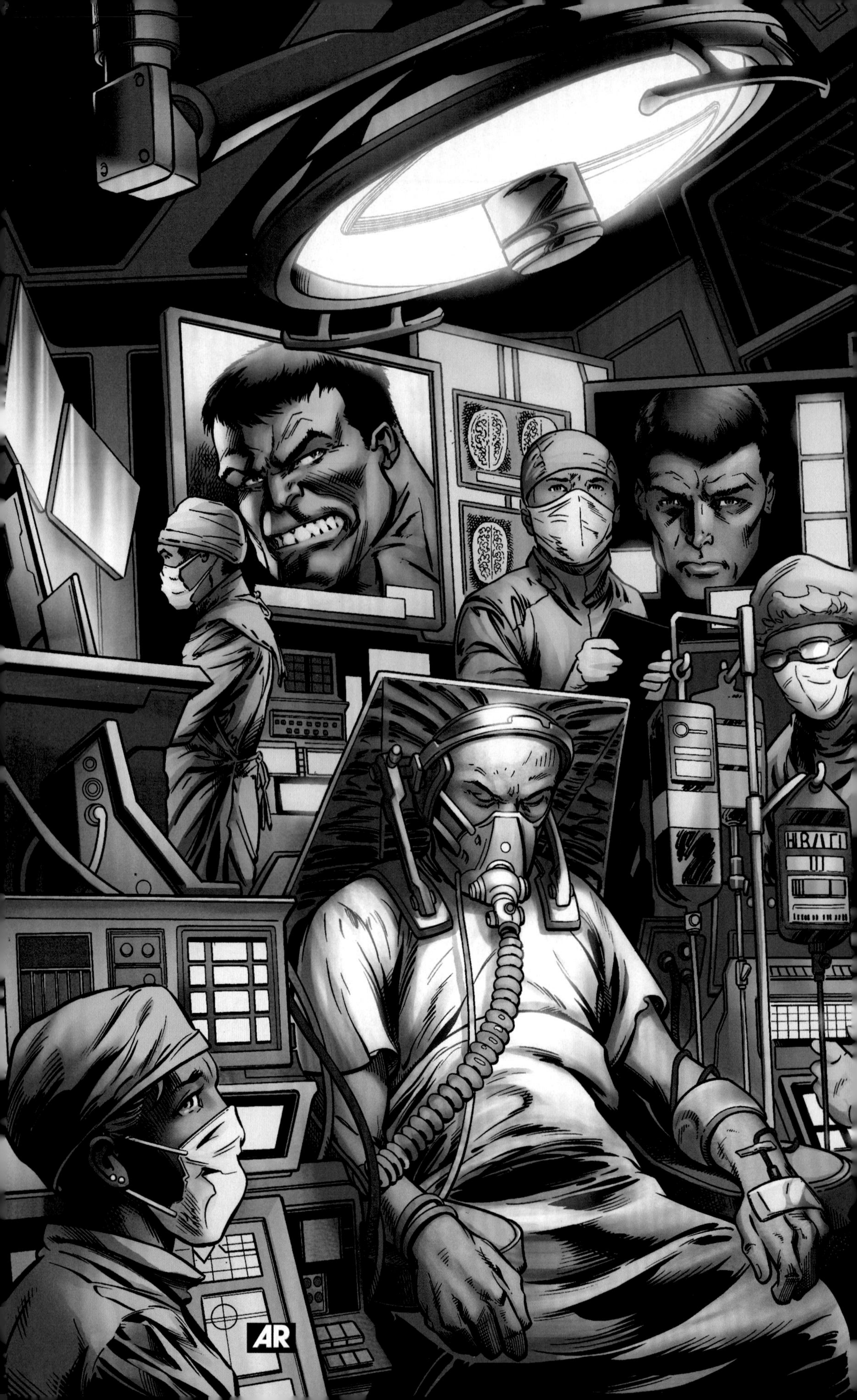

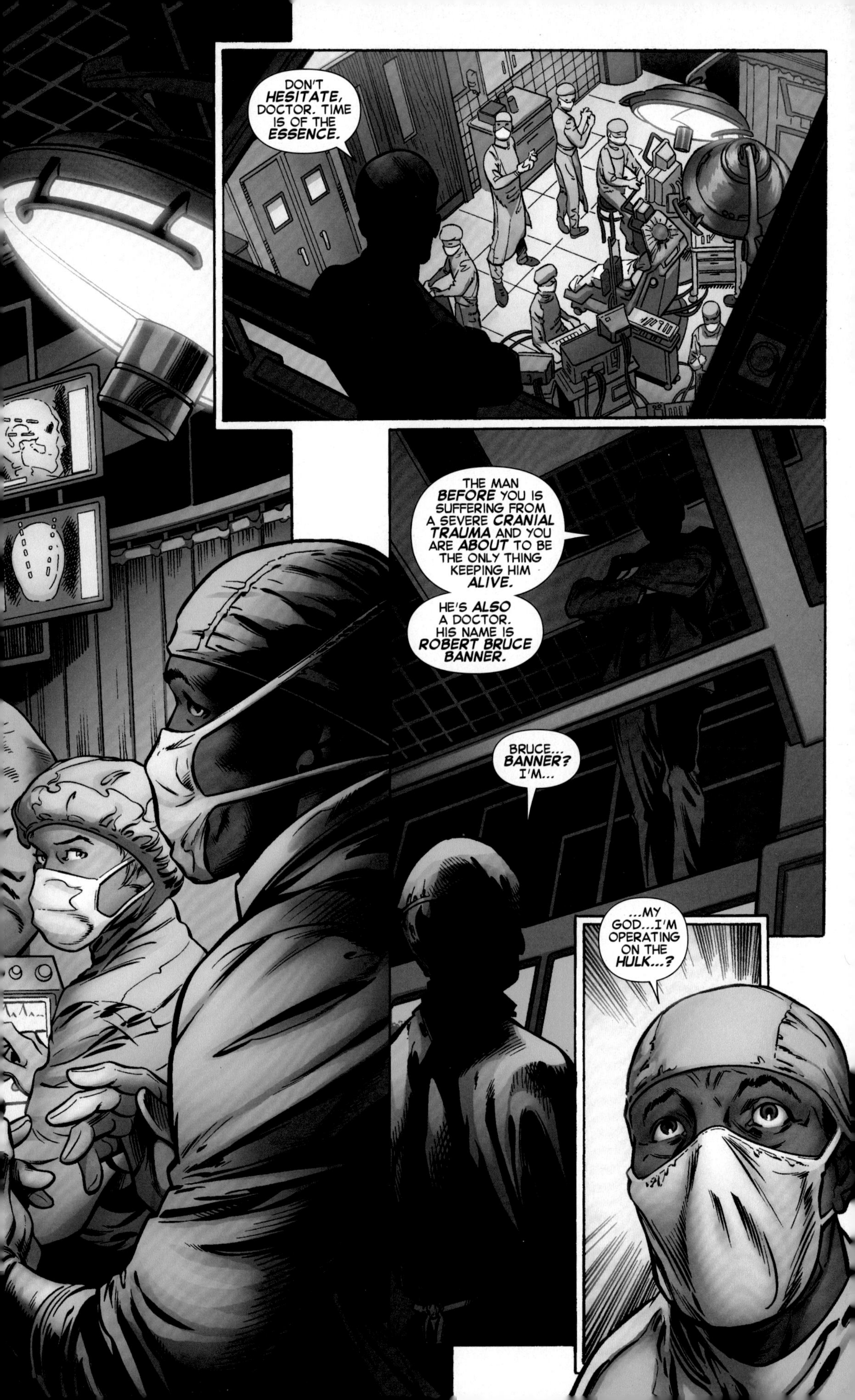
DON'T HESITATE, DOCTOR. TIME IS OF THE ESSENCE.
THE MAN BEFORE YOU IS SUFFERING FROM A SEVERE CRANIAL TRAUMA AND YOU ARE ABOUT TO BE THE ONLY THING KEEPING HIM ALIVE.
HE'S ALSO A DOCTOR. HIS NAME IS ROBERT BRUCE BANNER.
BRUCE... BANNER? I'M...
...MY GOD...I'M OPERATING ON THE HULK...?

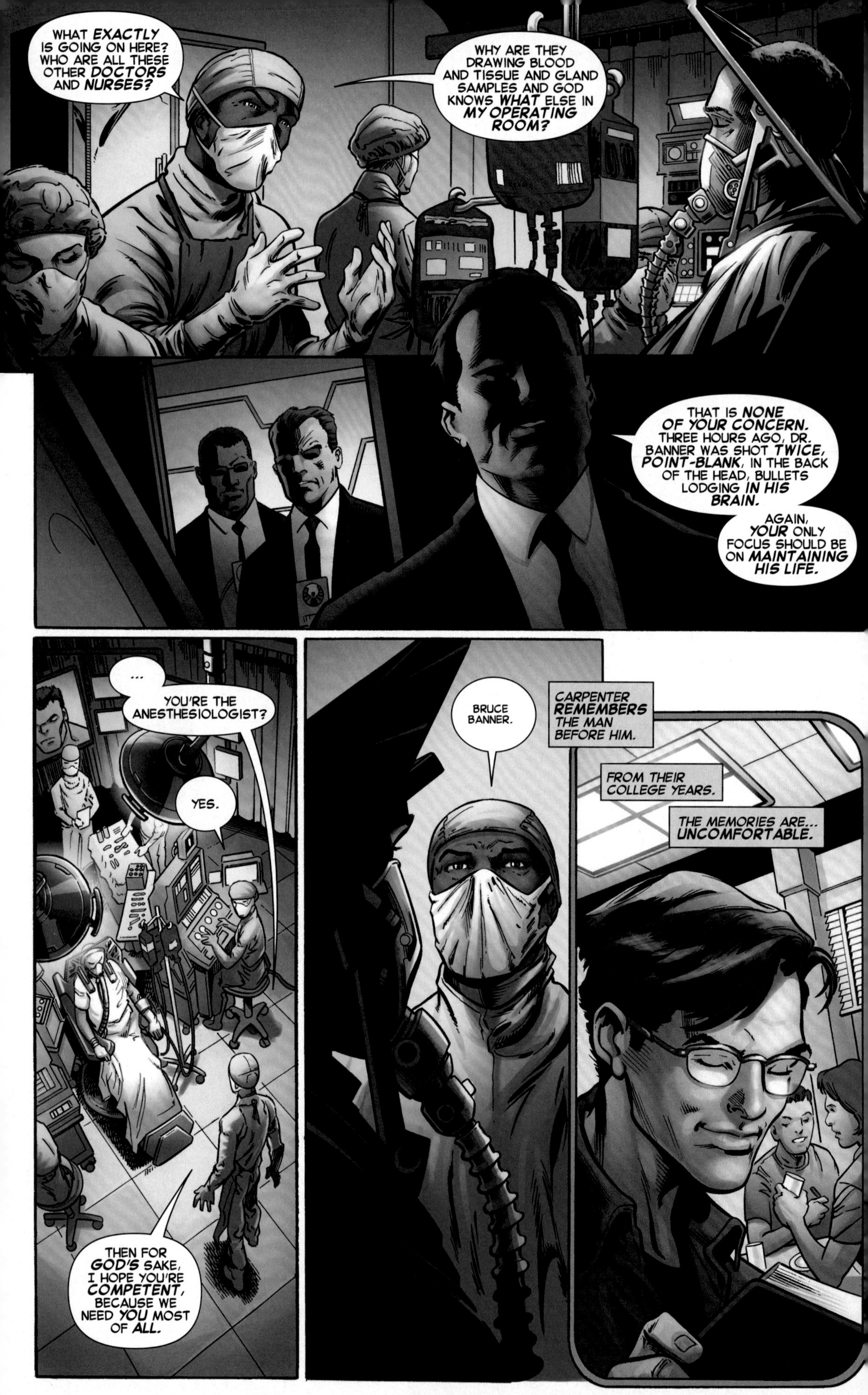
WHAT EXACTLY IS GOING ON HERE? WHO ARE ALL THESE OTHER DOCTORS AND NURSES?
WHY ARE THEY DRAWING BLOOD AND TISSUE AND GLAND SAMPLES AND GOD KNOWS WHAT ELSE IN MY OPERATING ROOM?
THAT IS NONE OF YOUR CONCERN. THREE HOURS AGO, DR. BANNER WAS SHOT TWICE, POINT-BLANK, IN THE BACK OF THE HEAD, BULLETS LODGING IN HIS BRAIN.
AGAIN, YOUR ONLY FOCUS SHOULD BE ON MAINTAINING HIS LIFE.
...
YOU'RE THE ANESTHESIOLOGIST?
YES.
THEN FOR GOD'S SAKE, I HOPE YOU'RE COMPETENT, BECAUSE WE NEED YOU MOST OF ALL.
BRUCE BANNER.
CARPENTER REMEMBERS THE MAN BEFORE HIM.
FROM THEIR COLLEGE YEARS.
THE MEMORIES ARE... UNCOMFORTABLE.

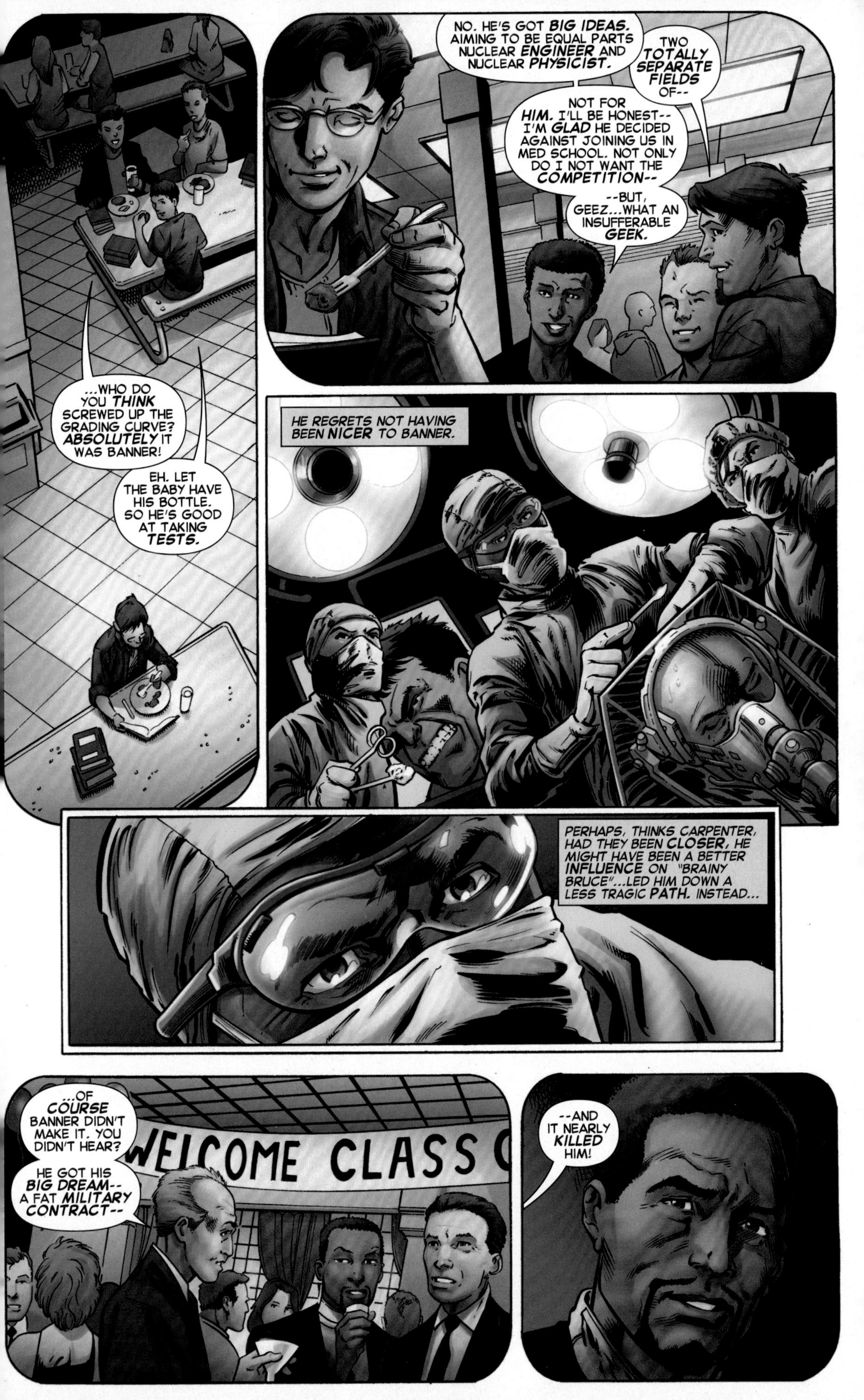
...WHO DO YOU THINK SCREWED UP THE GRADING CURVE? ABSOLUTELY IT WAS BANNER!
EH. LET THE BABY HAVE HIS BOTTLE. SO HE'S GOOD AT TAKING TESTS.
NO. HE'S GOT BIG IDEAS. AIMING TO BE EQUAL PARTS NUCLEAR ENGINEER AND NUCLEAR PHYSICIST.
TWO TOTALLY SEPARATE FIELDS OF--
NOT FOR HIM. I'LL BE HONEST--I'M GLAD HE DECIDED AGAINST JOINING US IN MED SCHOOL. NOT ONLY DO I NOT WANT THE COMPETITION--
--BUT, GEEZ...WHAT AN INSUFFERABLE GEEK.
HE REGRETS NOT HAVING BEEN NICER TO BANNER.
PERHAPS, THINKS CARPENTER, HAD THEY BEEN CLOSER, HE MIGHT HAVE BEEN A BETTER INFLUENCE ON "BRAINY BRUCE"...LED HIM DOWN A LESS TRAGIC PATH. INSTEAD...
...OF COURSE BANNER DIDN'T MAKE IT. YOU DIDN'T HEAR?
HE GOT HIS BIG DREAM--A FAT MILITARY CONTRACT--
WELCOME CLASS
--AND IT NEARLY KILLED HIM!

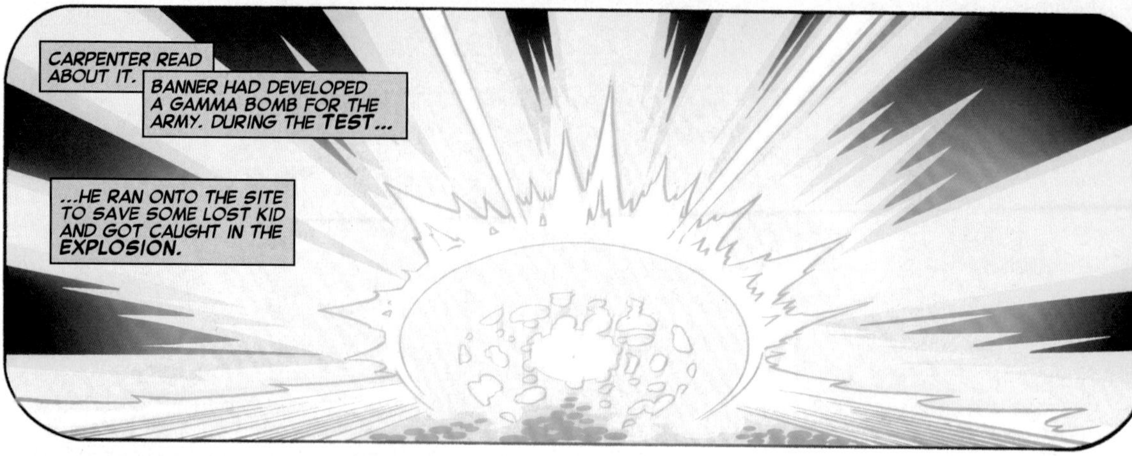

CARPENTER READ ABOUT IT.
BANNER HAD DEVELOPED A GAMMA BOMB FOR THE ARMY. DURING THE TEST...
...HE RAN ONTO THE SITE TO SAVE SOME LOST KID AND GOT CAUGHT IN THE EXPLOSION.

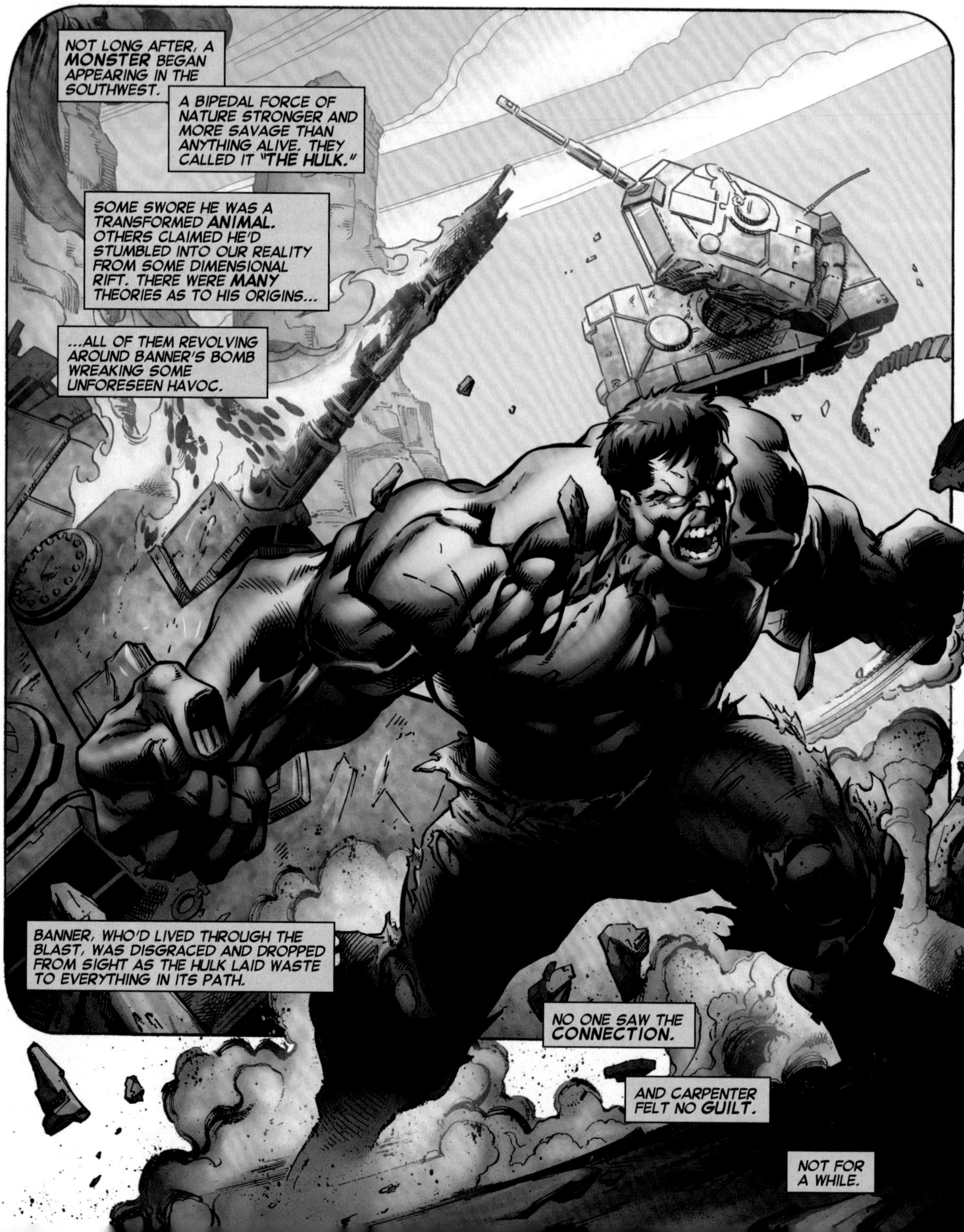

NOT LONG AFTER, A MONSTER BEGAN APPEARING IN THE SOUTHWEST.
A BIPEDAL FORCE OF NATURE STRONGER AND MORE SAVAGE THAN ANYTHING ALIVE. THEY CALLED IT "THE HULK."
SOME SWORE HE WAS A TRANSFORMED ANIMAL. OTHERS CLAIMED HE'D STUMBLED INTO OUR REALITY FROM SOME DIMENSIONAL RIFT. THERE WERE MANY THEORIES AS TO HIS ORIGINS...
...ALL OF THEM REVOLVING AROUND BANNER'S BOMB WREAKING SOME UNFORESEEN HAVOC.
BANNER, WHO'D LIVED THROUGH THE BLAST, WAS DISGRACED AND DROPPED FROM SIGHT AS THE HULK LAID WASTE TO EVERYTHING IN ITS PATH.
NO ONE SAW THE CONNECTION.
AND CARPENTER FELT NO GUILT.
NOT FOR A WHILE.

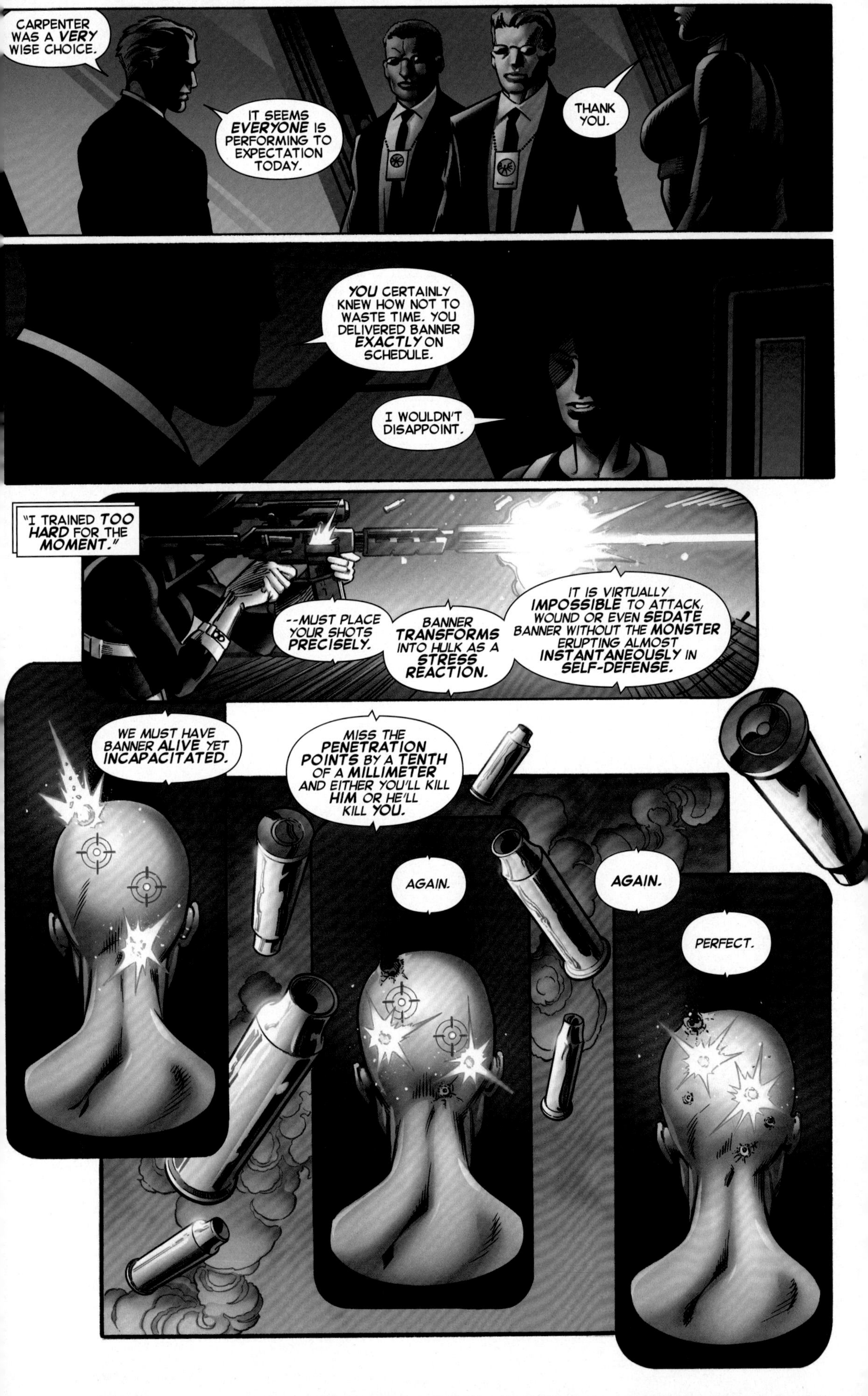
CARPENTER WAS A VERY WISE CHOICE.
IT SEEMS EVERYONE IS PERFORMING TO EXPECTATION TODAY.
THANK YOU.
YOU CERTAINLY KNEW HOW NOT TO WASTE TIME. YOU DELIVERED BANNER EXACTLY ON SCHEDULE.
I WOULDN'T DISAPPOINT.
"I TRAINED TOO HARD FOR THE MOMENT."
IT IS VIRTUALLY IMPOSSIBLE TO ATTACK, WOUND OR EVEN SEDATE BANNER WITHOUT THE MONSTER ERUPTING ALMOST INSTANTANEOUSLY IN SELF-DEFENSE.
BANNER TRANSFORMS INTO HULK AS A STRESS REACTION.
--MUST PLACE YOUR SHOTS PRECISELY.
WE MUST HAVE BANNER ALIVE YET INCAPACITATED.
MISS THE PENETRATION POINTS BY A TENTH OF A MILLIMETER AND EITHER YOU'LL KILL HIM OR HE'LL KILL YOU.
AGAIN.
AGAIN.
PERFECT.

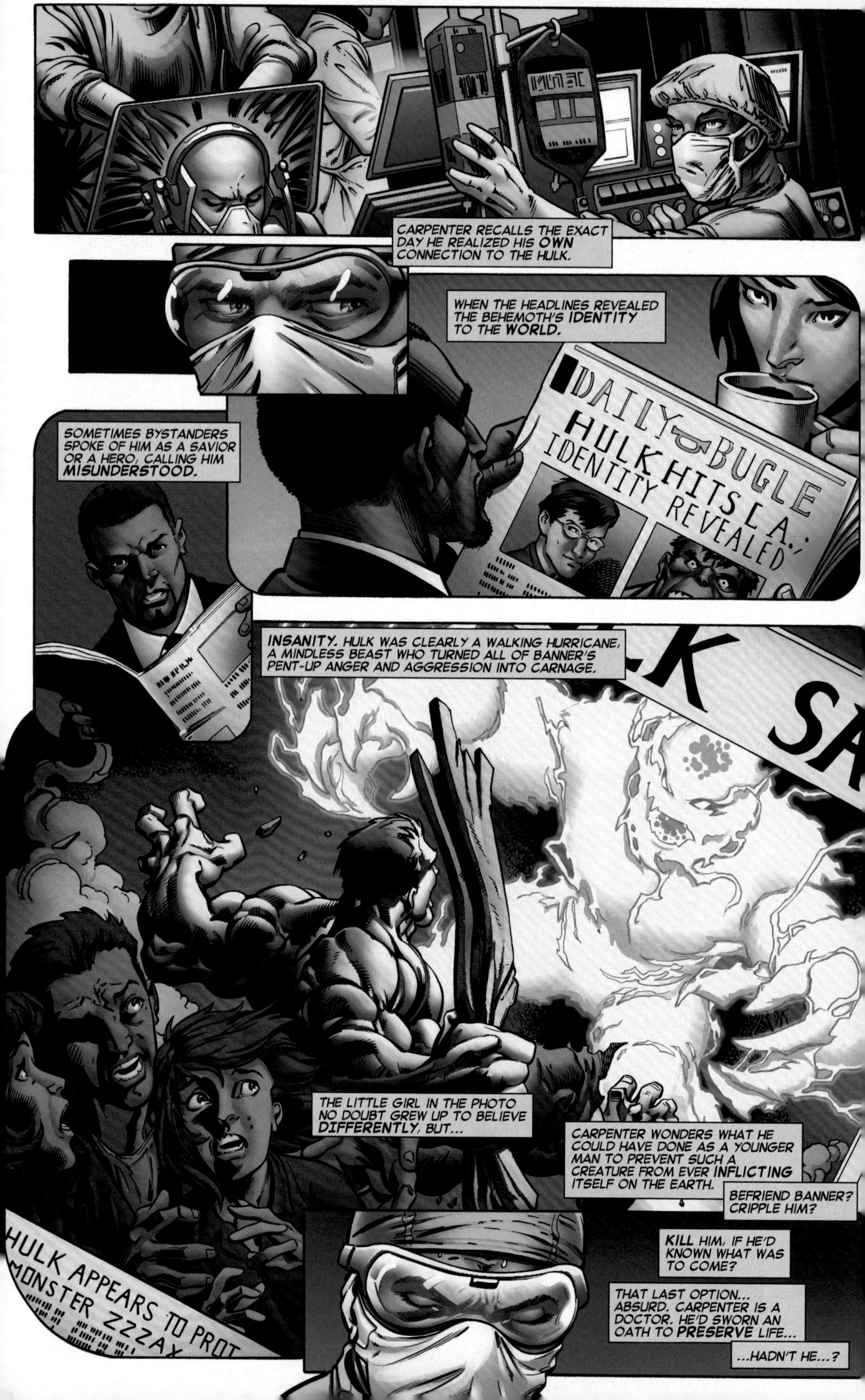

CARPENTER RECALLS THE EXACT DAY HE REALIZED HIS OWN CONNECTION TO THE HULK.
WHEN THE HEADLINES REVEALED THE BEHEMOTH'S IDENTITY TO THE WORLD.
DAILY BUGLE
HULK HITS L.A.
IDENTITY REVEALED
SOMETIMES BYSTANDERS SPOKE OF HIM AS A SAVIOR OR A HERO, CALLING HIM MISUNDERSTOOD.
INSANITY. HULK WAS CLEARLY A WALKING HURRICANE, A MINDLESS BEAST WHO TURNED ALL OF BANNER'S PENT-UP ANGER AND AGGRESSION INTO CARNAGE.
THE LITTLE GIRL IN THE PHOTO NO DOUBT GREW UP TO BELIEVE DIFFERENTLY, BUT...
CARPENTER WONDERS WHAT HE COULD HAVE DONE AS A YOUNGER MAN TO PREVENT SUCH A CREATURE FROM EVER INFLICTING ITSELF ON THE EARTH.
BEFRIEND BANNER? CRIPPLE HIM?
KILL HIM, IF HE'D KNOWN WHAT WAS TO COME?
HULK APPEARS TO PROT
MONSTER ZZZAX
THAT LAST OPTION... ABSURD. CARPENTER IS A DOCTOR. HE'D SWORN AN OATH TO PRESERVE LIFE...
...HADN'T HE...?

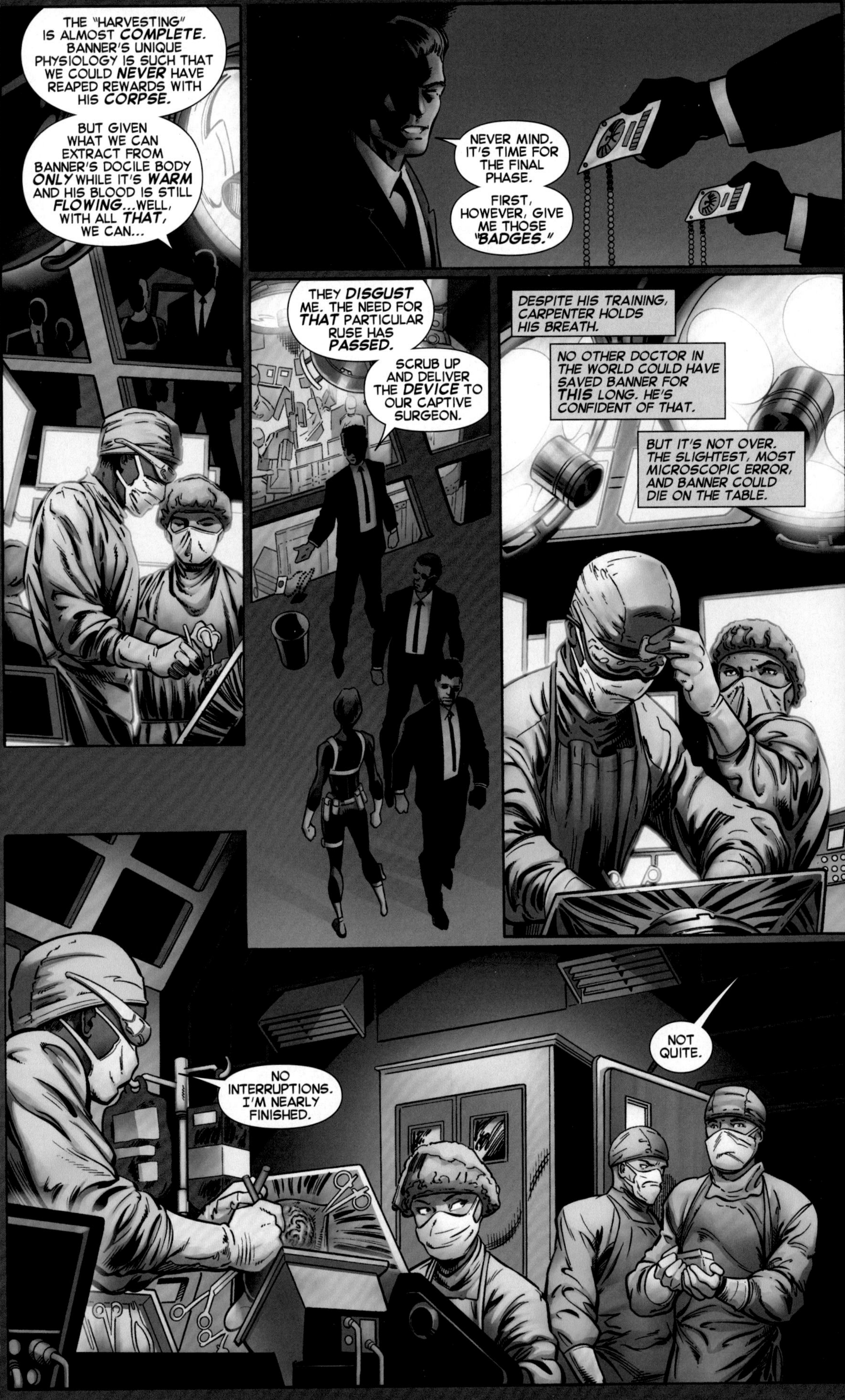
THE "HARVESTING" IS ALMOST COMPLETE. BANNER'S UNIQUE PHYSIOLOGY IS SUCH THAT WE COULD NEVER HAVE REAPED REWARDS WITH HIS CORPSE.
BUT GIVEN WHAT WE CAN EXTRACT FROM BANNER'S DOCILE BODY ONLY WHILE IT'S WARM AND HIS BLOOD IS STILL FLOWING...WELL, WITH ALL THAT, WE CAN...
NEVER MIND. IT'S TIME FOR THE FINAL PHASE.
FIRST, HOWEVER, GIVE ME THOSE "BADGES."
THEY DISGUST ME. THE NEED FOR THAT PARTICULAR RUSE HAS PASSED.
SCRUB UP AND DELIVER THE DEVICE TO OUR CAPTIVE SURGEON.
DESPITE HIS TRAINING, CARPENTER HOLDS HIS BREATH.
NO OTHER DOCTOR IN THE WORLD COULD HAVE SAVED BANNER FOR THIS LONG. HE'S CONFIDENT OF THAT.
BUT IT'S NOT OVER. THE SLIGHTEST, MOST MICROSCOPIC ERROR, AND BANNER COULD DIE ON THE TABLE.
NO INTERRUPTIONS. I'M NEARLY FINISHED.
NOT QUITE.

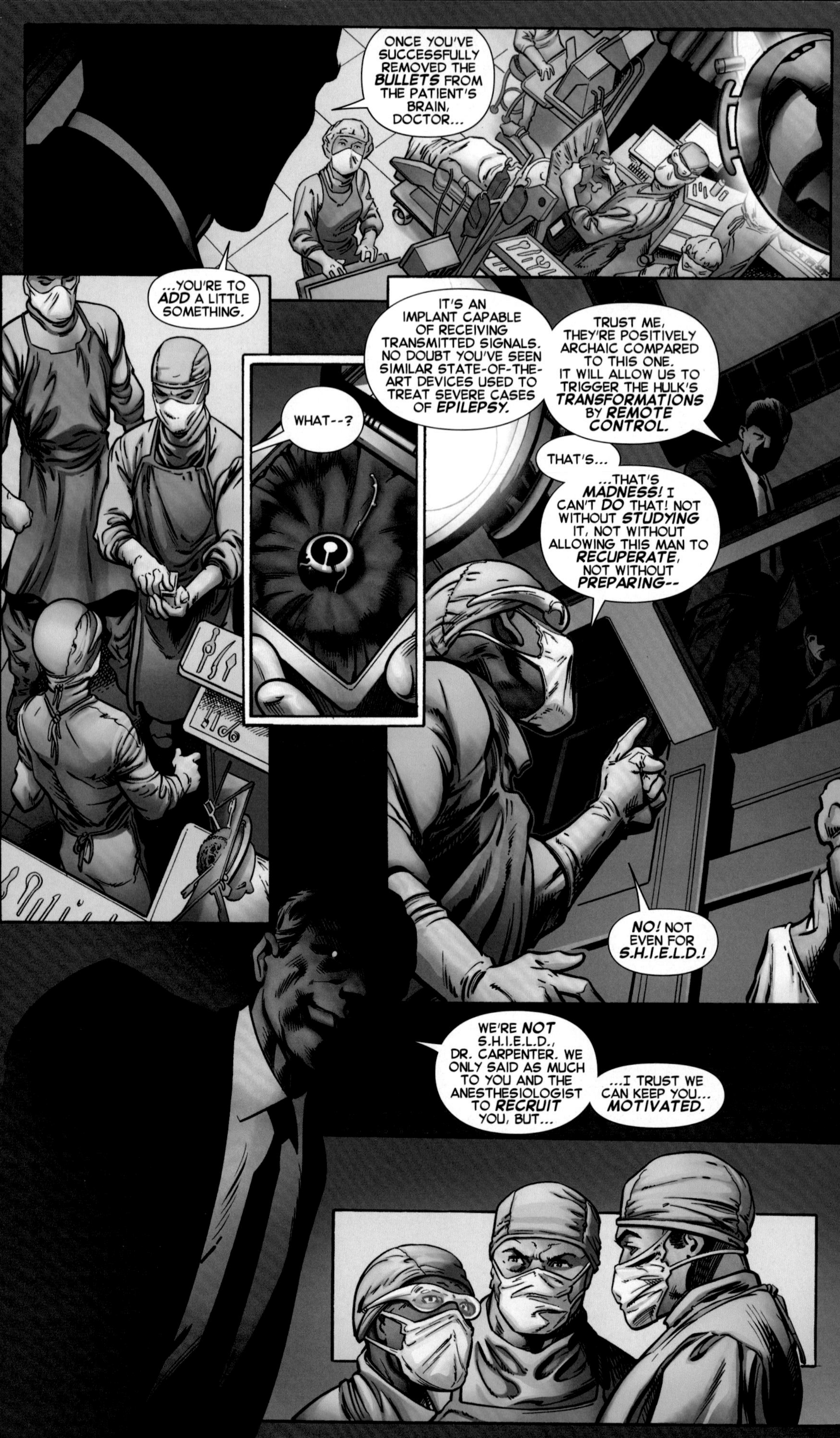
ONCE YOU'VE SUCCESSFULLY REMOVED THE BULLETS FROM THE PATIENT'S BRAIN, DOCTOR...
...YOU'RE TO ADD A LITTLE SOMETHING.
WHAT--?
IT'S AN IMPLANT CAPABLE OF RECEIVING TRANSMITTED SIGNALS. NO DOUBT YOU'VE SEEN SIMILAR STATE-OF-THE-ART DEVICES USED TO TREAT SEVERE CASES OF EPILEPSY.
TRUST ME, THEY'RE POSITIVELY ARCHAIC COMPARED TO THIS ONE. IT WILL ALLOW US TO TRIGGER THE HULK'S TRANSFORMATIONS BY REMOTE CONTROL.
THAT'S...
...THAT'S MADNESS! I CAN'T DO THAT! NOT WITHOUT STUDYING IT, NOT WITHOUT ALLOWING THIS MAN TO RECUPERATE, NOT WITHOUT PREPARING--
NO! NOT EVEN FOR S.H.I.E.L.D.!
WE'RE NOT S.H.I.E.L.D., DR. CARPENTER. WE ONLY SAID AS MUCH TO YOU AND THE ANESTHESIOLOGIST TO RECRUIT YOU, BUT...
...I TRUST WE CAN KEEP YOU... MOTIVATED.

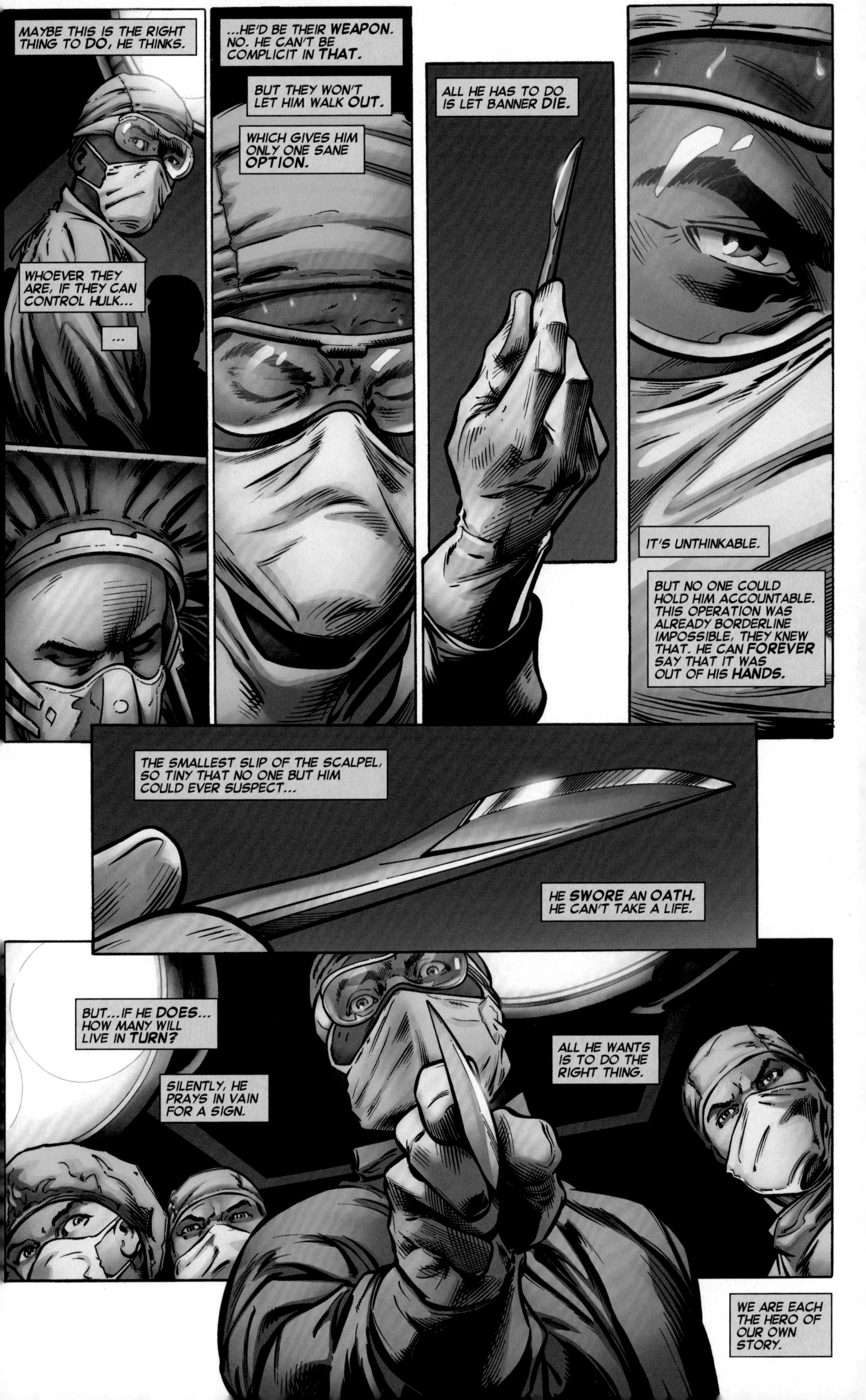
MAYBE THIS IS THE RIGHT THING TO DO, HE THINKS.
WHOEVER THEY ARE, IF THEY CAN CONTROL HULK...
...
...HE'D BE THEIR WEAPON. NO. HE CAN'T BE COMPLICIT IN THAT.
BUT THEY WON'T LET HIM WALK OUT.
WHICH GIVES HIM ONLY ONE SANE OPTION.
ALL HE HAS TO DO IS LET BANNER DIE.
IT'S UNTHINKABLE.
BUT NO ONE COULD HOLD HIM ACCOUNTABLE. THIS OPERATION WAS ALREADY BORDERLINE IMPOSSIBLE, THEY KNEW THAT. HE CAN FOREVER SAY THAT IT WAS OUT OF HIS HANDS.
THE SMALLEST SLIP OF THE SCALPEL, SO TINY THAT NO ONE BUT HIM COULD EVER SUSPECT...
HE SWORE AN OATH. HE CAN'T TAKE A LIFE.
BUT...IF HE DOES... HOW MANY WILL LIVE IN TURN?
SILENTLY, HE PRAYS IN VAIN FOR A SIGN.
ALL HE WANTS IS TO DO THE RIGHT THING.
WE ARE EACH THE HERO OF OUR OWN STORY.

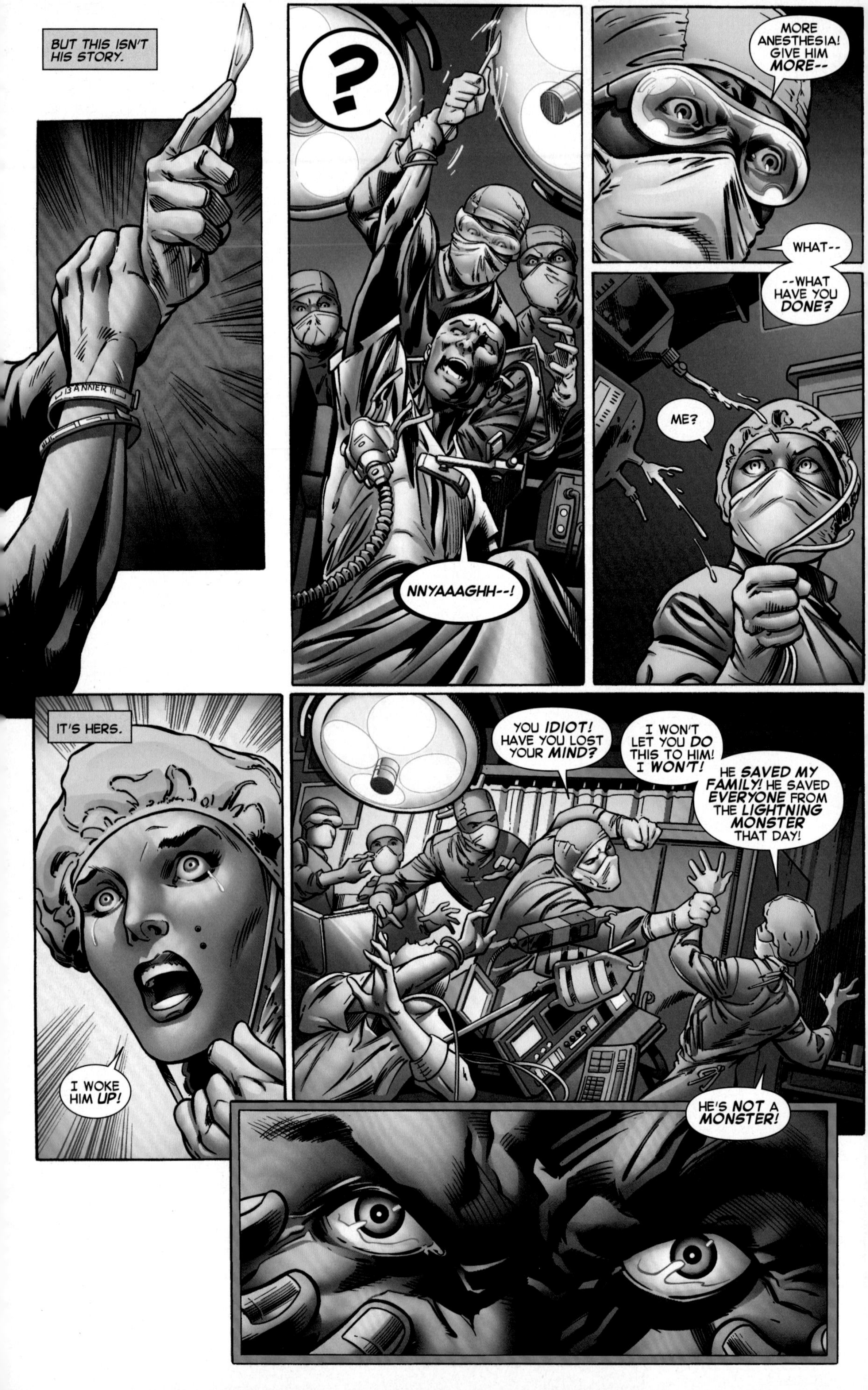
BUT THIS ISN'T HIS STORY.
BANNER
?
NNYAAAGHH--!
MORE ANESTHESIA! GIVE HIM MORE--
WHAT--
--WHAT HAVE YOU DONE?
ME?
IT'S HERS.
I WOKE HIM UP!
YOU IDIOT! HAVE YOU LOST YOUR MIND?
I WON'T LET YOU DO THIS TO HIM! I WON'T!
HE SAVED MY FAMILY! HE SAVED EVERYONE FROM THE LIGHTNING MONSTER THAT DAY!
HE'S NOT A MONSTER!

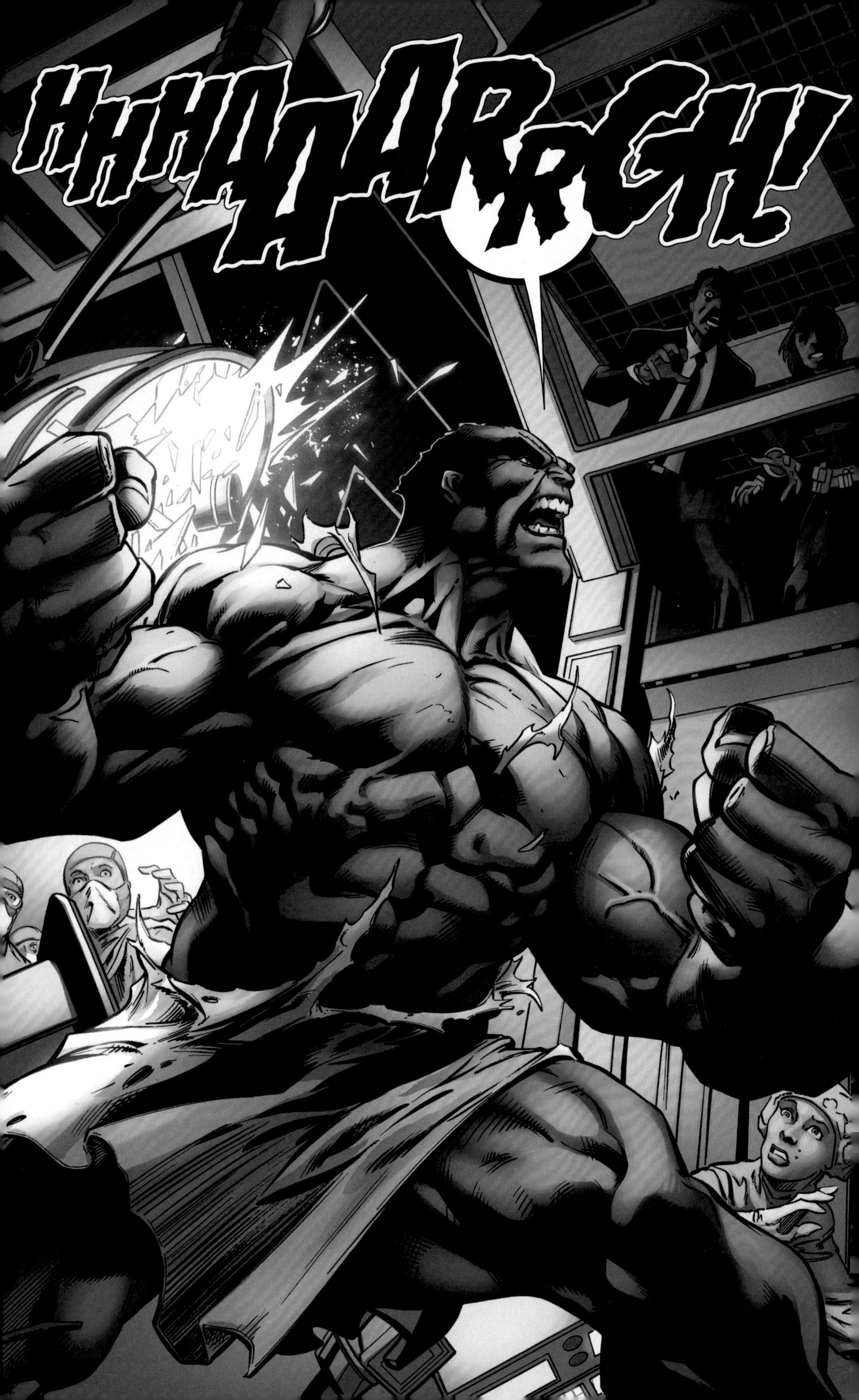
HHHAAARRRGH!

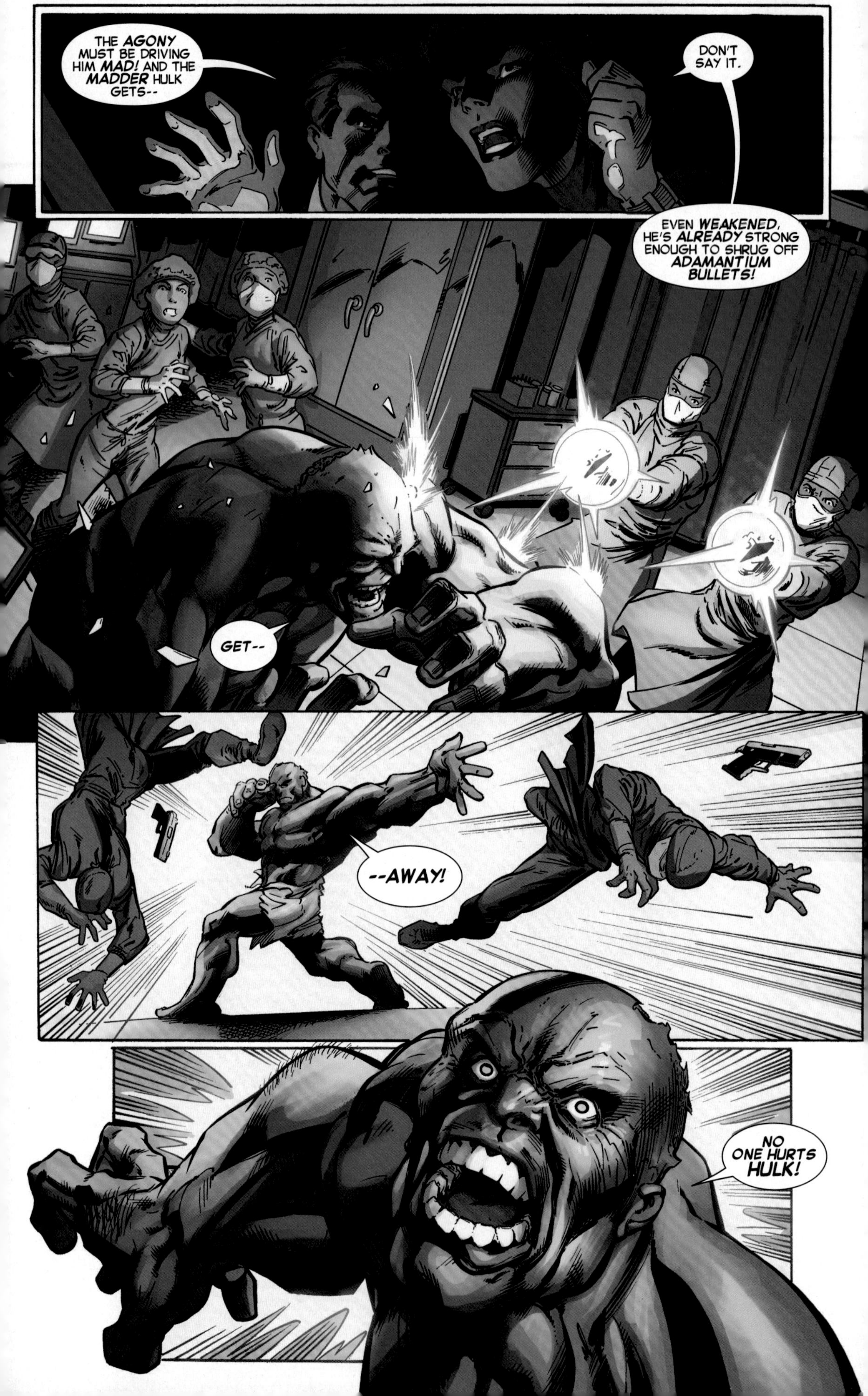
THE AGONY MUST BE DRIVING HIM MAD! AND THE MADDER HULK GETS--
DON'T SAY IT.
EVEN WEAKENED, HE'S ALREADY STRONG ENOUGH TO SHRUG OFF ADAMANTIUM BULLETS!
GET--
--AWAY!
NO ONE HURTS HULK!

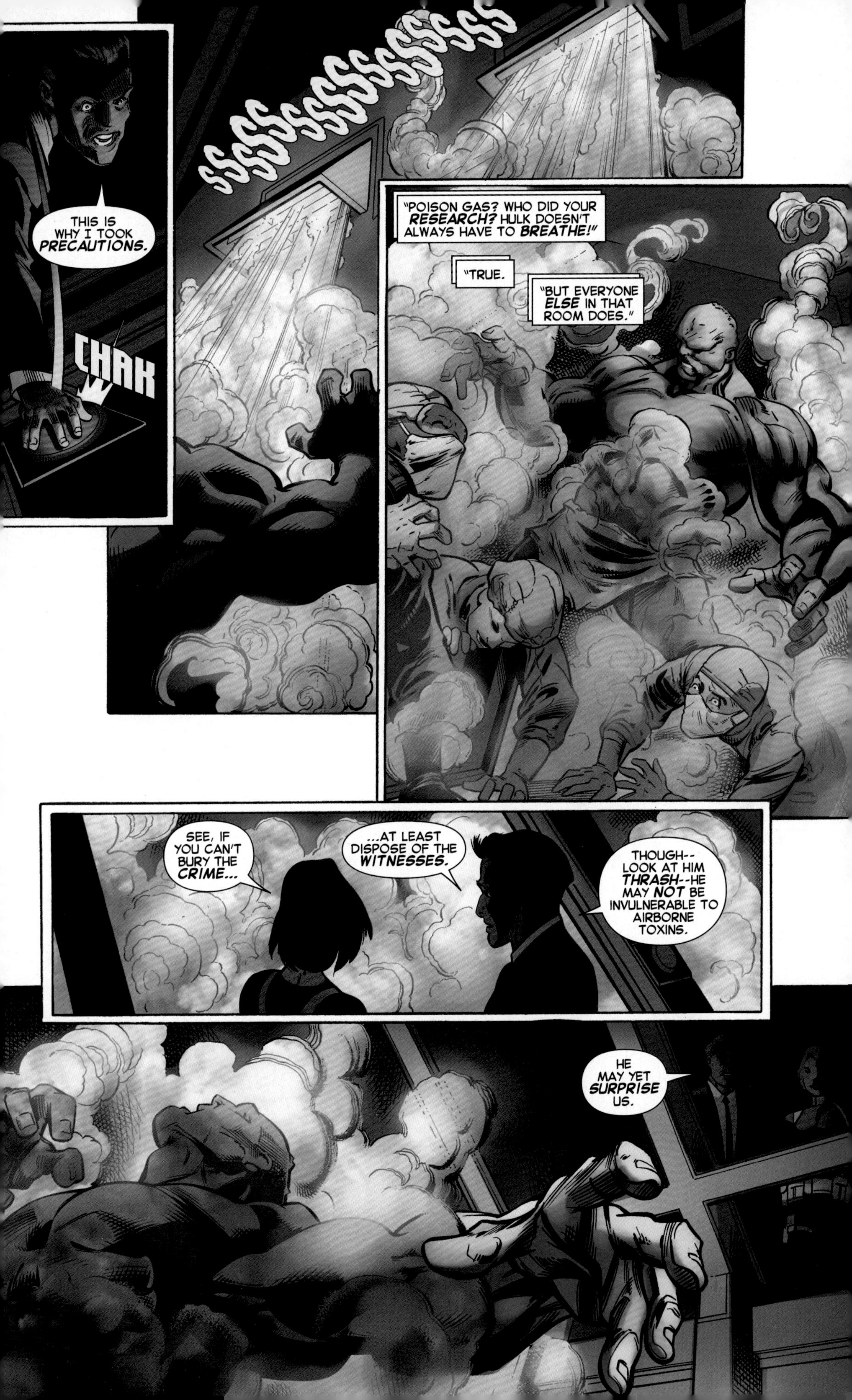

SSSSSSSSSSSSSSSSSSS
THIS IS WHY I TOOK PRECAUTIONS.
CHAK
"POISON GAS? WHO DID YOUR RESEARCH? HULK DOESN'T ALWAYS HAVE TO BREATHE!"
"TRUE.
"BUT EVERYONE ELSE IN THAT ROOM DOES."
SEE, IF YOU CAN'T BURY THE CRIME...
...AT LEAST DISPOSE OF THE WITNESSES.
THOUGH-- LOOK AT HIM THRASH--HE MAY NOT BE INVULNERABLE TO AIRBORNE TOXINS.
HE MAY YET SURPRISE US.

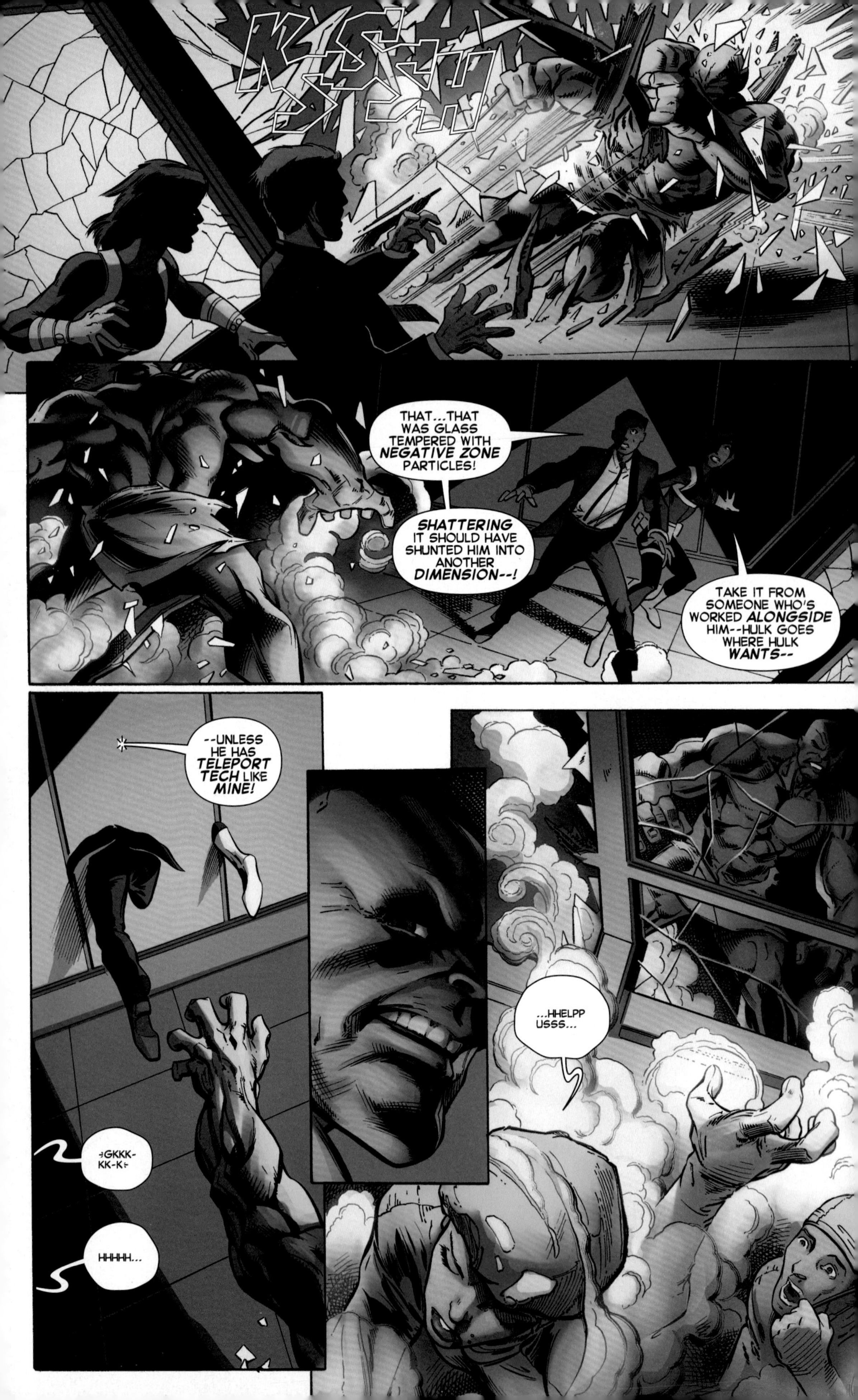
THAT...THAT WAS GLASS TEMPERED WITH NEGATIVE ZONE PARTICLES!
SHATTERING IT SHOULD HAVE SHUNTED HIM INTO ANOTHER DIMENSION--!
TAKE IT FROM SOMEONE WHO'S WORKED ALONGSIDE HIM--HULK GOES WHERE HULK WANTS--
--UNLESS HE HAS TELEPORT TECH LIKE MINE!
...HHELPP USSS...
GKKK-KK-K
HHHHH...

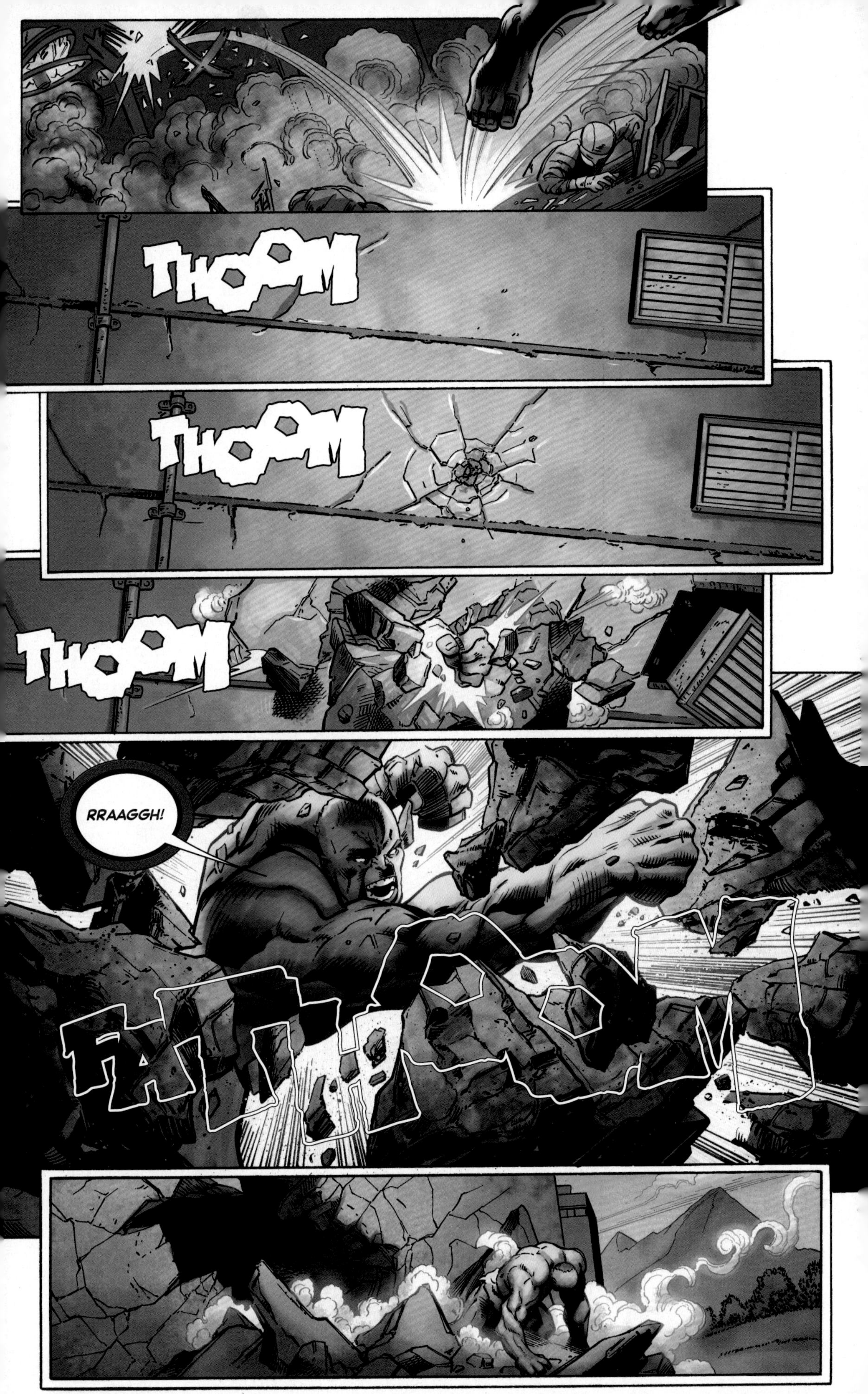
THOOM
THOOM
THOOM
RRAAGGH!
FATHOOM

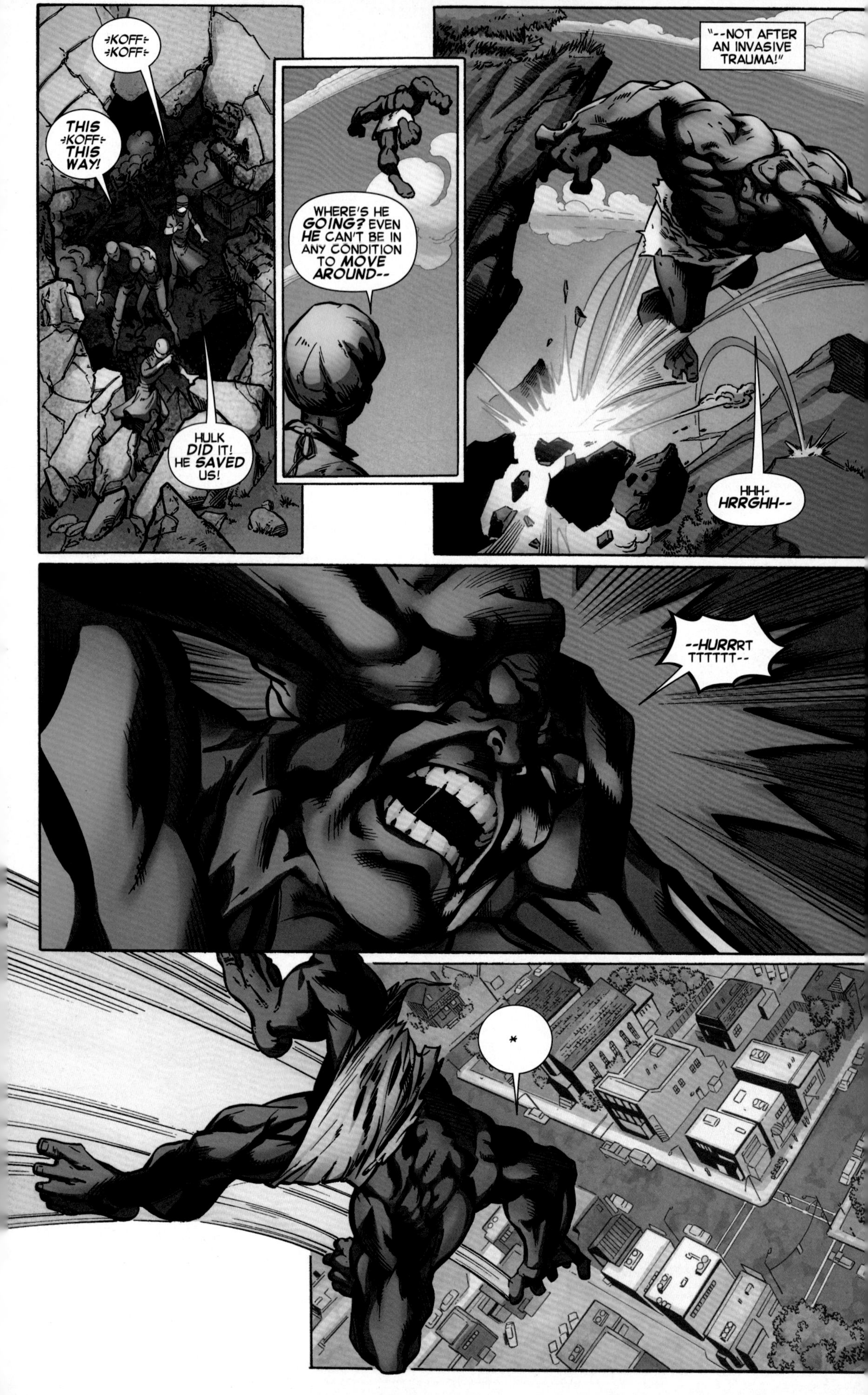

⫩KOFF⫩ ⫩KOFF⫩
THIS ⫩KOFF⫩ THIS WAY!
HULK DID IT! HE SAVED US!
WHERE'S HE GOING? EVEN HE CAN'T BE IN ANY CONDITION TO MOVE AROUND--
"--NOT AFTER AN INVASIVE TRAUMA!"
HHH-HRRGHH--
--HURRRT TTTTTT--
*

TWO WEEKS LATER

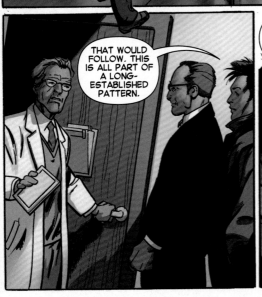

...SURE THIS IS THE FELLA YOU'RE *AFTER*, MISS...?

AGENT. SHE'S HILL, I'M *COULSON,* AND OUR MAN VANISHED FOURTEEN LONG DAYS AGO, SO IF YOU COULD PLEASE SPARE US ANY FURTHER DELAYS...?

HE DOES FIT THE *DESCRIPTION* TO A TEE, DOCTOR. NAKED AND PALE...?

HIS HEAD CUT HALF-OPEN... NO I.D., ALL CONFUSED...

THAT WOULD FOLLOW. THIS IS ALL PART OF A LONG-ESTABLISHED PATTERN.

S.H.I.E.L.D. THANKS YOU FOR YOUR *CARE.* YOU MAY NOT REALIZE IT--

--BUT YOU'VE LIKELY SAVED THE LIFE OF ONE OF THE MOST BRILLIANT MINDS ON THE PLANET.

DON'T BE TOO QUICK WITH YOUR *GRATITUDE.*

DIDN'T YOU HEAR ME? I SAID HIS BRAIN WAS PRACTICALLY HANGING OUT OF HIS *SKULL* WHEN WE FOUND HIM.

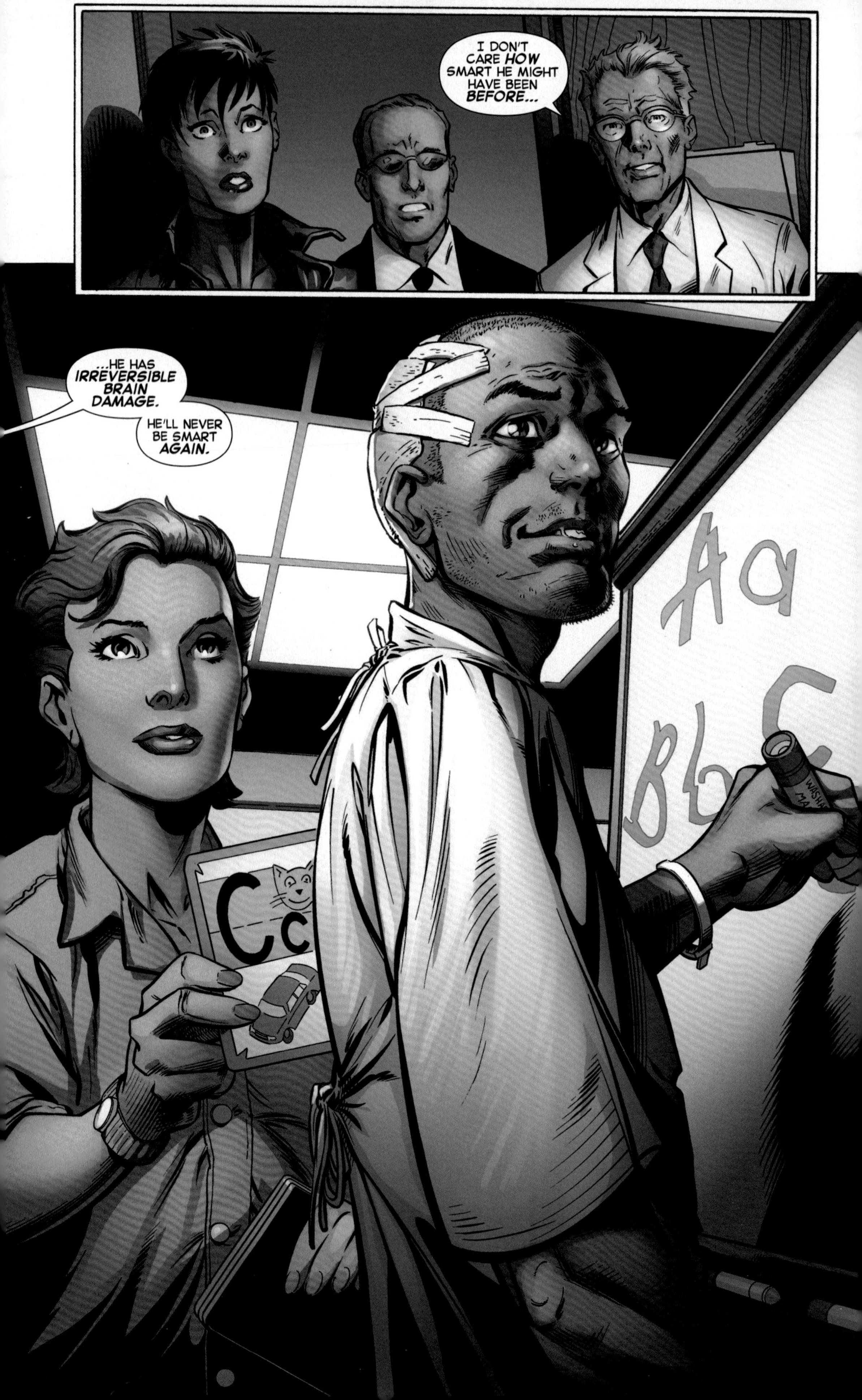
I DON'T CARE *HOW* SMART HE MIGHT HAVE BEEN *BEFORE*...
...HE HAS *IRREVERSIBLE BRAIN DAMAGE.*
HE'LL NEVER BE SMART *AGAIN.*
Aa
Bb
C
Cc

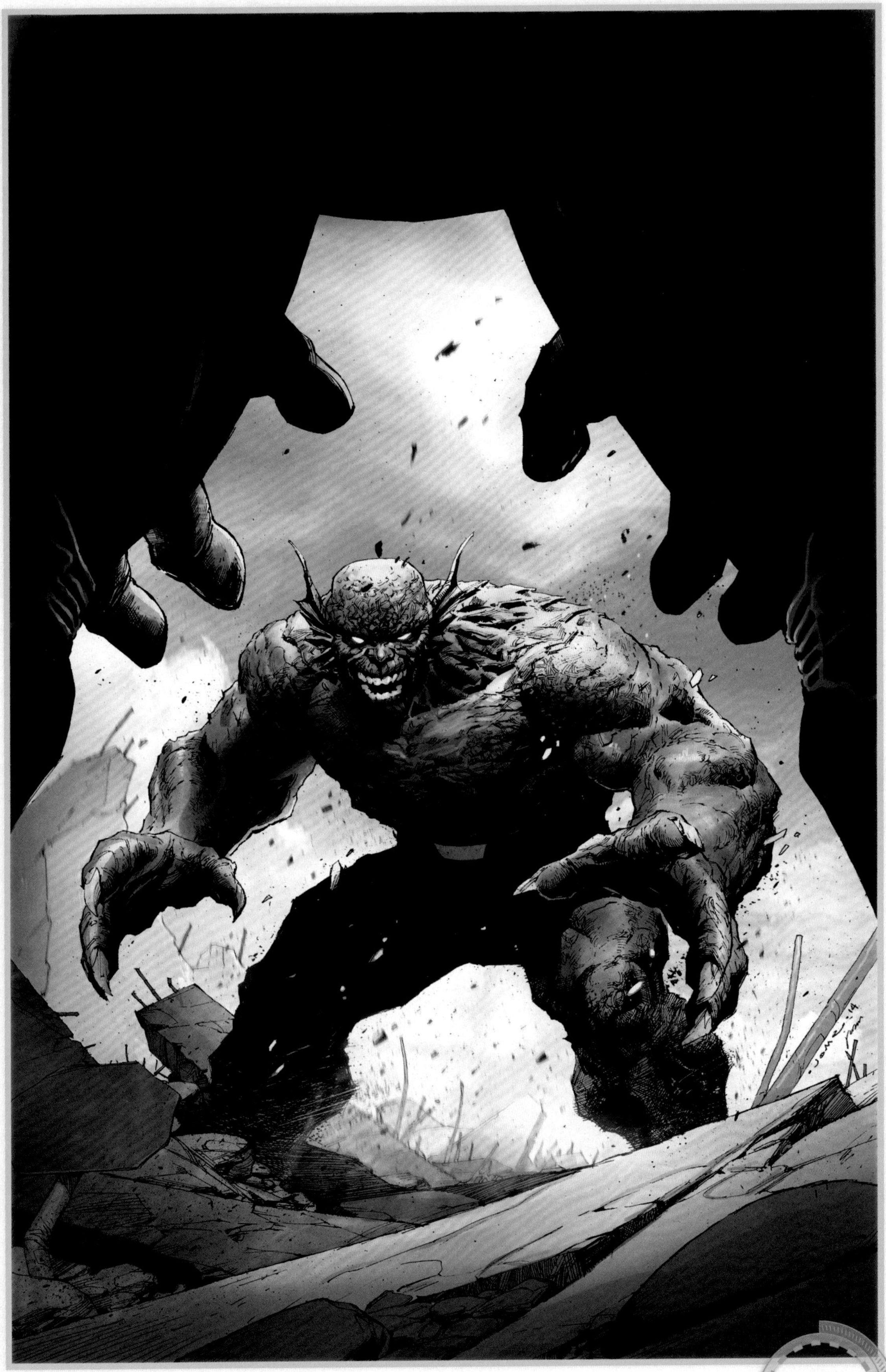

2

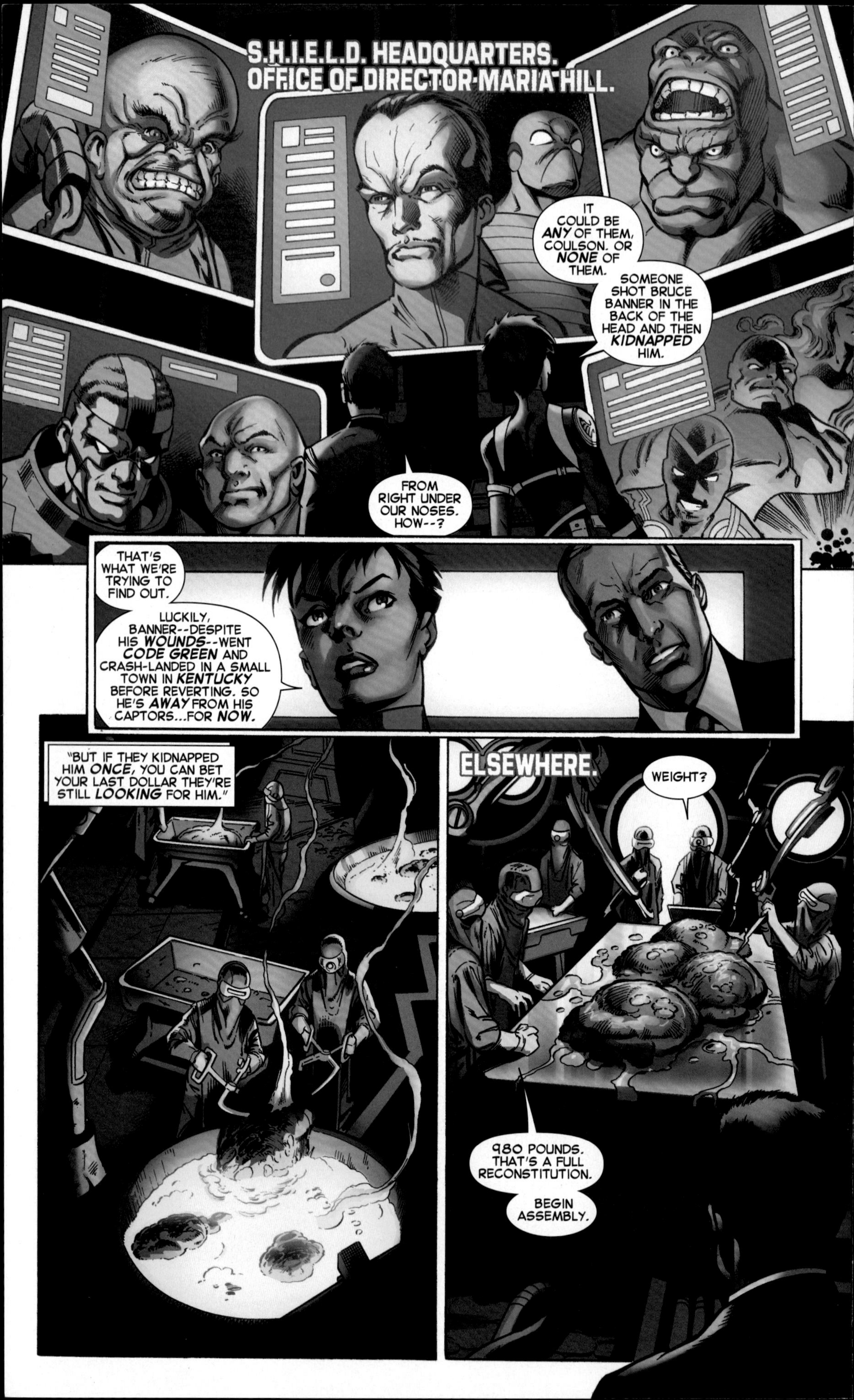
S.H.I.E.L.D. HEADQUARTERS. OFFICE OF DIRECTOR MARIA HILL.
IT COULD BE ANY OF THEM, COULSON. OR NONE OF THEM.
SOMEONE SHOT BRUCE BANNER IN THE BACK OF THE HEAD AND THEN KIDNAPPED HIM.
FROM RIGHT UNDER OUR NOSES. HOW--?
THAT'S WHAT WE'RE TRYING TO FIND OUT.
LUCKILY, BANNER--DESPITE HIS WOUNDS--WENT CODE GREEN AND CRASH-LANDED IN A SMALL TOWN IN KENTUCKY BEFORE REVERTING. SO HE'S AWAY FROM HIS CAPTORS...FOR NOW.
"BUT IF THEY KIDNAPPED HIM ONCE, YOU CAN BET YOUR LAST DOLLAR THEY'RE STILL LOOKING FOR HIM."
ELSEWHERE.
WEIGHT?
980 POUNDS. THAT'S A FULL RECONSTITUTION.
BEGIN ASSEMBLY.

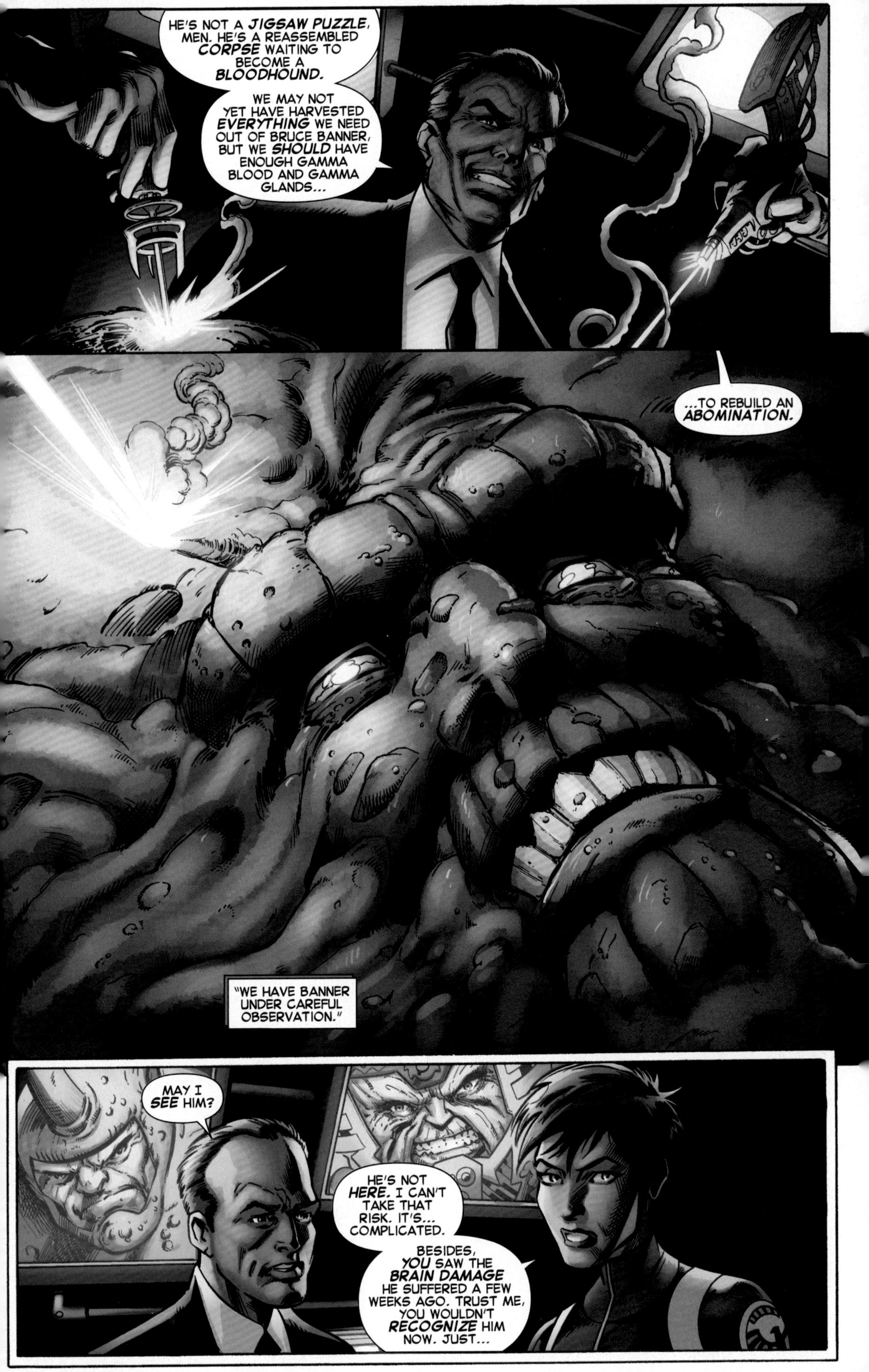
HE'S NOT A JIGSAW PUZZLE, MEN. HE'S A REASSEMBLED CORPSE WAITING TO BECOME A BLOODHOUND.
WE MAY NOT YET HAVE HARVESTED EVERYTHING WE NEED OUT OF BRUCE BANNER, BUT WE SHOULD HAVE ENOUGH GAMMA BLOOD AND GAMMA GLANDS...
...TO REBUILD AN ABOMINATION.
"WE HAVE BANNER UNDER CAREFUL OBSERVATION."
MAY I SEE HIM?
HE'S NOT HERE. I CAN'T TAKE THAT RISK. IT'S... COMPLICATED.
BESIDES, YOU SAW THE BRAIN DAMAGE HE SUFFERED A FEW WEEKS AGO. TRUST ME, YOU WOULDN'T RECOGNIZE HIM NOW. JUST...

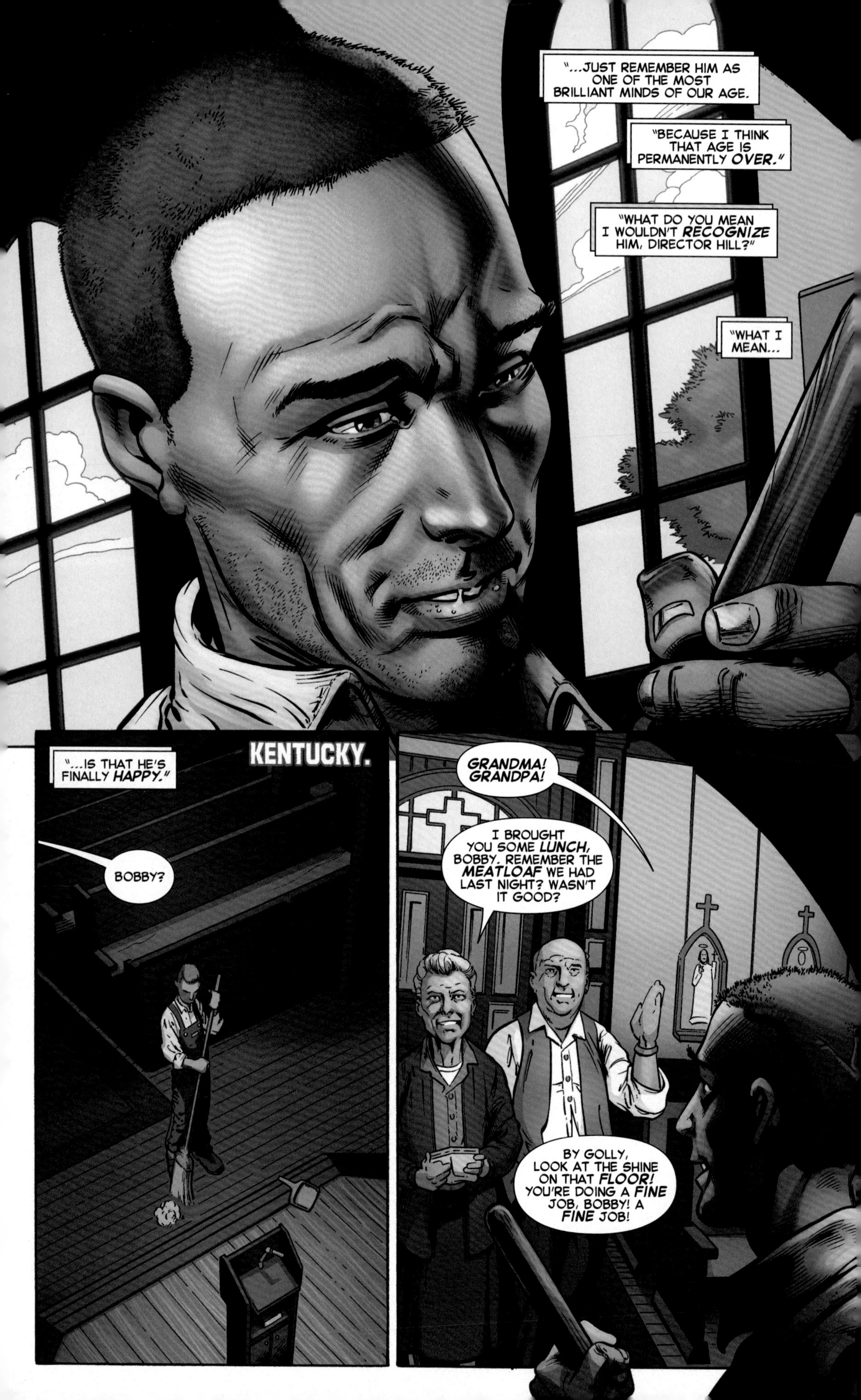
"...JUST REMEMBER HIM AS ONE OF THE MOST BRILLIANT MINDS OF OUR AGE.
"BECAUSE I THINK THAT AGE IS PERMANENTLY OVER."
"WHAT DO YOU MEAN I WOULDN'T RECOGNIZE HIM, DIRECTOR HILL?"
"WHAT I MEAN...
"...IS THAT HE'S FINALLY HAPPY."
KENTUCKY.
BOBBY?
GRANDMA! GRANDPA!
I BROUGHT YOU SOME LUNCH, BOBBY. REMEMBER THE MEATLOAF WE HAD LAST NIGHT? WASN'T IT GOOD?
BY GOLLY, LOOK AT THE SHINE ON THAT FLOOR! YOU'RE DOING A FINE JOB, BOBBY! A FINE JOB!

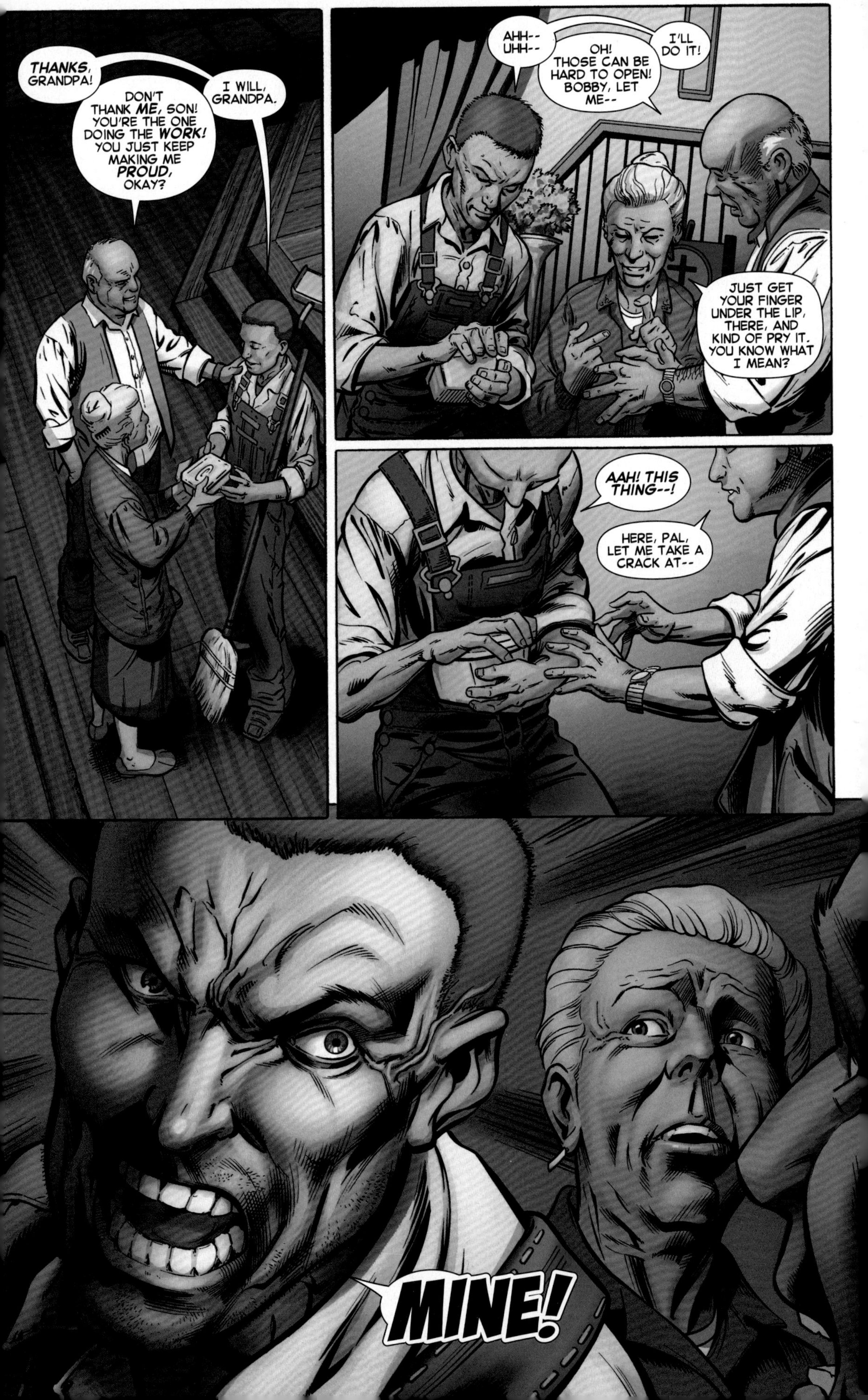
THANKS, GRANDPA!
DON'T THANK ME, SON! YOU'RE THE ONE DOING THE WORK! YOU JUST KEEP MAKING ME PROUD, OKAY?
I WILL, GRANDPA.
AHH-- UHH--
OH! THOSE CAN BE HARD TO OPEN! BOBBY, LET ME--
I'LL DO IT!
JUST GET YOUR FINGER UNDER THE LIP, THERE, AND KIND OF PRY IT. YOU KNOW WHAT I MEAN?
AAH! THIS THING--!
HERE, PAL, LET ME TAKE A CRACK AT--
MINE!

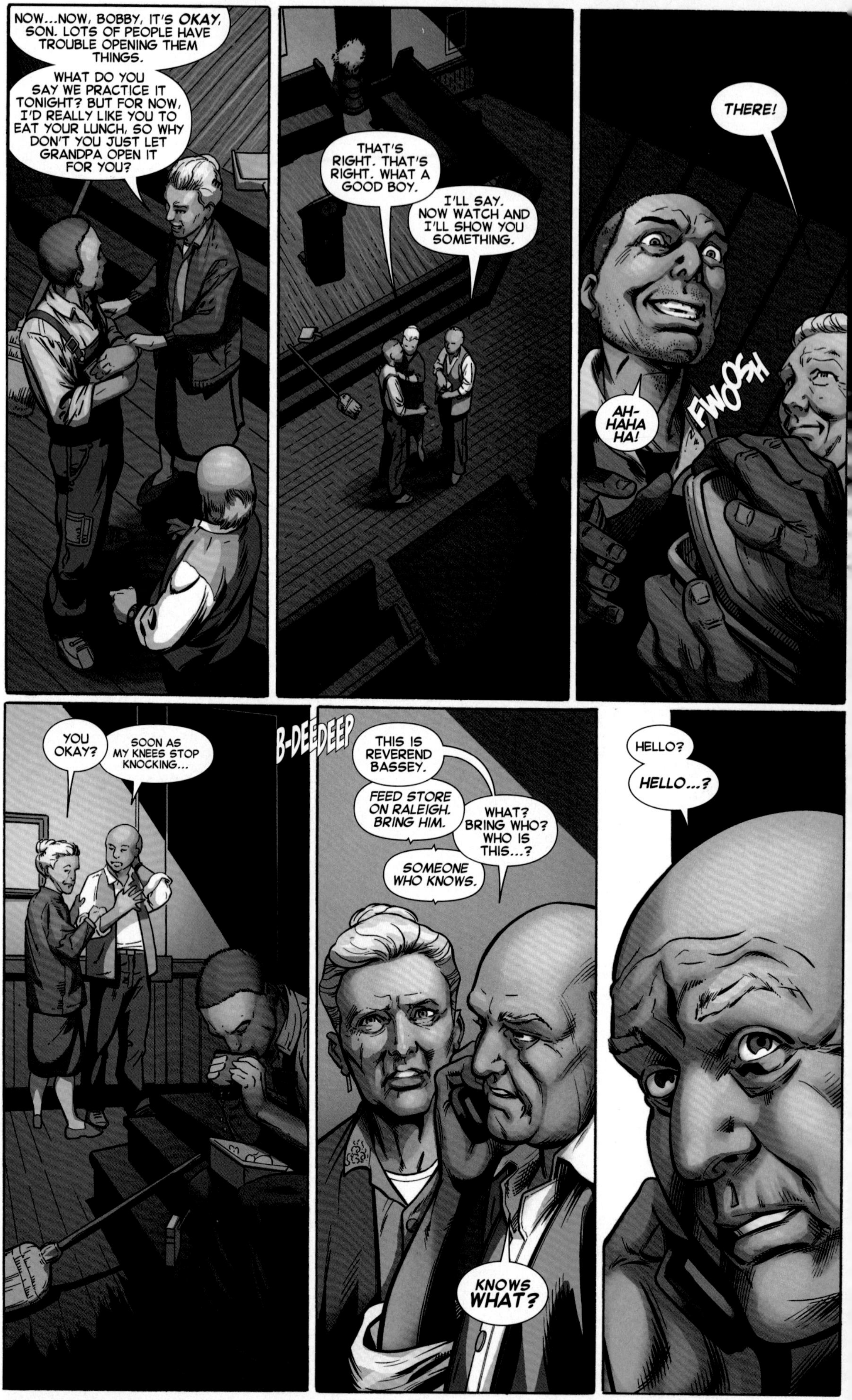
NOW...NOW, BOBBY, IT'S OKAY, SON. LOTS OF PEOPLE HAVE TROUBLE OPENING THEM THINGS.
WHAT DO YOU SAY WE PRACTICE IT TONIGHT? BUT FOR NOW, I'D REALLY LIKE YOU TO EAT YOUR LUNCH, SO WHY DON'T YOU JUST LET GRANDPA OPEN IT FOR YOU?
THAT'S RIGHT. THAT'S RIGHT. WHAT A GOOD BOY.
I'LL SAY. NOW WATCH AND I'LL SHOW YOU SOMETHING.
THERE!
AH-HAHA HA!
FWOOSH
YOU OKAY?
SOON AS MY KNEES STOP KNOCKING...
B-DEEDEEP
THIS IS REVEREND BASSEY.
FEED STORE ON RALEIGH. BRING HIM.
WHAT? BRING WHO? WHO IS THIS...?
SOMEONE WHO KNOWS.
KNOWS WHAT?
HELLO?
HELLO...?

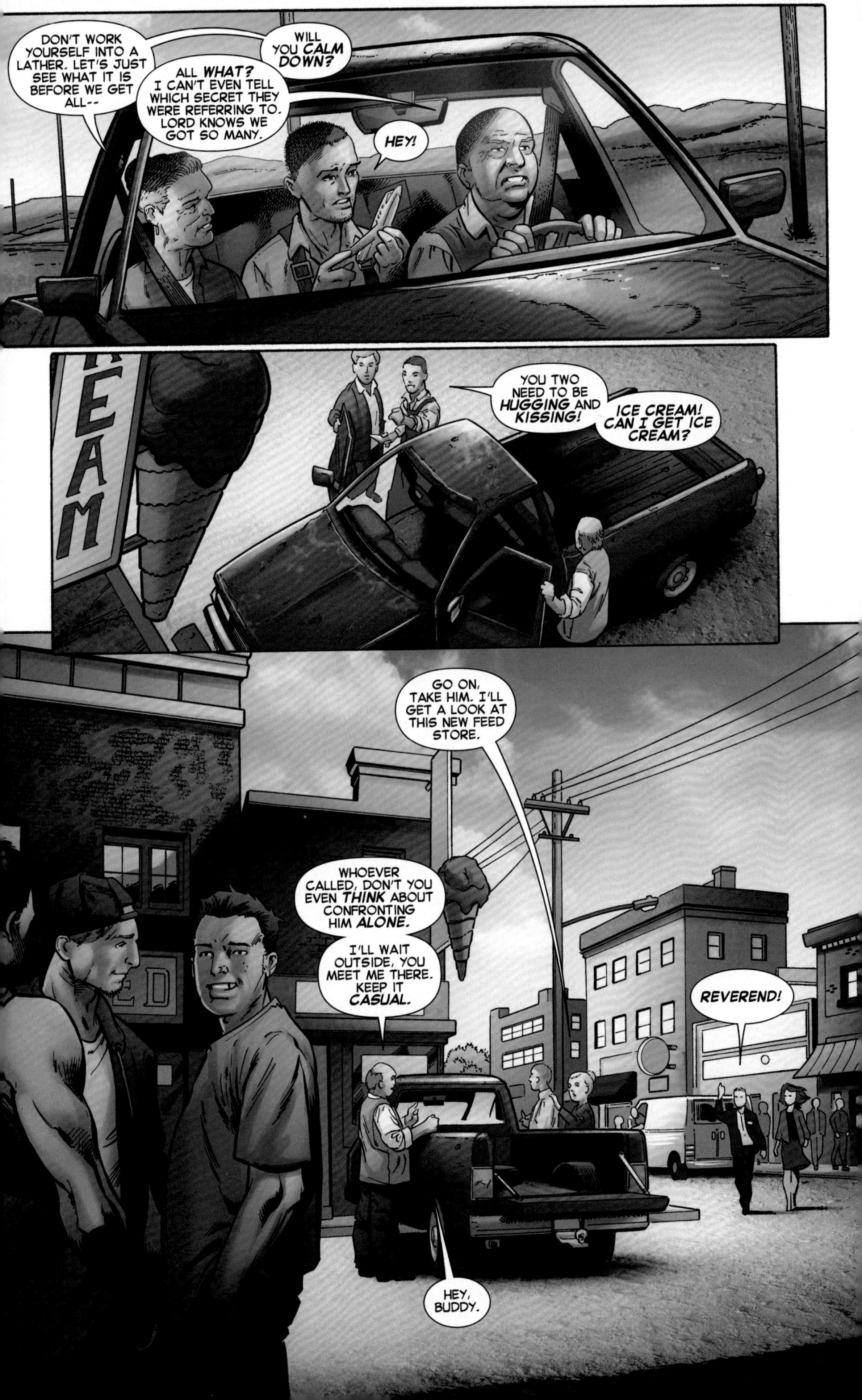

DON'T WORK YOURSELF INTO A LATHER. LET'S JUST SEE WHAT IT IS BEFORE WE GET ALL--
WILL YOU CALM DOWN?
ALL WHAT? I CAN'T EVEN TELL WHICH SECRET THEY WERE REFERRING TO. LORD KNOWS WE GOT SO MANY.
HEY!
EAM
YOU TWO NEED TO BE HUGGING AND KISSING!
ICE CREAM! CAN I GET ICE CREAM?
GO ON, TAKE HIM. I'LL GET A LOOK AT THIS NEW FEED STORE.
WHOEVER CALLED, DON'T YOU EVEN THINK ABOUT CONFRONTING HIM ALONE.
I'LL WAIT OUTSIDE, YOU MEET ME THERE. KEEP IT CASUAL.
REVEREND!
HEY, BUDDY.

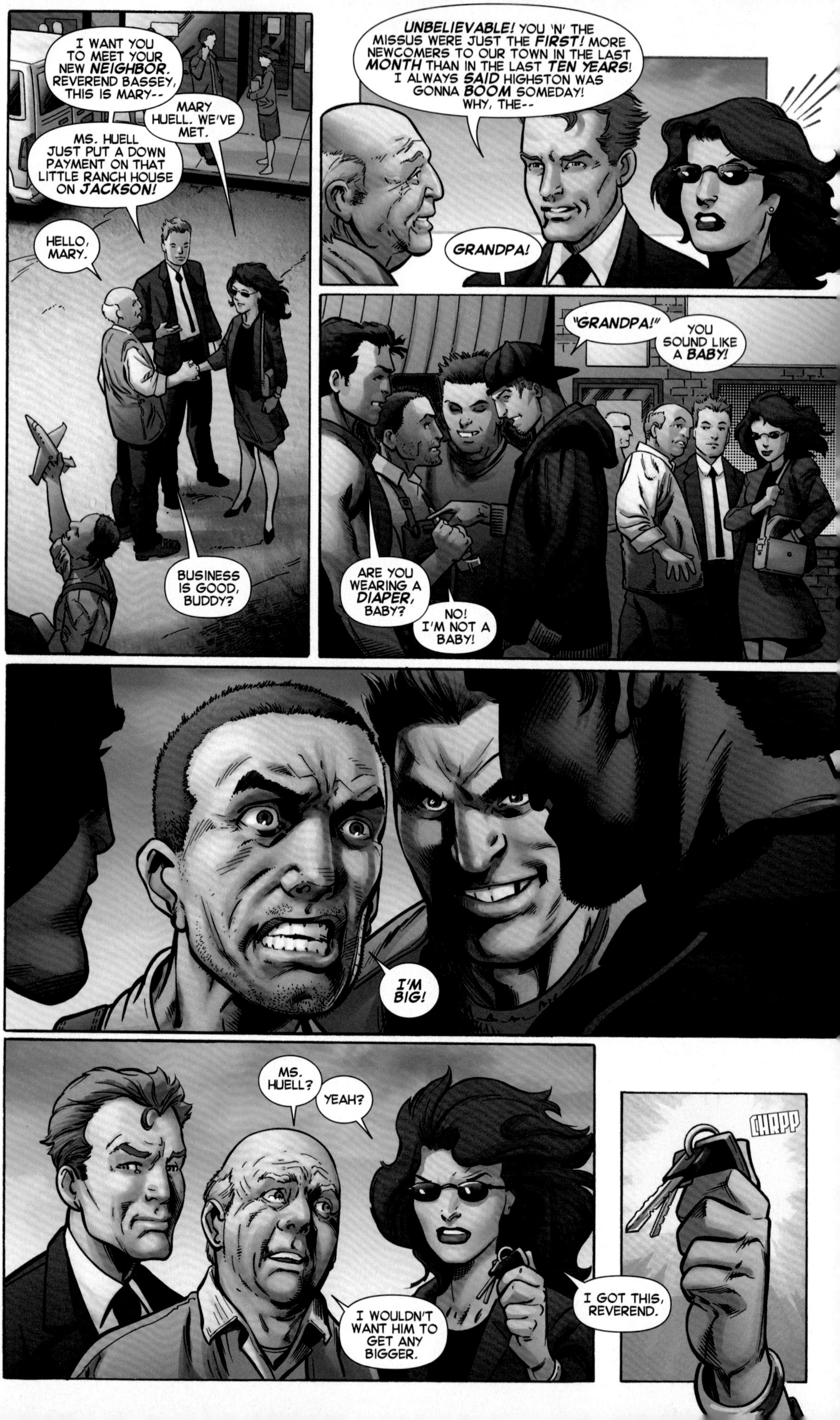
I WANT YOU TO MEET YOUR NEW NEIGHBOR. REVEREND BASSEY, THIS IS MARY--
MARY HUELL. WE'VE MET.
MS. HUELL JUST PUT A DOWN PAYMENT ON THAT LITTLE RANCH HOUSE ON JACKSON!
HELLO, MARY.
BUSINESS IS GOOD, BUDDY?
UNBELIEVABLE! YOU 'N' THE MISSUS WERE JUST THE FIRST! MORE NEWCOMERS TO OUR TOWN IN THE LAST MONTH THAN IN THE LAST TEN YEARS! I ALWAYS SAID HIGHSTON WAS GONNA BOOM SOMEDAY! WHY, THE--
GRANDPA!
"GRANDPA!"
YOU SOUND LIKE A BABY!
ARE YOU WEARING A DIAPER, BABY?
NO! I'M NOT A BABY!
I'M BIG!
MS. HUELL?
YEAH?
I WOULDN'T WANT HIM TO GET ANY BIGGER.
I GOT THIS, REVEREND.
CHRPP

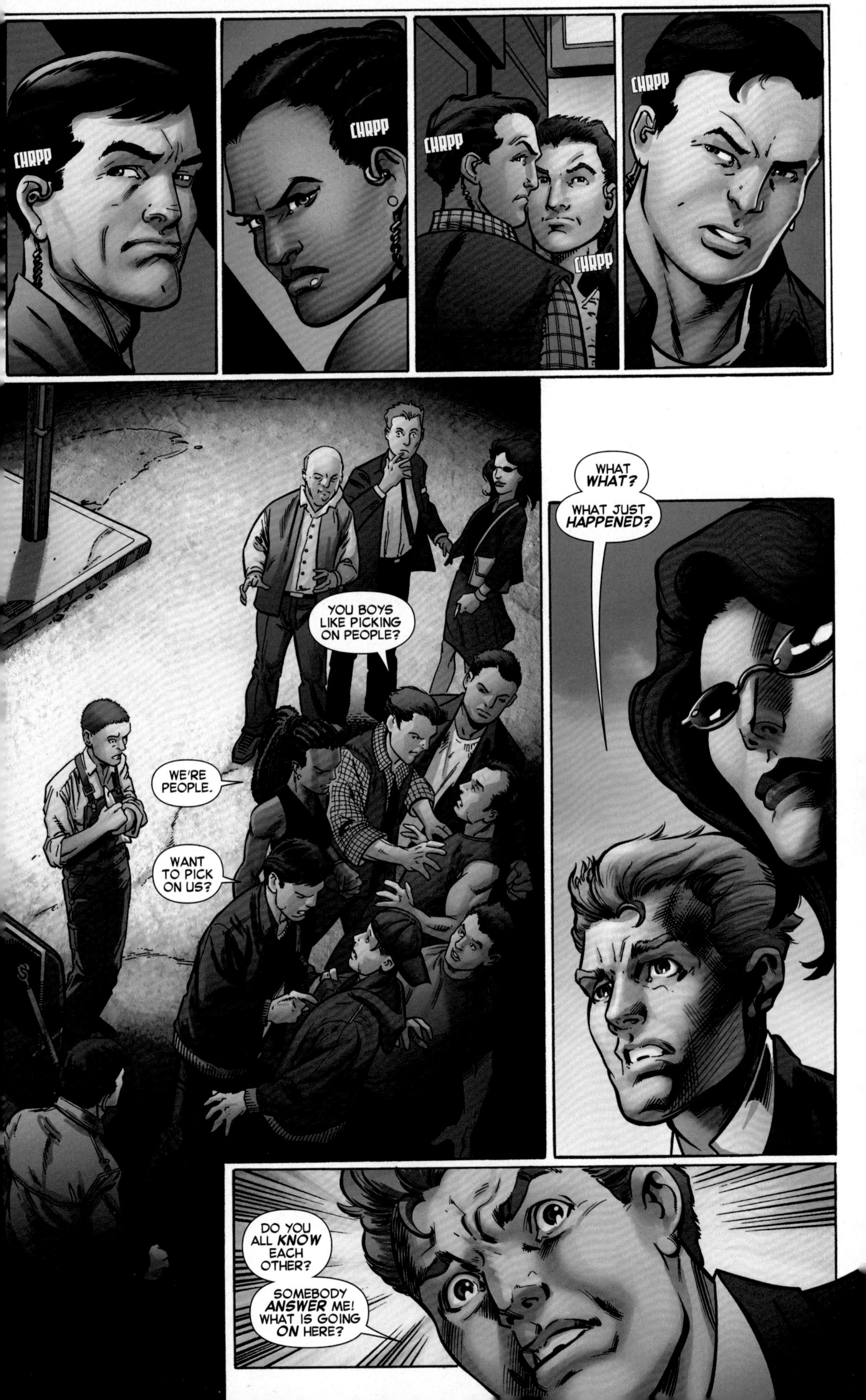
CHRPP
CHRPP
CHRPP
CHRPP
CHRPP
YOU BOYS LIKE PICKING ON PEOPLE?
WE'RE PEOPLE.
WANT TO PICK ON US?
WHAT WHAT?
WHAT JUST HAPPENED?
DO YOU ALL KNOW EACH OTHER?
SOMEBODY ANSWER ME! WHAT IS GOING ON HERE?

ARE YOU THE COWARD WHO MADE THREATS ON THE PHONE?

I DIDN'T MEAN TO DO THAT, MS. BASSEY. YOU AND I ARE ON THE SAME TEAM. MY NAME IS HAYES.

WALLET'S ON THE COUNTER. GO AHEAD. TAKE A LOOK.

DO YOU KNOW WHY THERE'S SO MANY OF US IN A BACKWATER LIKE HIGHSTON, "MRS. BASSEY"?

THE SHOOTING OF ROBERT BRUCE BANNER WAS AN INSIDE JOB.

UNTIL DIRECTOR HILL CAN FIND THE PERP, THOSE OF US WITH A CLEAN *ALIBI* HAVE BEEN ASSIGNED HERE TO MONITOR HIM OFF-SITE.

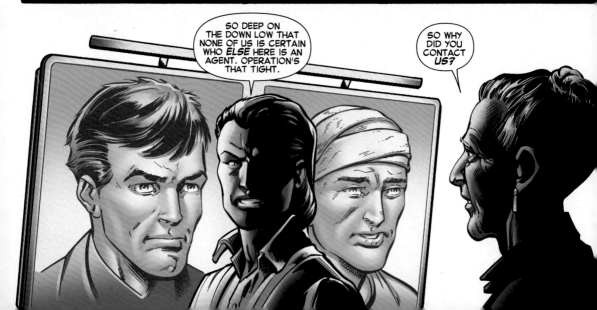

SO DEEP ON THE DOWN LOW THAT NONE OF US IS CERTAIN WHO *ELSE* HERE IS AN AGENT. OPERATION'S THAT TIGHT.

SO WHY DID YOU CONTACT *US*?

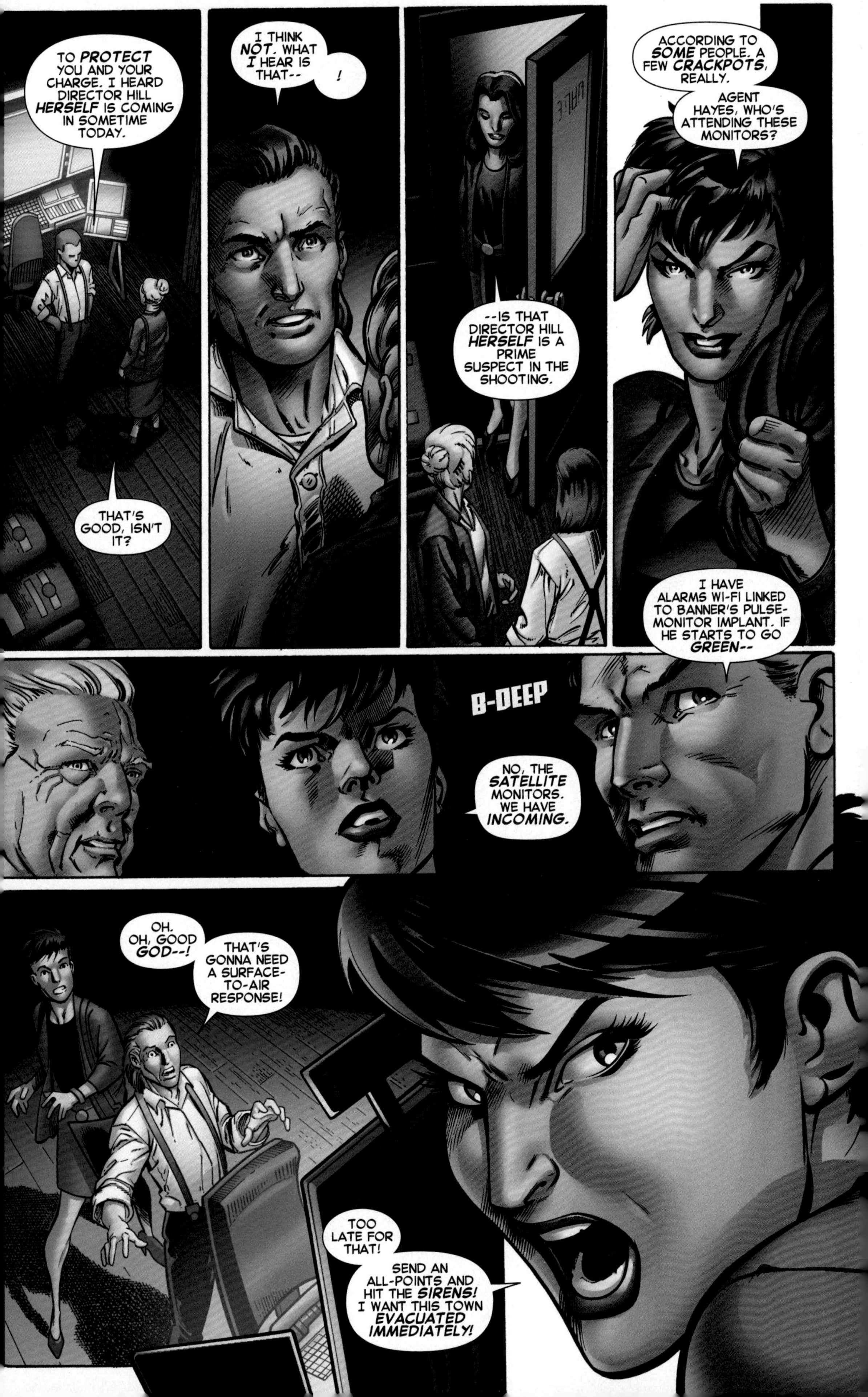
TO PROTECT YOU AND YOUR CHARGE. I HEARD DIRECTOR HILL HERSELF IS COMING IN SOMETIME TODAY.
THAT'S GOOD, ISN'T IT?
I THINK NOT. WHAT I HEAR IS THAT--
!
--IS THAT DIRECTOR HILL HERSELF IS A PRIME SUSPECT IN THE SHOOTING.
ACCORDING TO SOME PEOPLE. A FEW CRACKPOTS, REALLY.
AGENT HAYES, WHO'S ATTENDING THESE MONITORS?
I HAVE ALARMS WI-FI LINKED TO BANNER'S PULSE-MONITOR IMPLANT. IF HE STARTS TO GO GREEN--
B-DEEP
NO, THE SATELLITE MONITORS. WE HAVE INCOMING.
OH. OH, GOOD GOD--!
THAT'S GONNA NEED A SURFACE-TO-AIR RESPONSE!
TOO LATE FOR THAT!
SEND AN ALL-POINTS AND HIT THE SIRENS! I WANT THIS TOWN EVACUATED IMMEDIATELY!

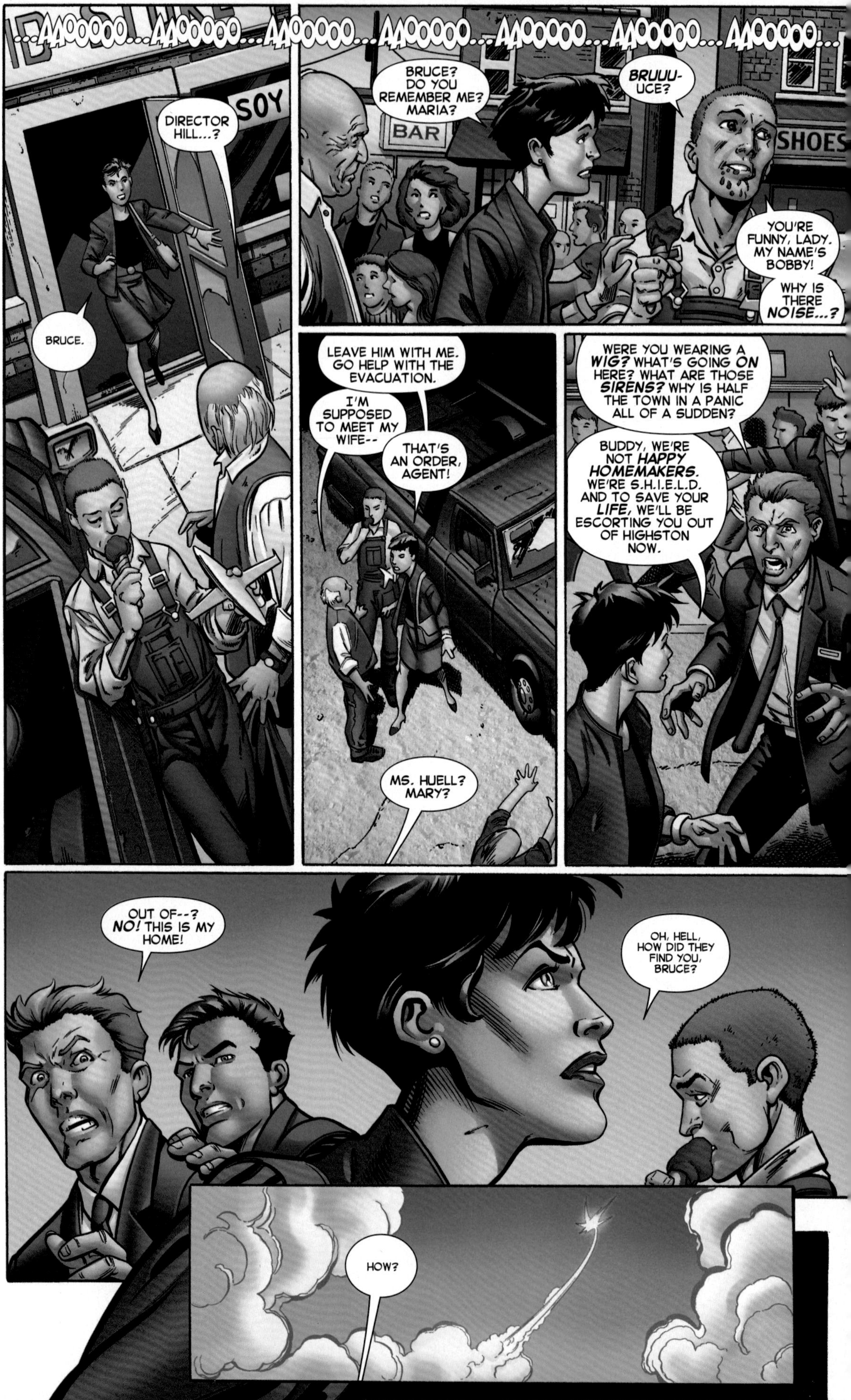
...AAOOOOO...AAOOOOO...AAOOOOO...AAOOOOO...AAOOOOO...AAOOOOO...AAOOOOO...
DIRECTOR HILL...?
BRUCE.
BRUCE? DO YOU REMEMBER ME? MARIA?
BRUUU-UCE?
YOU'RE FUNNY, LADY. MY NAME'S BOBBY!
WHY IS THERE NOISE...?
LEAVE HIM WITH ME. GO HELP WITH THE EVACUATION.
I'M SUPPOSED TO MEET MY WIFE--
THAT'S AN ORDER, AGENT!
MS. HUELL? MARY?
WERE YOU WEARING A WIG? WHAT'S GOING ON HERE? WHAT ARE THOSE SIRENS? WHY IS HALF THE TOWN IN A PANIC ALL OF A SUDDEN?
BUDDY, WE'RE NOT HAPPY HOMEMAKERS. WE'RE S.H.I.E.L.D. AND TO SAVE YOUR LIFE, WE'LL BE ESCORTING YOU OUT OF HIGHSTON NOW.
OUT OF--? NO! THIS IS MY HOME!
OH, HELL, HOW DID THEY FIND YOU, BRUCE?
HOW?

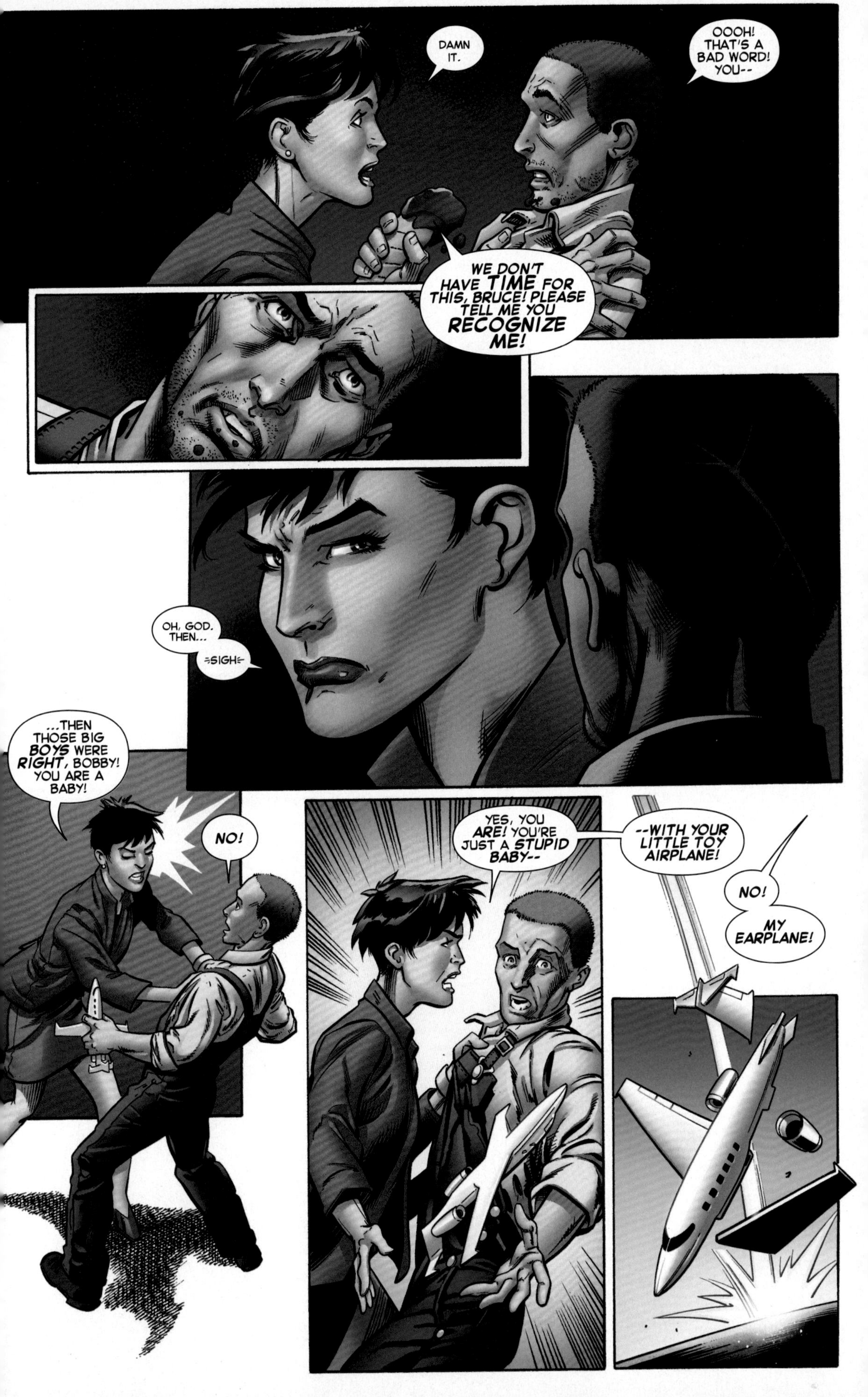
DAMN IT.
OOOH! THAT'S A BAD WORD! YOU--
WE DON'T HAVE TIME FOR THIS, BRUCE! PLEASE TELL ME YOU RECOGNIZE ME!
OH, GOD. THEN...
=SIGH=
...THEN THOSE BIG BOYS WERE RIGHT, BOBBY! YOU ARE A BABY!
NO!
YES, YOU ARE! YOU'RE JUST A STUPID BABY--
--WITH YOUR LITTLE TOY AIRPLANE!
NO!
MY EARPLANE!

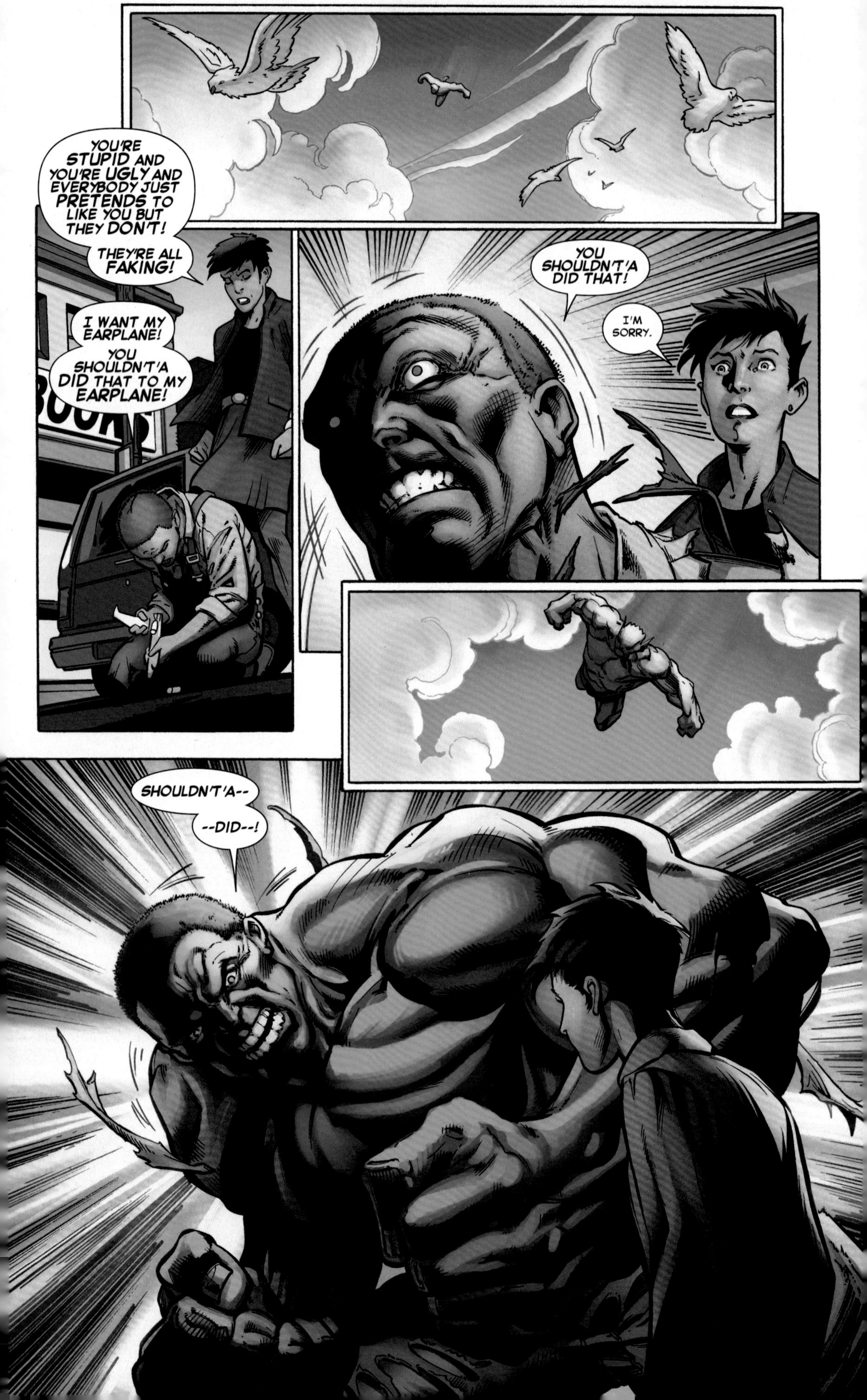
YOU'RE STUPID AND YOU'RE UGLY AND EVERYBODY JUST PRETENDS TO LIKE YOU BUT THEY DON'T!
THEY'RE ALL FAKING!
I WANT MY EARPLANE!
YOU SHOULDN'T'A DID THAT TO MY EARPLANE!
YOU SHOULDN'T'A DID THAT!
I'M SORRY.
SHOULDN'T'A--
--DID--!

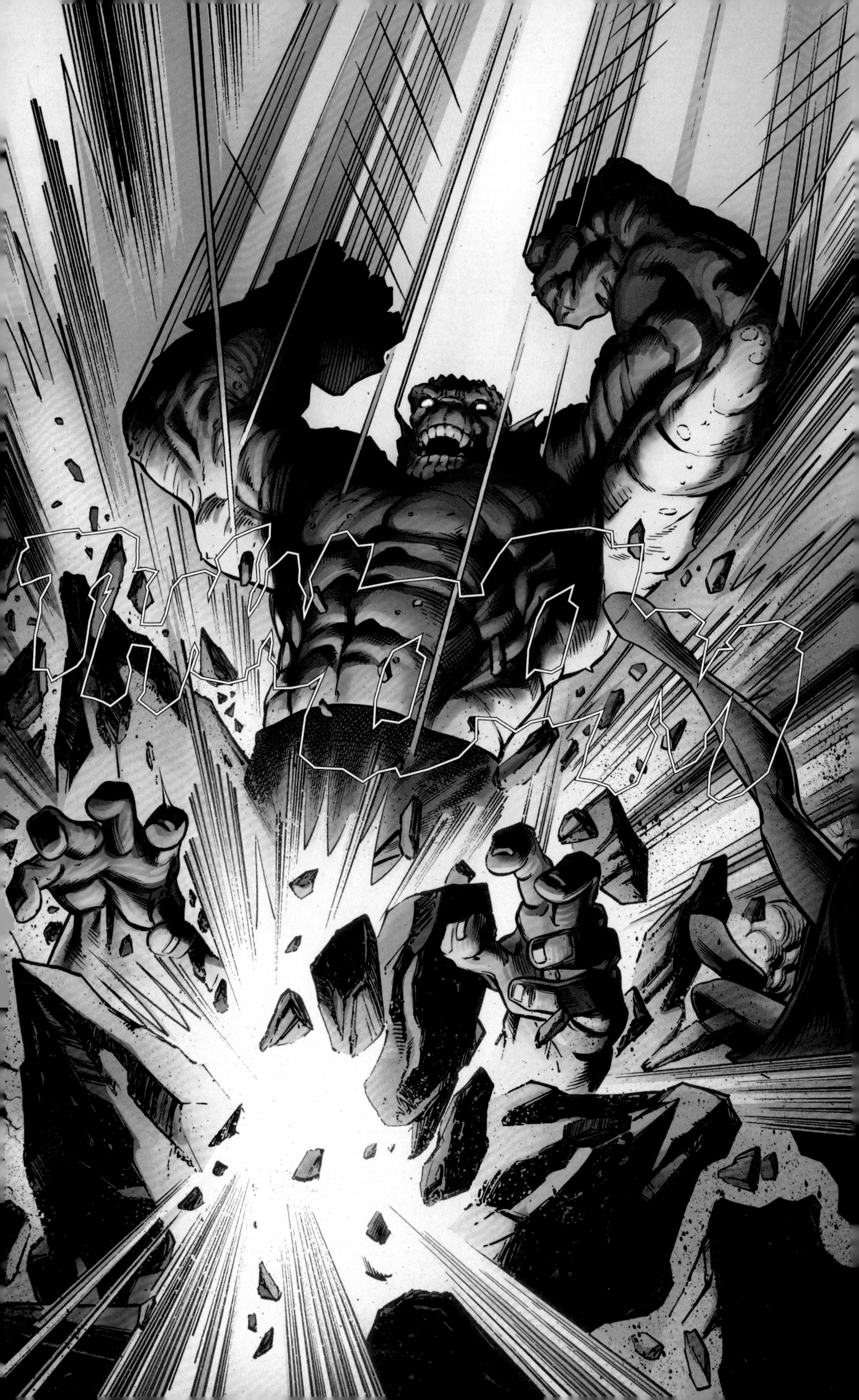

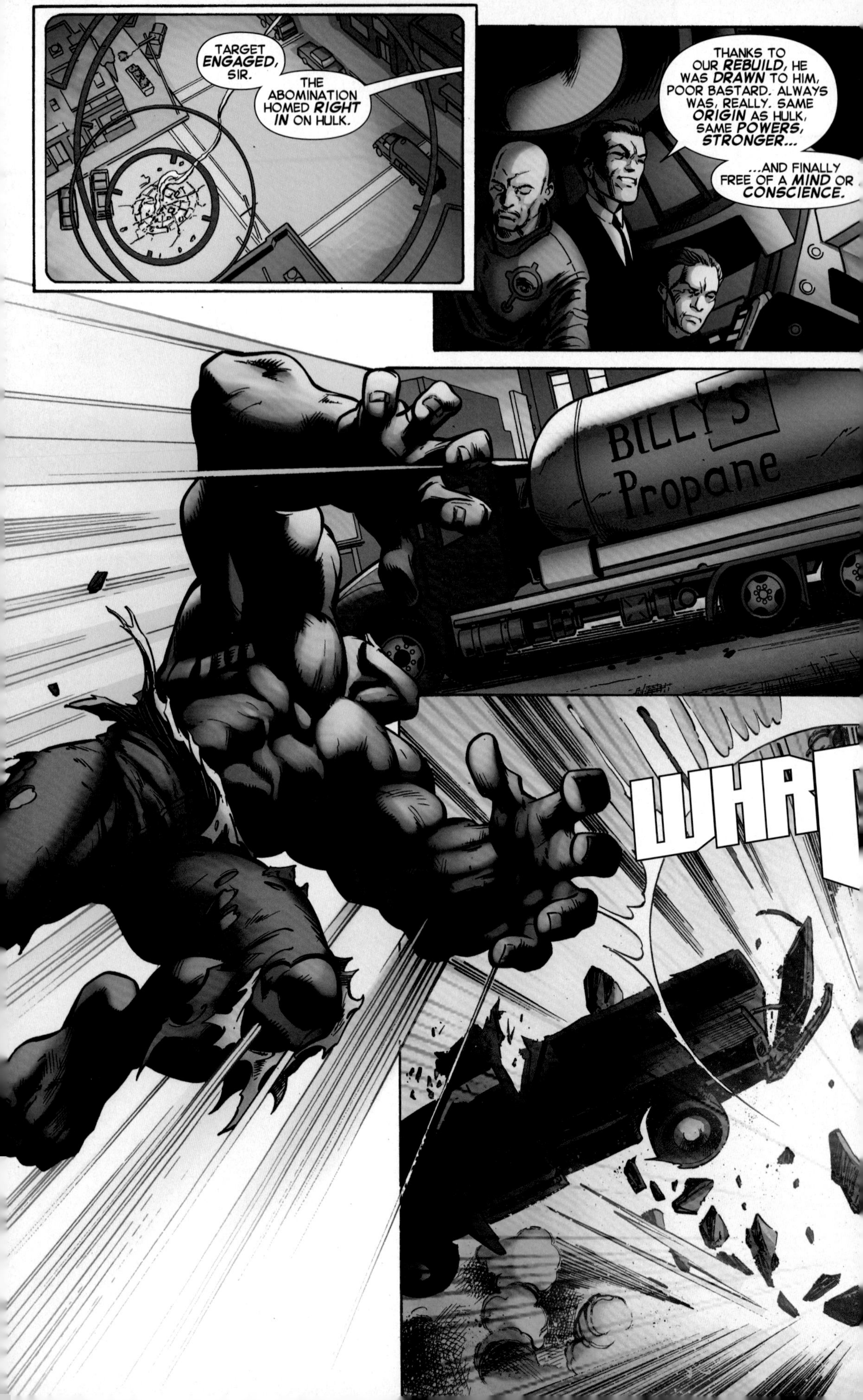
TARGET ENGAGED, SIR.
THE ABOMINATION HOMED RIGHT IN ON HULK.
THANKS TO OUR REBUILD, HE WAS DRAWN TO HIM, POOR BASTARD. ALWAYS WAS, REALLY. SAME ORIGIN AS HULK, SAME POWERS, STRONGER...
...AND FINALLY FREE OF A MIND OR CONSCIENCE.
BILLY'S Propane

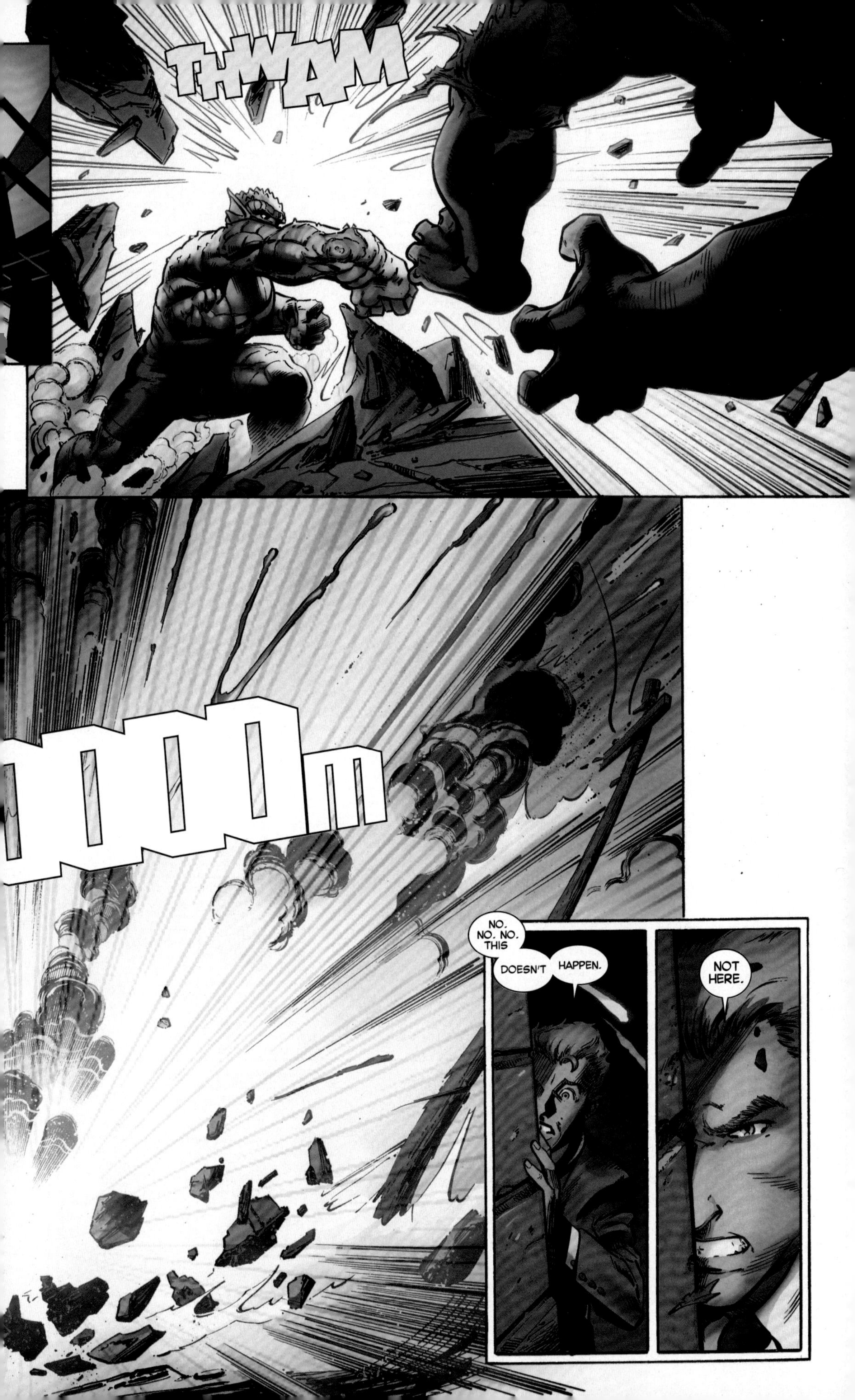
THWAM
NO. NO. NO. THIS
DOESN'T
HAPPEN.
NOT HERE.

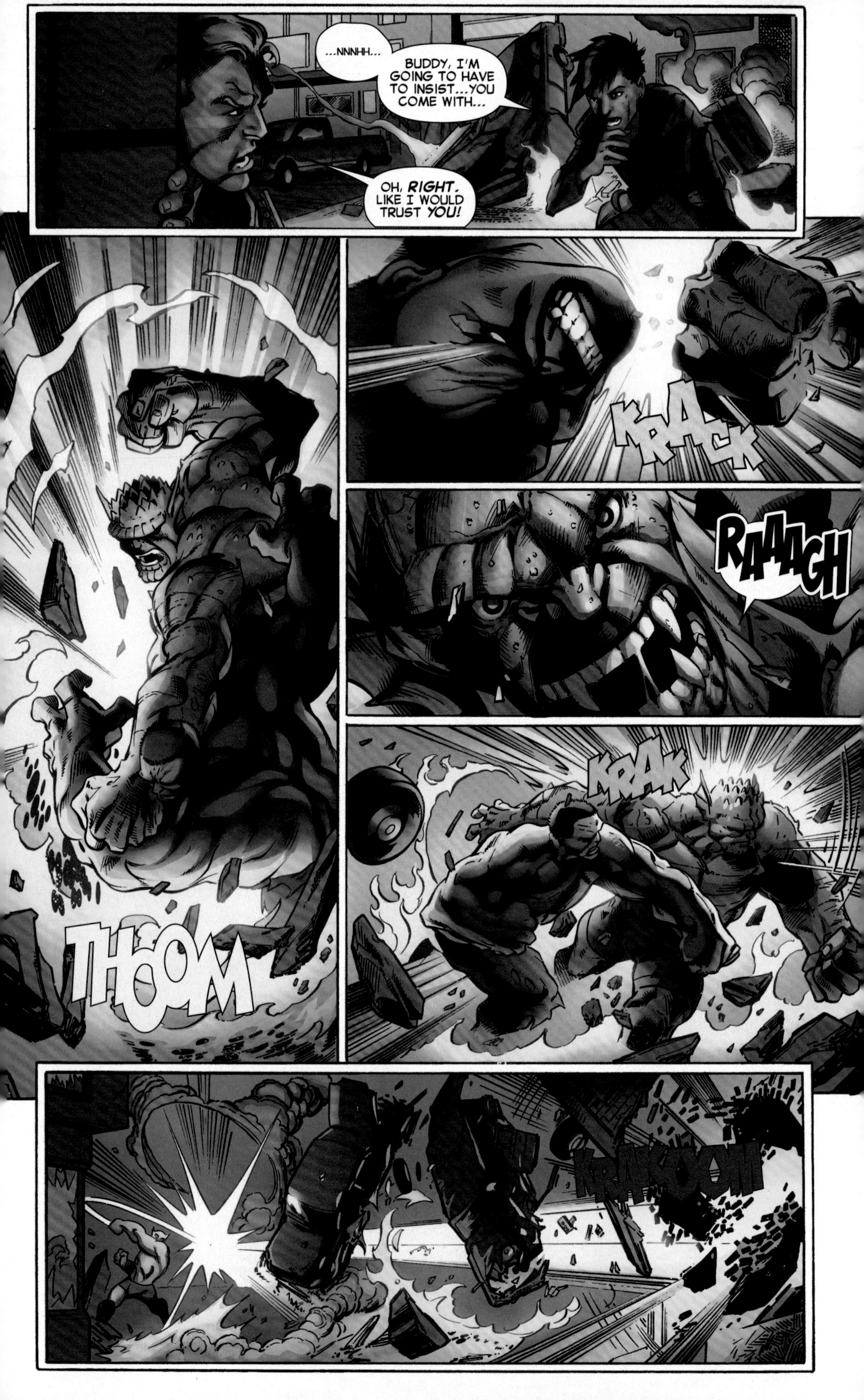
...NNNHH...
BUDDY, I'M GOING TO HAVE TO INSIST...YOU COME WITH...
OH, RIGHT. LIKE I WOULD TRUST YOU!
THOOM
KRACK
RAAAGH
KRAK
KRAKOOM

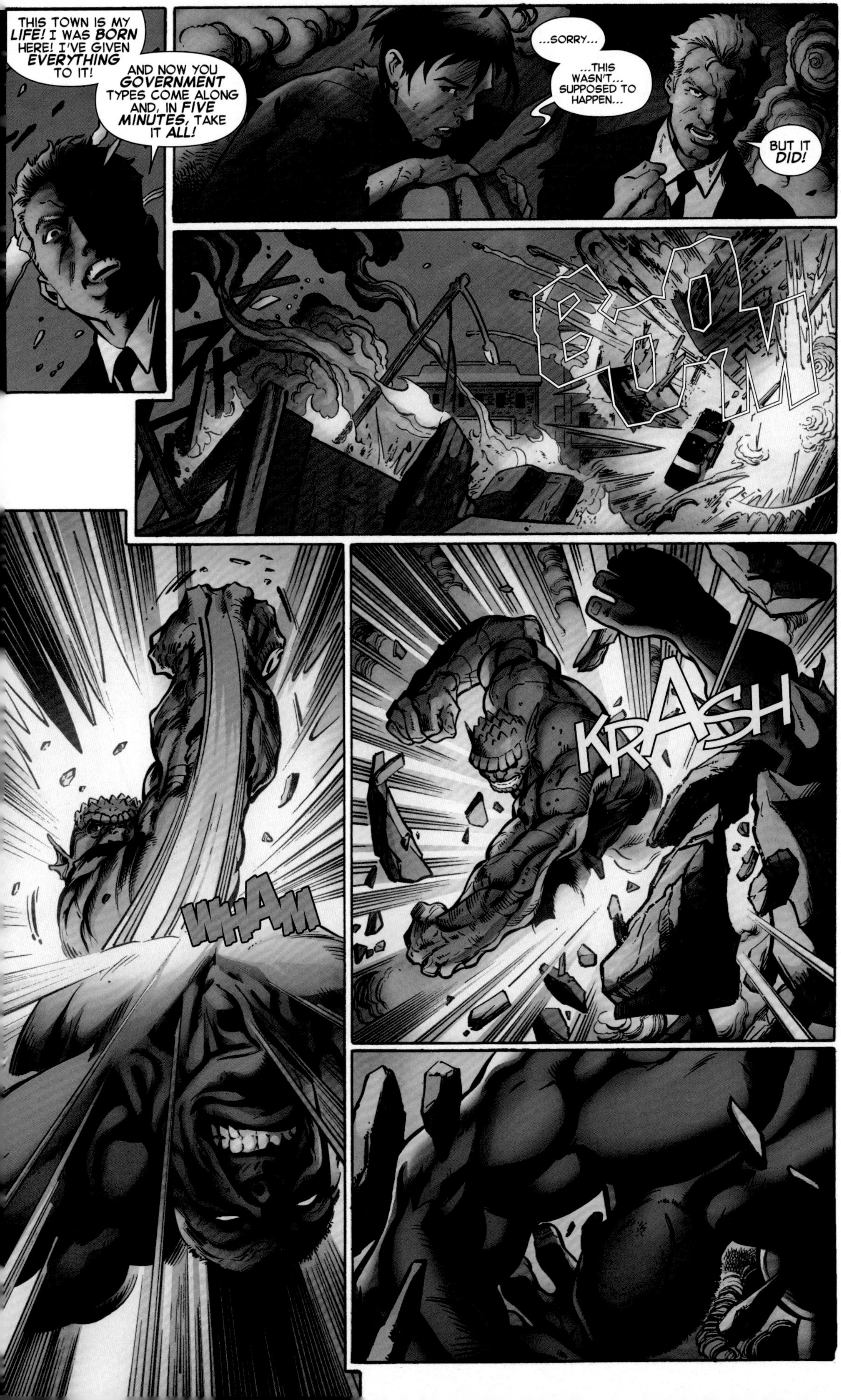
THIS TOWN IS MY LIFE! I WAS BORN HERE! I'VE GIVEN EVERYTHING TO IT!
AND NOW YOU GOVERNMENT TYPES COME ALONG AND, IN FIVE MINUTES, TAKE IT ALL!
...SORRY...
...THIS WASN'T... SUPPOSED TO HAPPEN...
BUT IT DID!
BOOOM
WHAM
KRASH

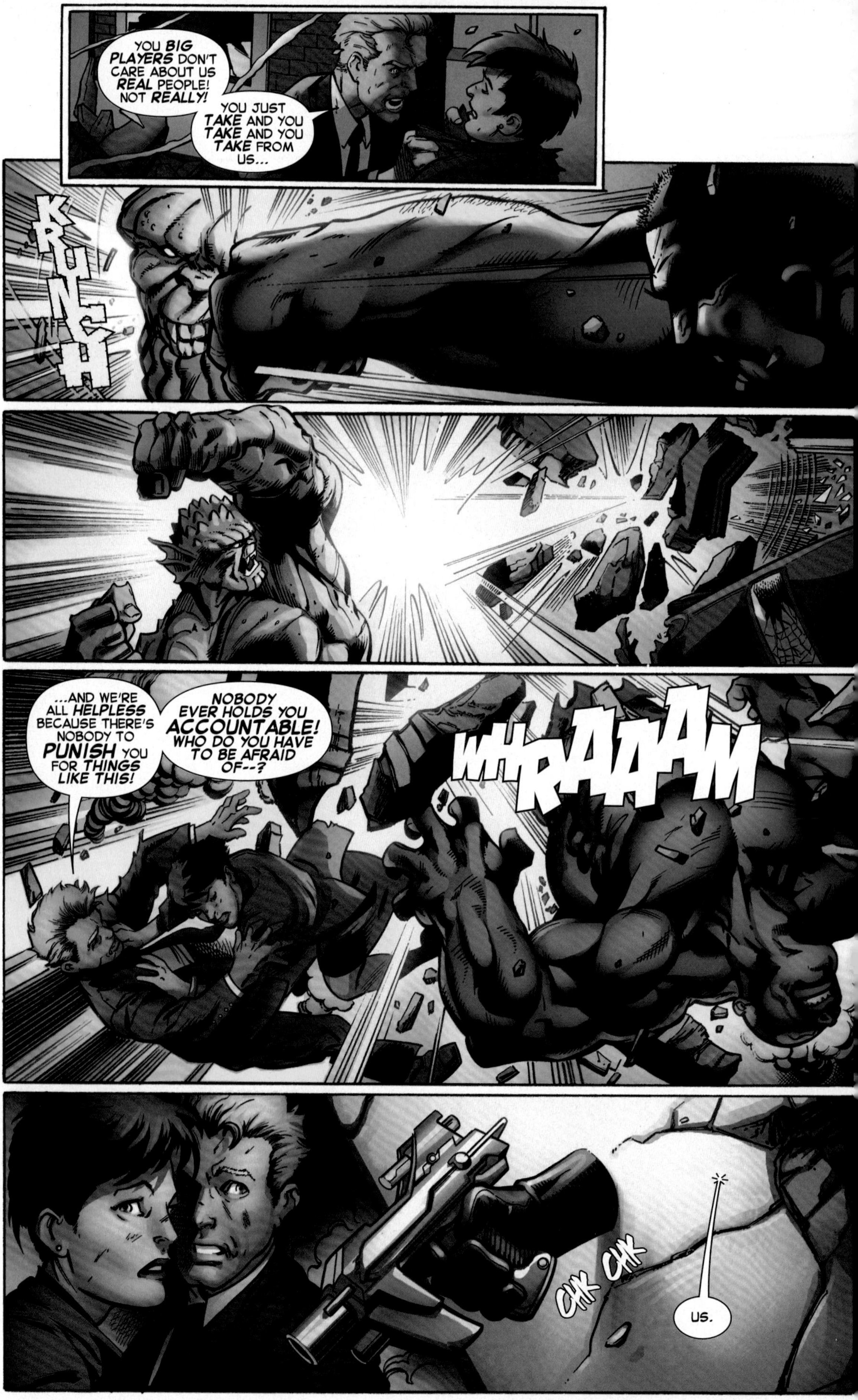
YOU BIG PLAYERS DON'T CARE ABOUT US REAL PEOPLE! NOT REALLY!
YOU JUST TAKE AND YOU TAKE AND YOU TAKE FROM US...
KRUNCH
...AND WE'RE ALL HELPLESS BECAUSE THERE'S NOBODY TO PUNISH YOU FOR THINGS LIKE THIS!
NOBODY EVER HOLDS YOU ACCOUNTABLE! WHO DO YOU HAVE TO BE AFRAID OF--?
WHRAAAAM
CHK CHK
US.

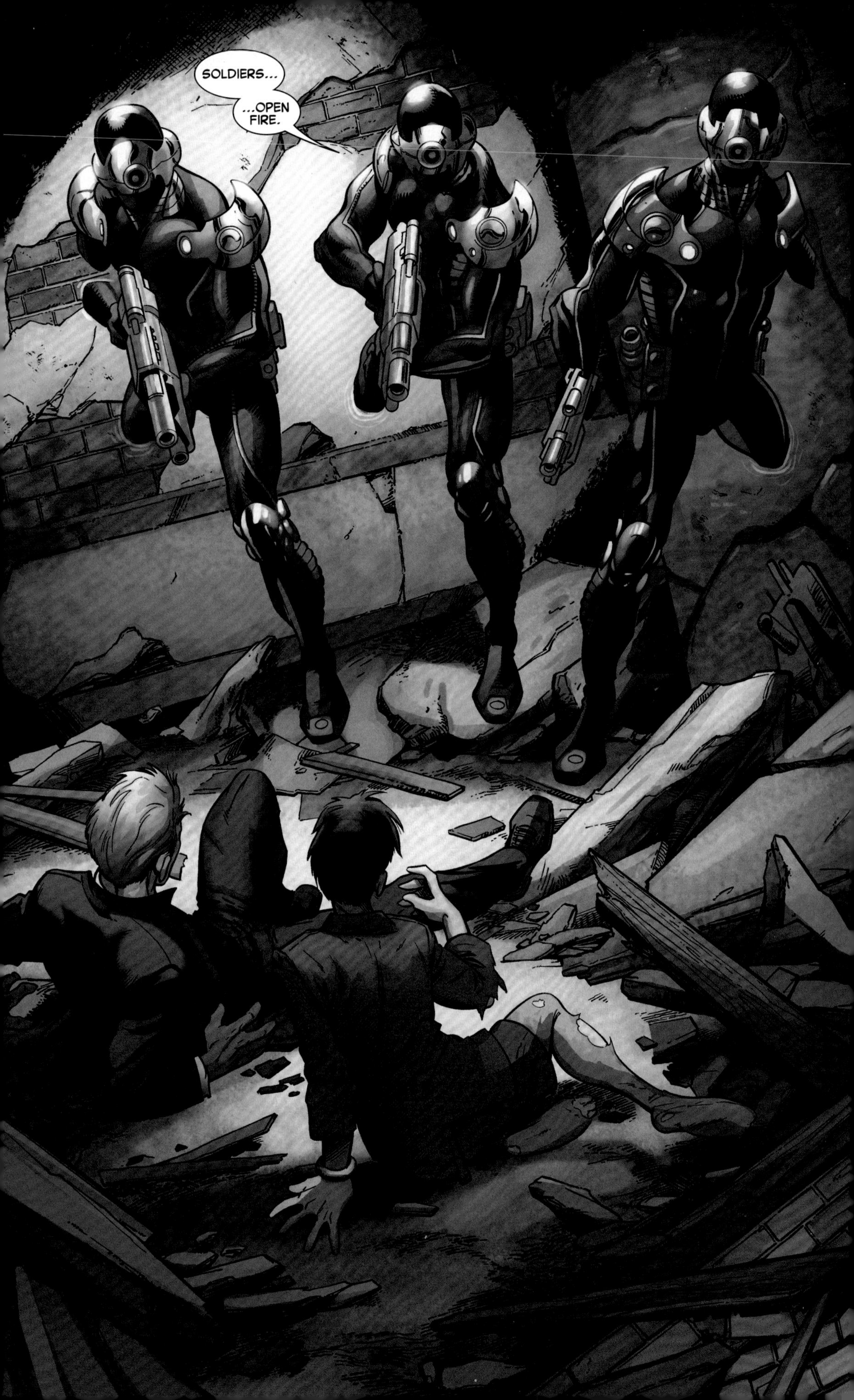
SOLDIERS...
...OPEN FIRE.

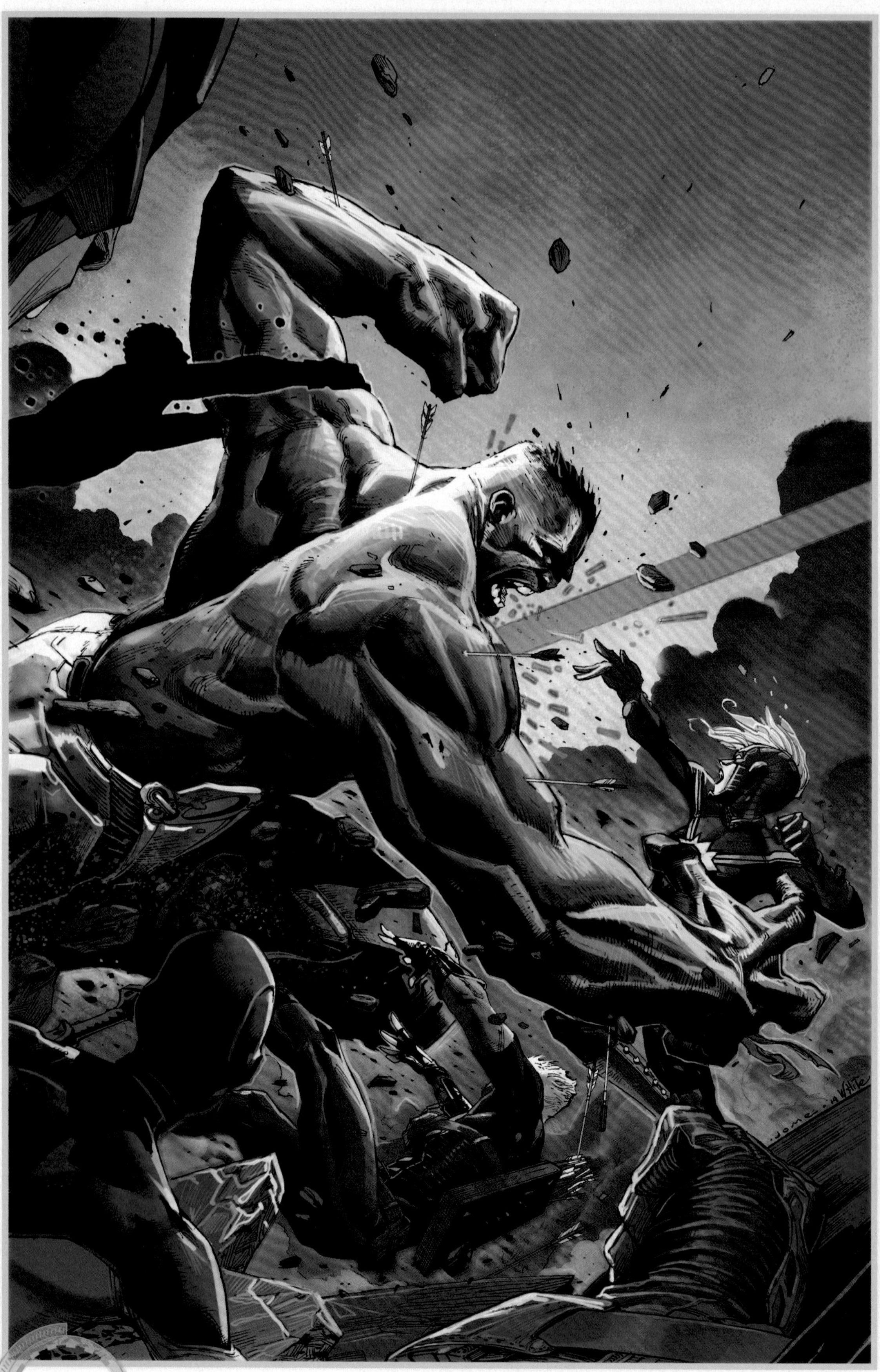

3

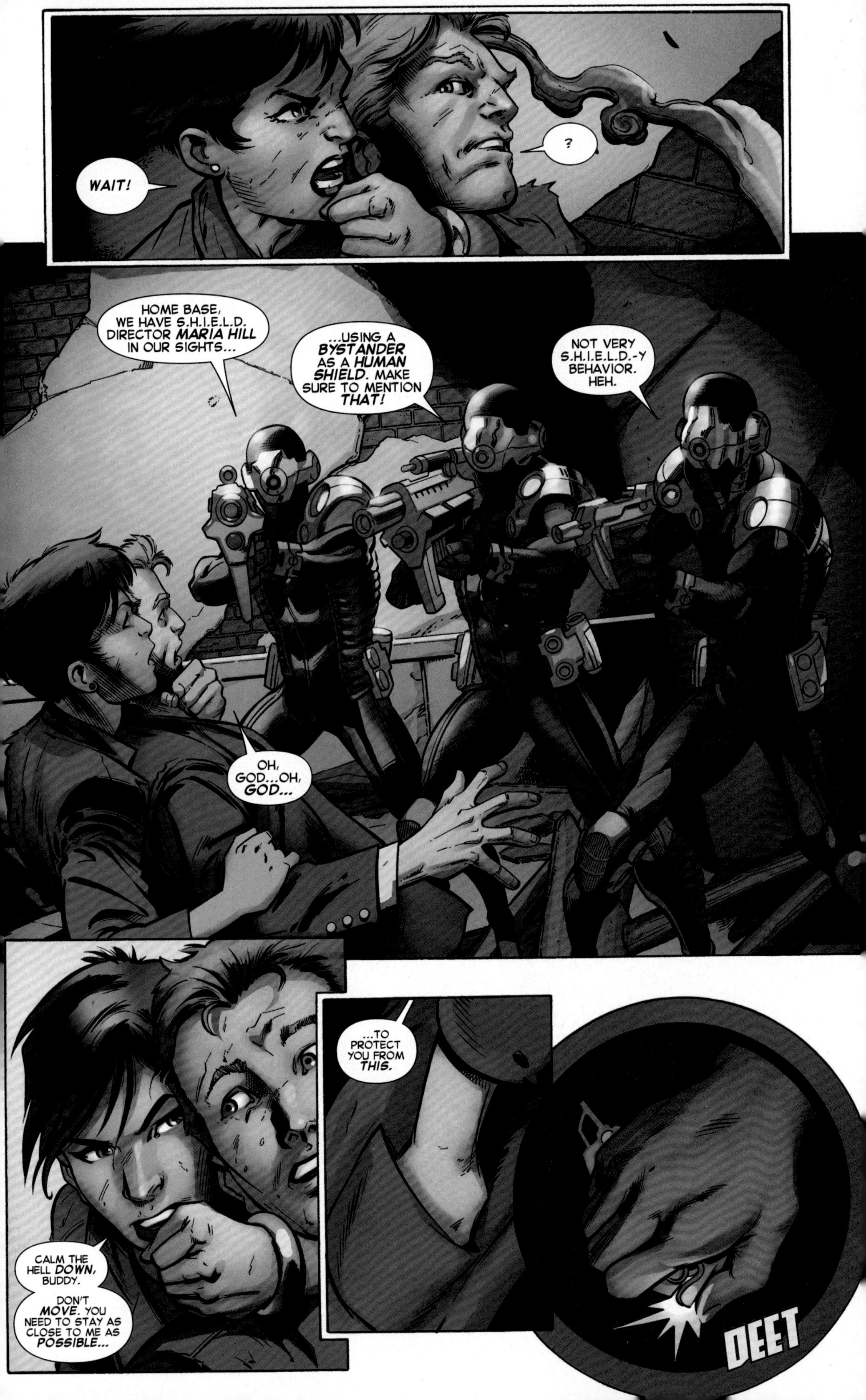
WAIT!
?
HOME BASE, WE HAVE S.H.I.E.L.D. DIRECTOR MARIA HILL IN OUR SIGHTS...
...USING A BYSTANDER AS A HUMAN SHIELD. MAKE SURE TO MENTION THAT!
NOT VERY S.H.I.E.L.D.-Y BEHAVIOR. HEH.
OH, GOD...OH, GOD...
CALM THE HELL DOWN, BUDDY.
DON'T MOVE. YOU NEED TO STAY AS CLOSE TO ME AS POSSIBLE...
...TO PROTECT YOU FROM THIS.
DEET

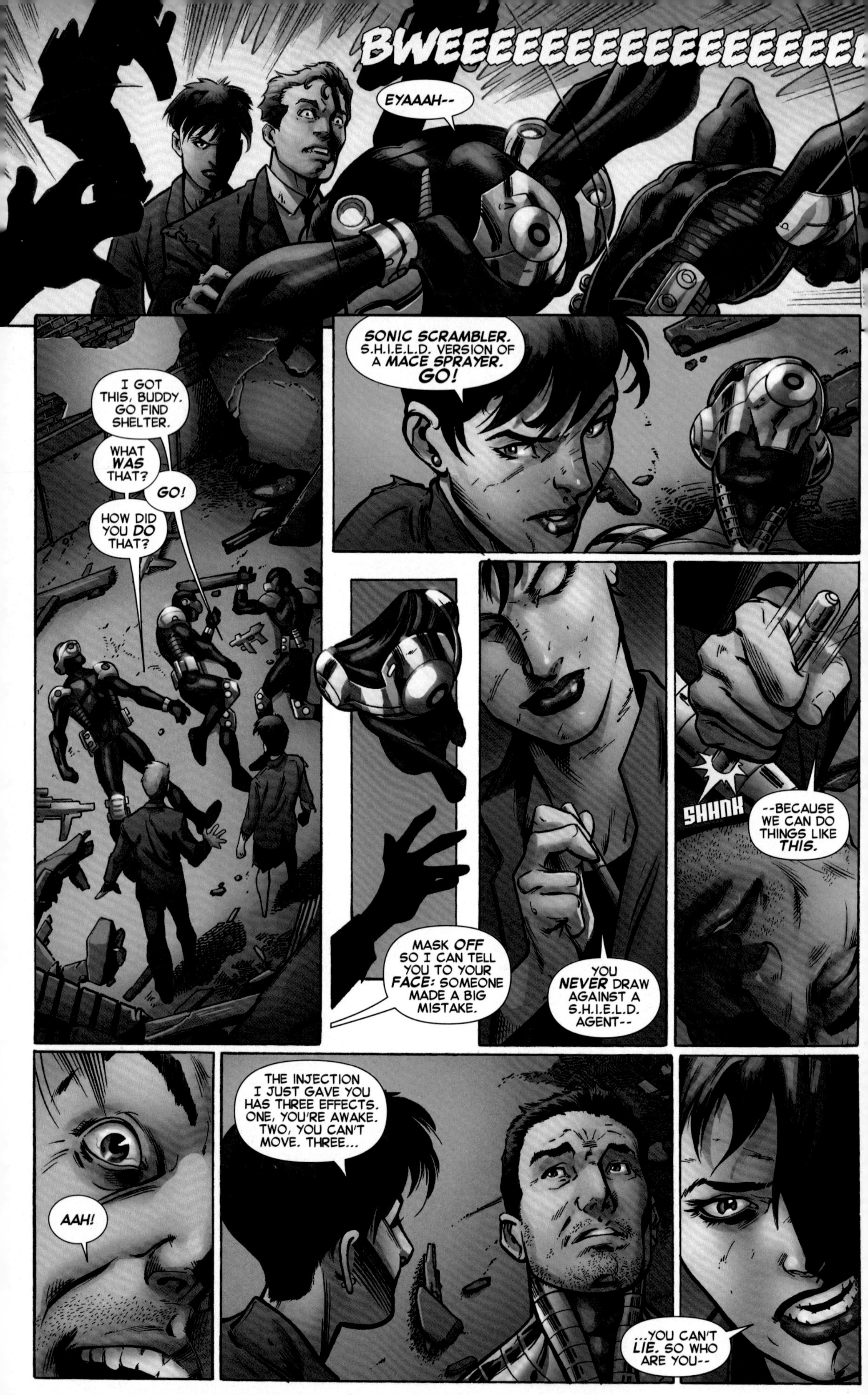
BWEEEEEEEEEEEEEEEE
EYAAAH--
I GOT THIS, BUDDY. GO FIND SHELTER.
WHAT WAS THAT?
GO!
HOW DID YOU DO THAT?
SONIC SCRAMBLER. S.H.I.E.L.D. VERSION OF A MACE SPRAYER. GO!
MASK OFF SO I CAN TELL YOU TO YOUR FACE: SOMEONE MADE A BIG MISTAKE.
YOU NEVER DRAW AGAINST A S.H.I.E.L.D. AGENT--
SHHNK
--BECAUSE WE CAN DO THINGS LIKE THIS.
AAH!
THE INJECTION I JUST GAVE YOU HAS THREE EFFECTS. ONE, YOU'RE AWAKE. TWO, YOU CAN'T MOVE. THREE...
...YOU CAN'T LIE. SO WHO ARE YOU--

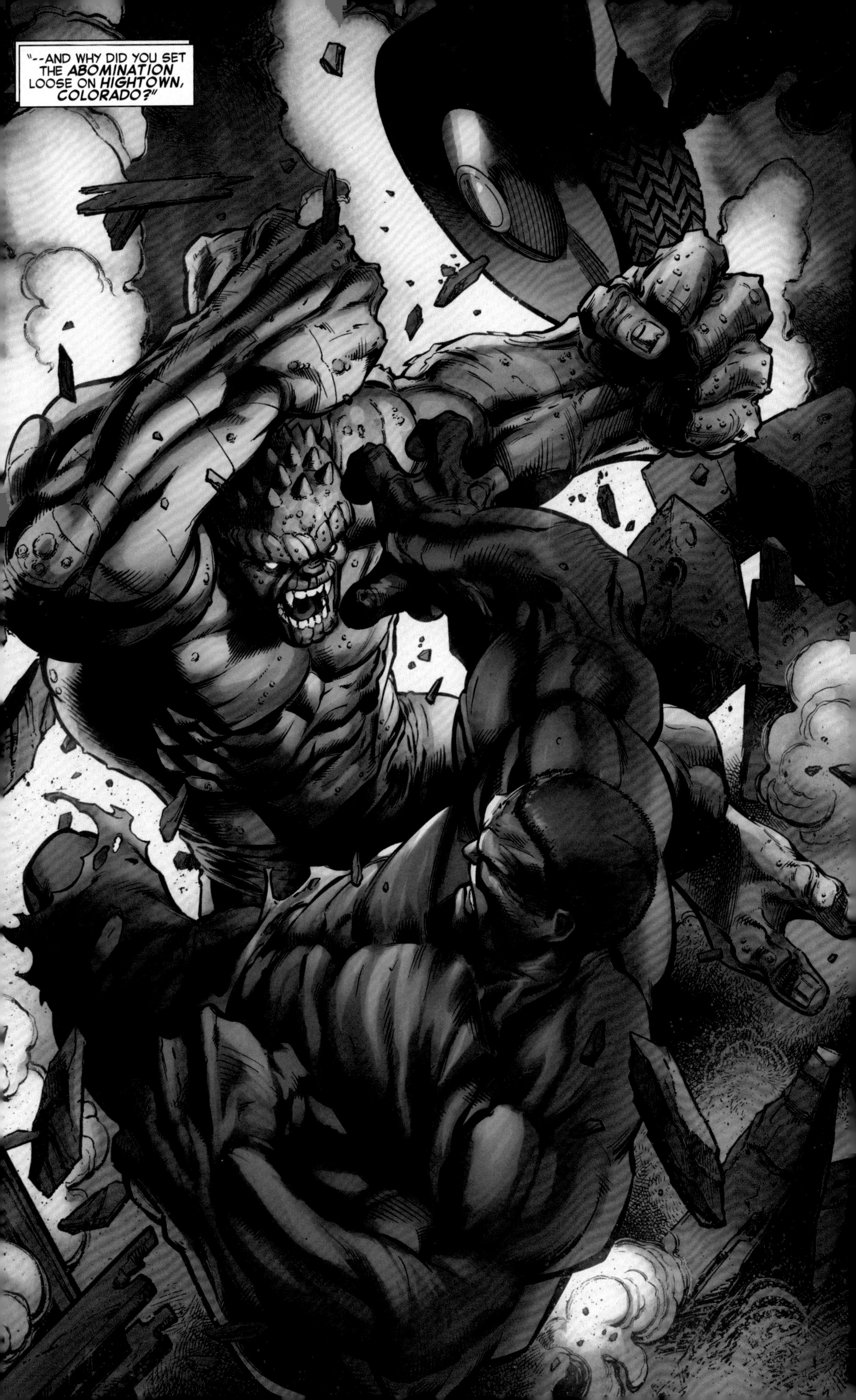
"--AND WHY DID YOU SET THE ABOMINATION LOOSE ON HIGHTOWN, COLORADO?"

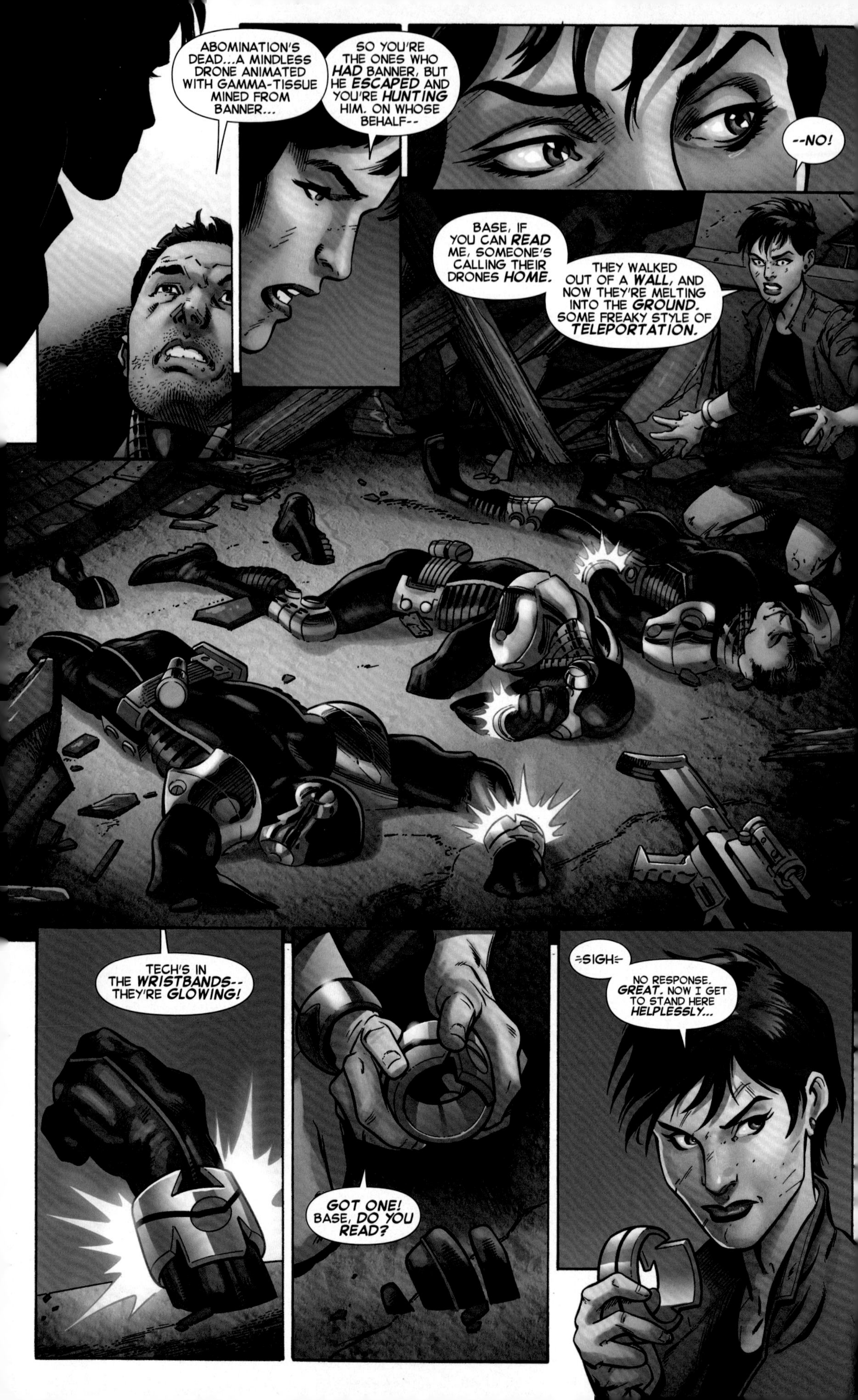
ABOMINATION'S DEAD...A MINDLESS DRONE ANIMATED WITH GAMMA-TISSUE MINED FROM BANNER...
SO YOU'RE THE ONES WHO HAD BANNER, BUT HE ESCAPED AND YOU'RE HUNTING HIM. ON WHOSE BEHALF--
--NO!
BASE, IF YOU CAN READ ME, SOMEONE'S CALLING THEIR DRONES HOME.
THEY WALKED OUT OF A WALL, AND NOW THEY'RE MELTING INTO THE GROUND. SOME FREAKY STYLE OF TELEPORTATION.
TECH'S IN THE WRISTBANDS-- THEY'RE GLOWING!
GOT ONE! BASE, DO YOU READ?
=SIGH=
NO RESPONSE. GREAT. NOW I GET TO STAND HERE HELPLESSLY...

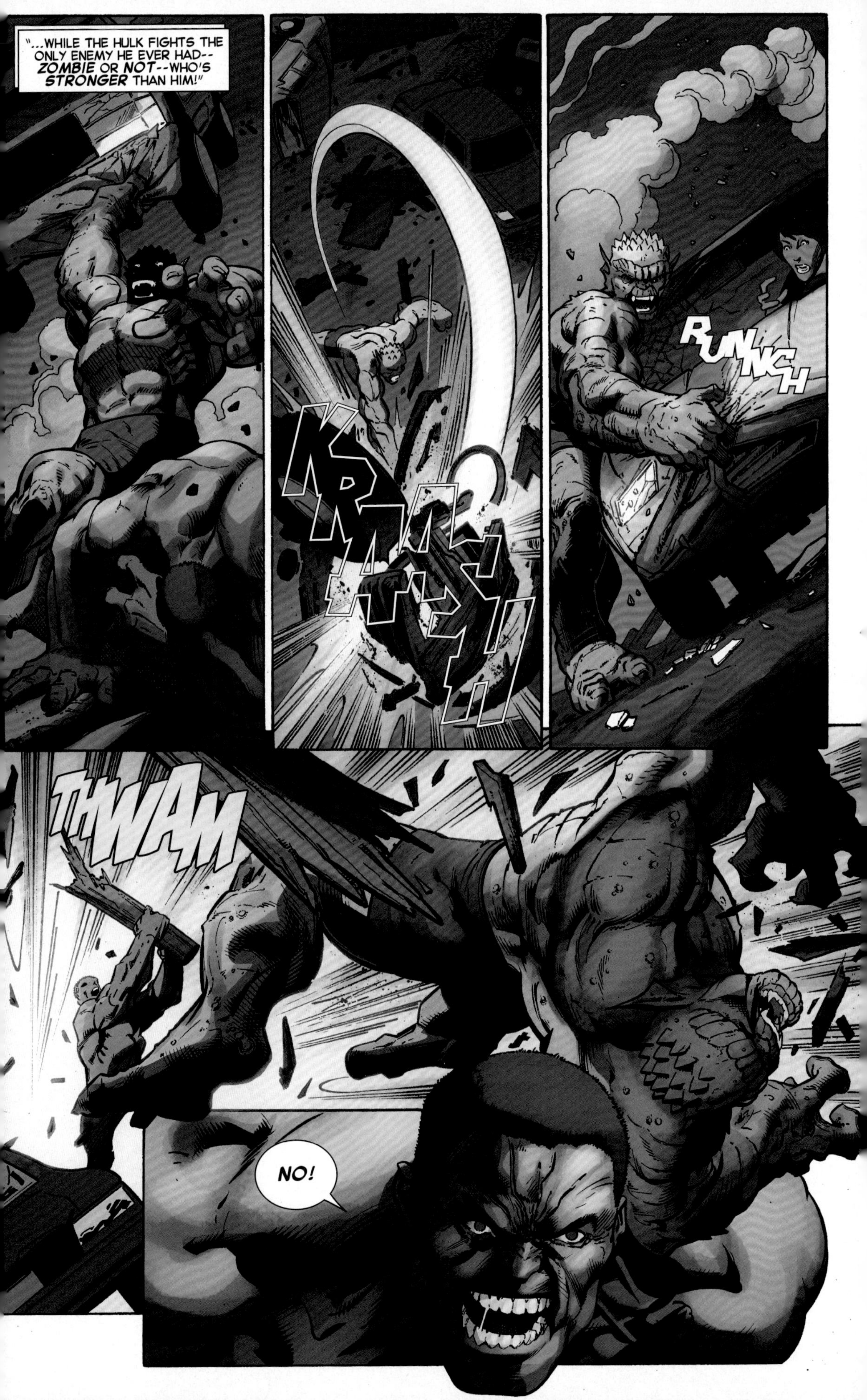
"...WHILE THE HULK FIGHTS THE ONLY ENEMY HE EVER HAD-- ZOMBIE OR NOT--WHO'S STRONGER THAN HIM!"
KRAASH
RUNNCH
THWAM
NO!

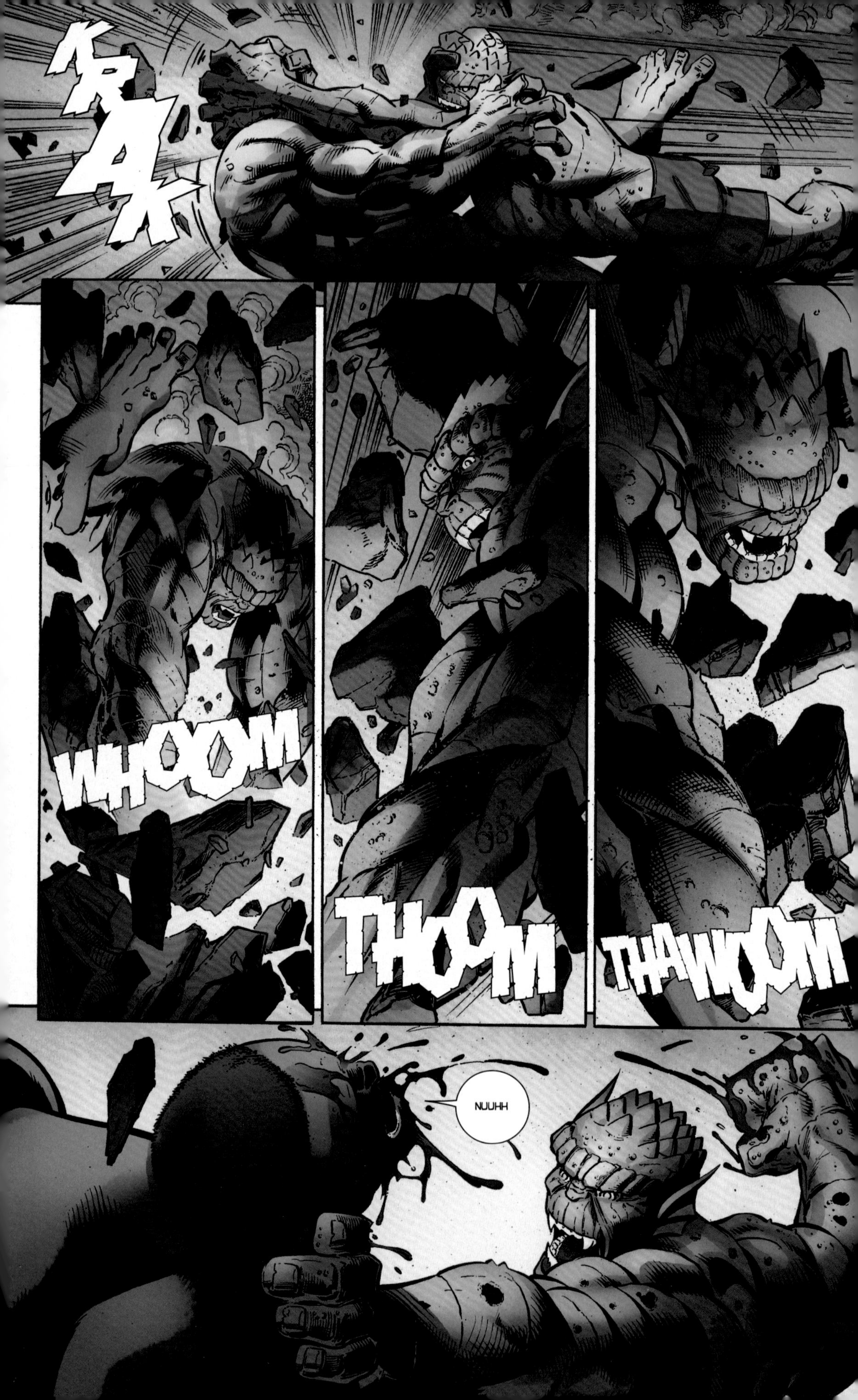

KRAK
WHOOM
THOOM
THAWOOM
NUUHH

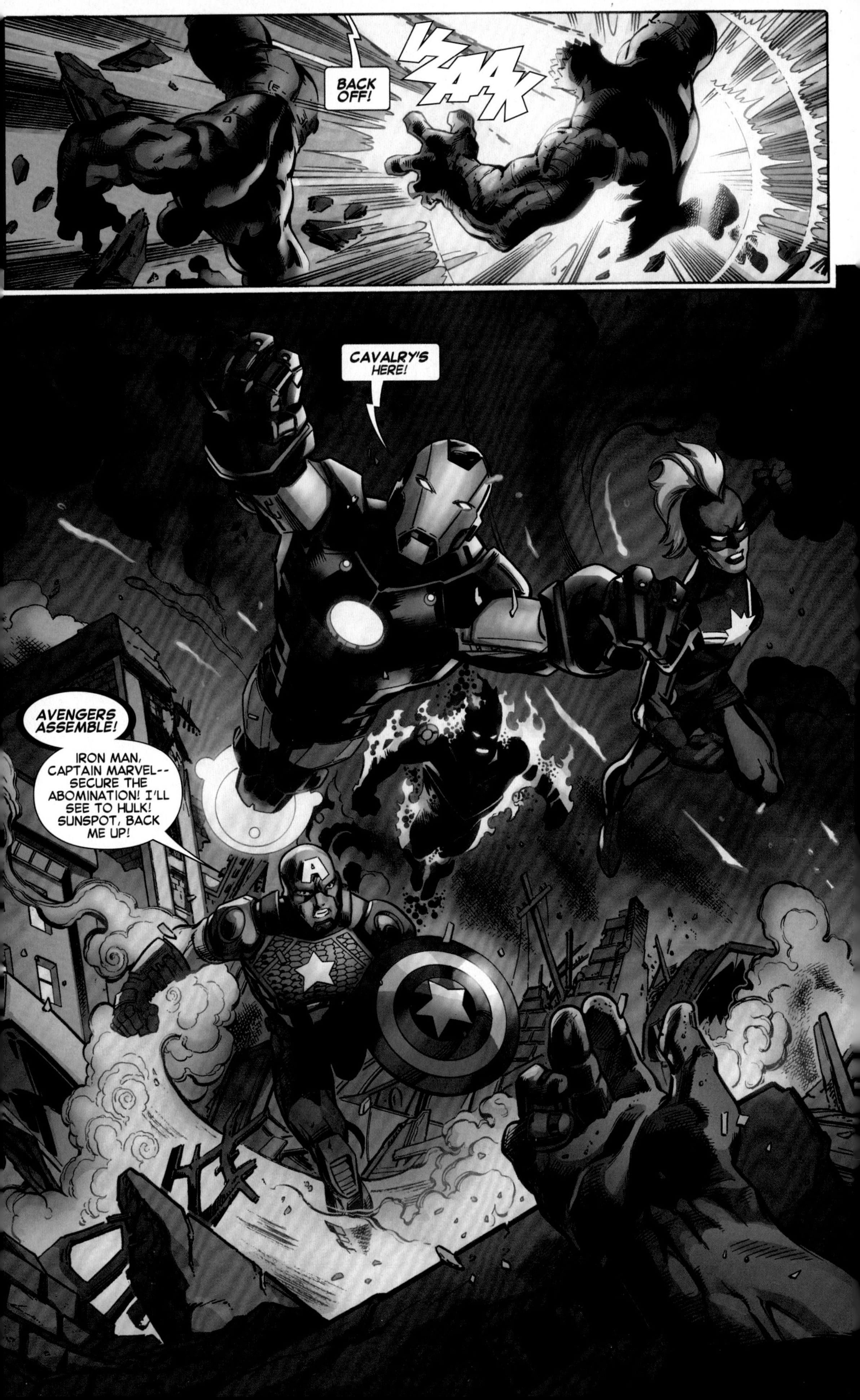
BACK OFF!
VZAAK
CAVALRY'S HERE!
AVENGERS ASSEMBLE!
IRON MAN, CAPTAIN MARVEL-- SECURE THE ABOMINATION! I'LL SEE TO HULK! SUNSPOT, BACK ME UP!

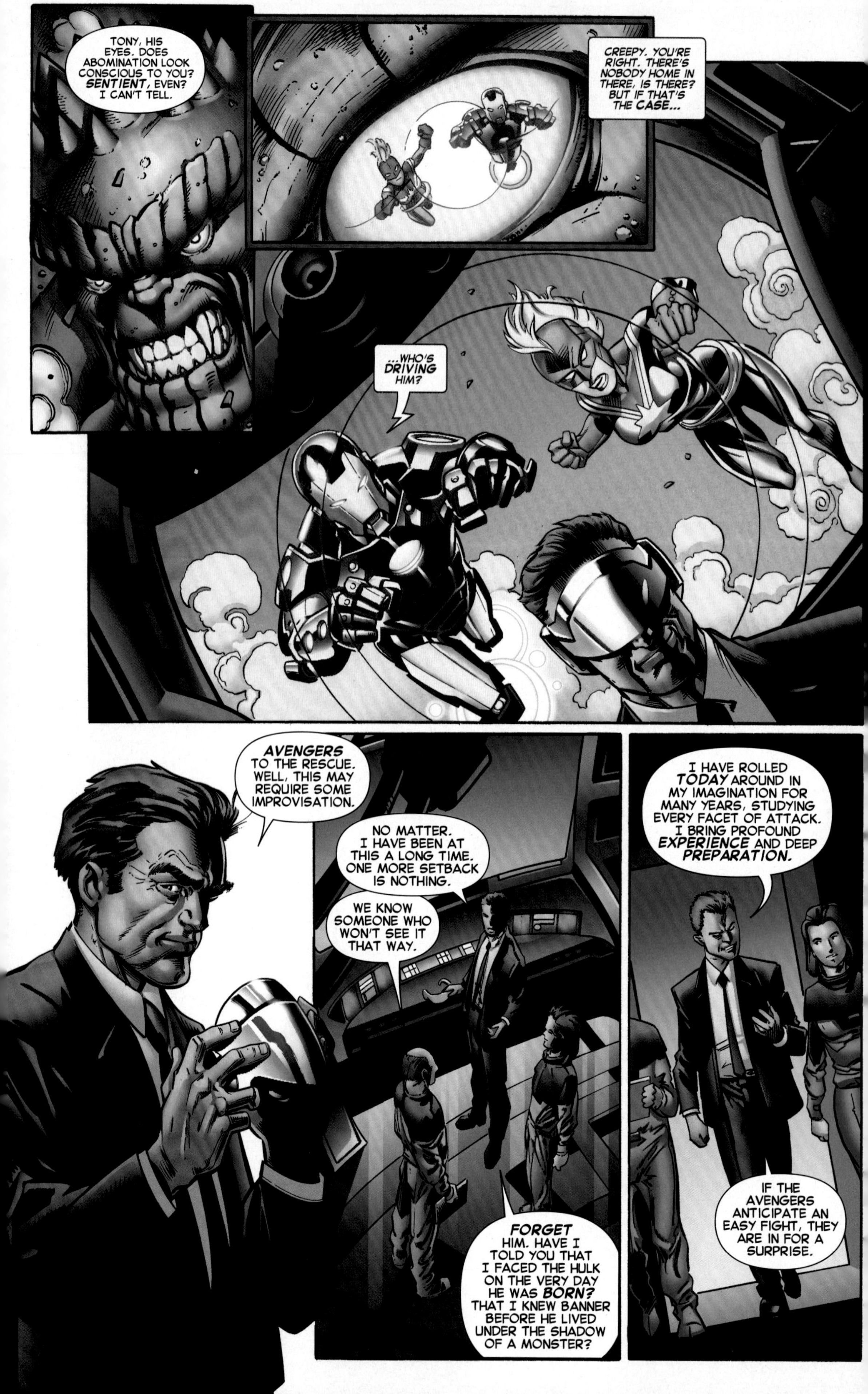
TONY, HIS EYES. DOES ABOMINATION LOOK CONSCIOUS TO YOU? SENTIENT, EVEN? I CAN'T TELL.
CREEPY. YOU'RE RIGHT. THERE'S NOBODY HOME IN THERE, IS THERE? BUT IF THAT'S THE CASE...
...WHO'S DRIVING HIM?
AVENGERS TO THE RESCUE. WELL, THIS MAY REQUIRE SOME IMPROVISATION.
NO MATTER. I HAVE BEEN AT THIS A LONG TIME. ONE MORE SETBACK IS NOTHING.
WE KNOW SOMEONE WHO WON'T SEE IT THAT WAY.
FORGET HIM. HAVE I TOLD YOU THAT I FACED THE HULK ON THE VERY DAY HE WAS BORN? THAT I KNEW BANNER BEFORE HE LIVED UNDER THE SHADOW OF A MONSTER?
I HAVE ROLLED TODAY AROUND IN MY IMAGINATION FOR MANY YEARS, STUDYING EVERY FACET OF ATTACK. I BRING PROFOUND EXPERIENCE AND DEEP PREPARATION.
IF THE AVENGERS ANTICIPATE AN EASY FIGHT, THEY ARE IN FOR A SURPRISE.

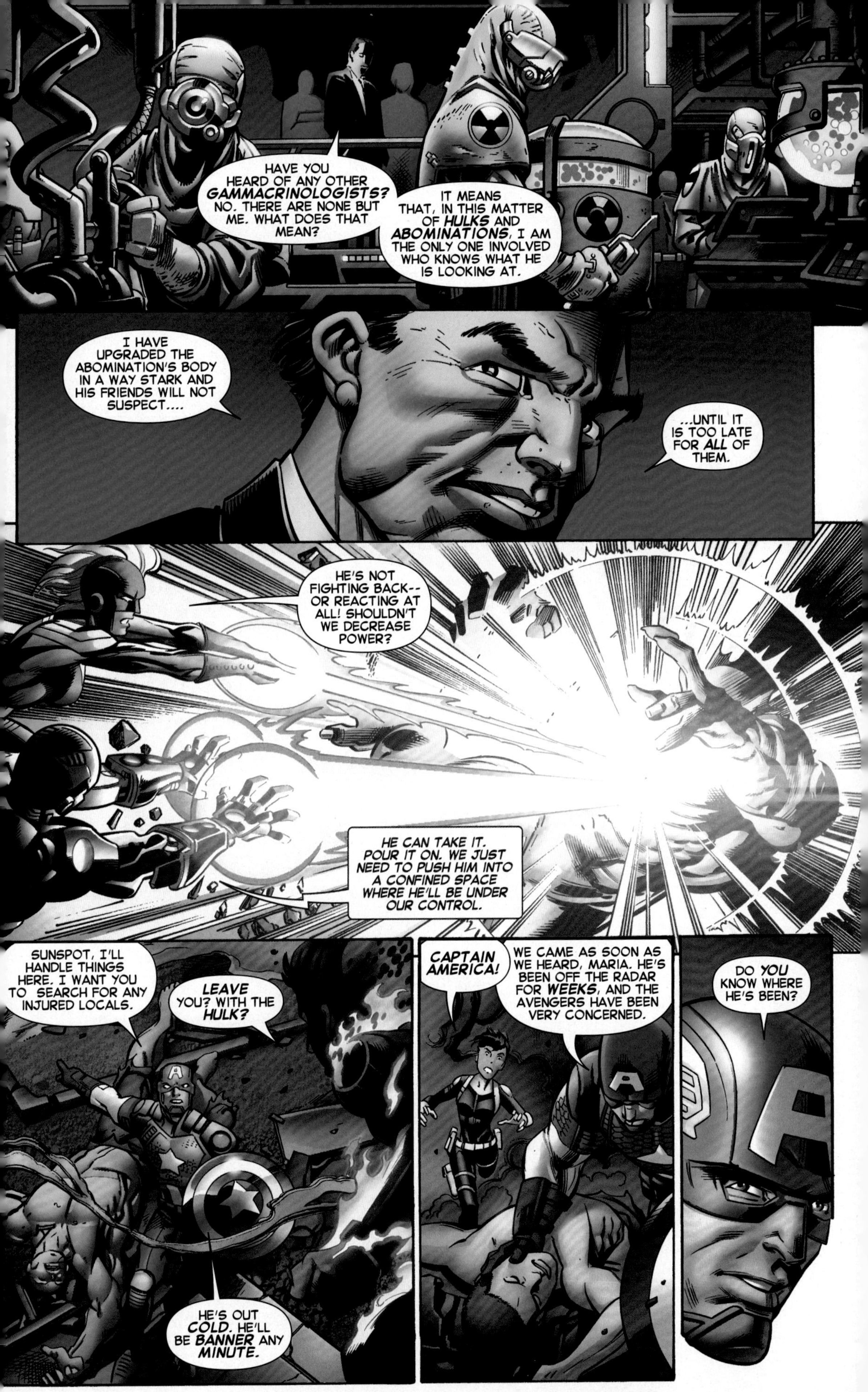
HAVE YOU HEARD OF ANY OTHER GAMMACRINOLOGISTS? NO. THERE ARE NONE BUT ME. WHAT DOES THAT MEAN?
IT MEANS THAT, IN THIS MATTER OF HULKS AND ABOMINATIONS, I AM THE ONLY ONE INVOLVED WHO KNOWS WHAT HE IS LOOKING AT.
I HAVE UPGRADED THE ABOMINATION'S BODY IN A WAY STARK AND HIS FRIENDS WILL NOT SUSPECT....
...UNTIL IT IS TOO LATE FOR ALL OF THEM.
HE'S NOT FIGHTING BACK-- OR REACTING AT ALL! SHOULDN'T WE DECREASE POWER?
HE CAN TAKE IT. POUR IT ON. WE JUST NEED TO PUSH HIM INTO A CONFINED SPACE WHERE HE'LL BE UNDER OUR CONTROL.
SUNSPOT, I'LL HANDLE THINGS HERE. I WANT YOU TO SEARCH FOR ANY INJURED LOCALS.
LEAVE YOU? WITH THE HULK?
HE'S OUT COLD. HE'LL BE BANNER ANY MINUTE.
CAPTAIN AMERICA!
WE CAME AS SOON AS WE HEARD, MARIA. HE'S BEEN OFF THE RADAR FOR WEEKS, AND THE AVENGERS HAVE BEEN VERY CONCERNED.
DO YOU KNOW WHERE HE'S BEEN?

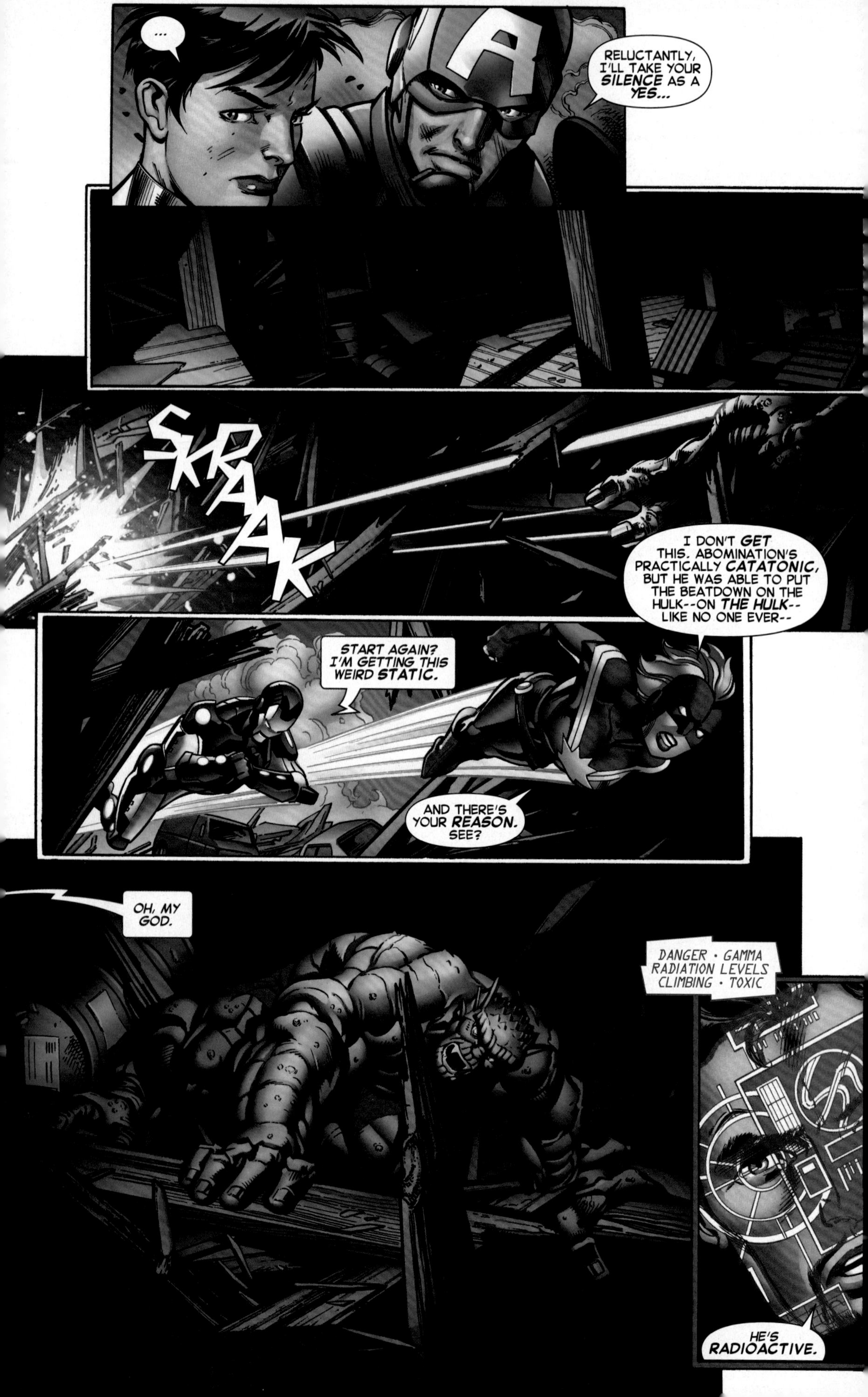
...
RELUCTANTLY, I'LL TAKE YOUR SILENCE AS A YES...
SKRAAK
I DON'T GET THIS. ABOMINATION'S PRACTICALLY CATATONIC, BUT HE WAS ABLE TO PUT THE BEATDOWN ON THE HULK--ON THE HULK--LIKE NO ONE EVER--
START AGAIN? I'M GETTING THIS WEIRD STATIC.
AND THERE'S YOUR REASON. SEE?
OH, MY GOD.
DANGER • GAMMA RADIATION LEVELS CLIMBING • TOXIC
HE'S RADIOACTIVE.

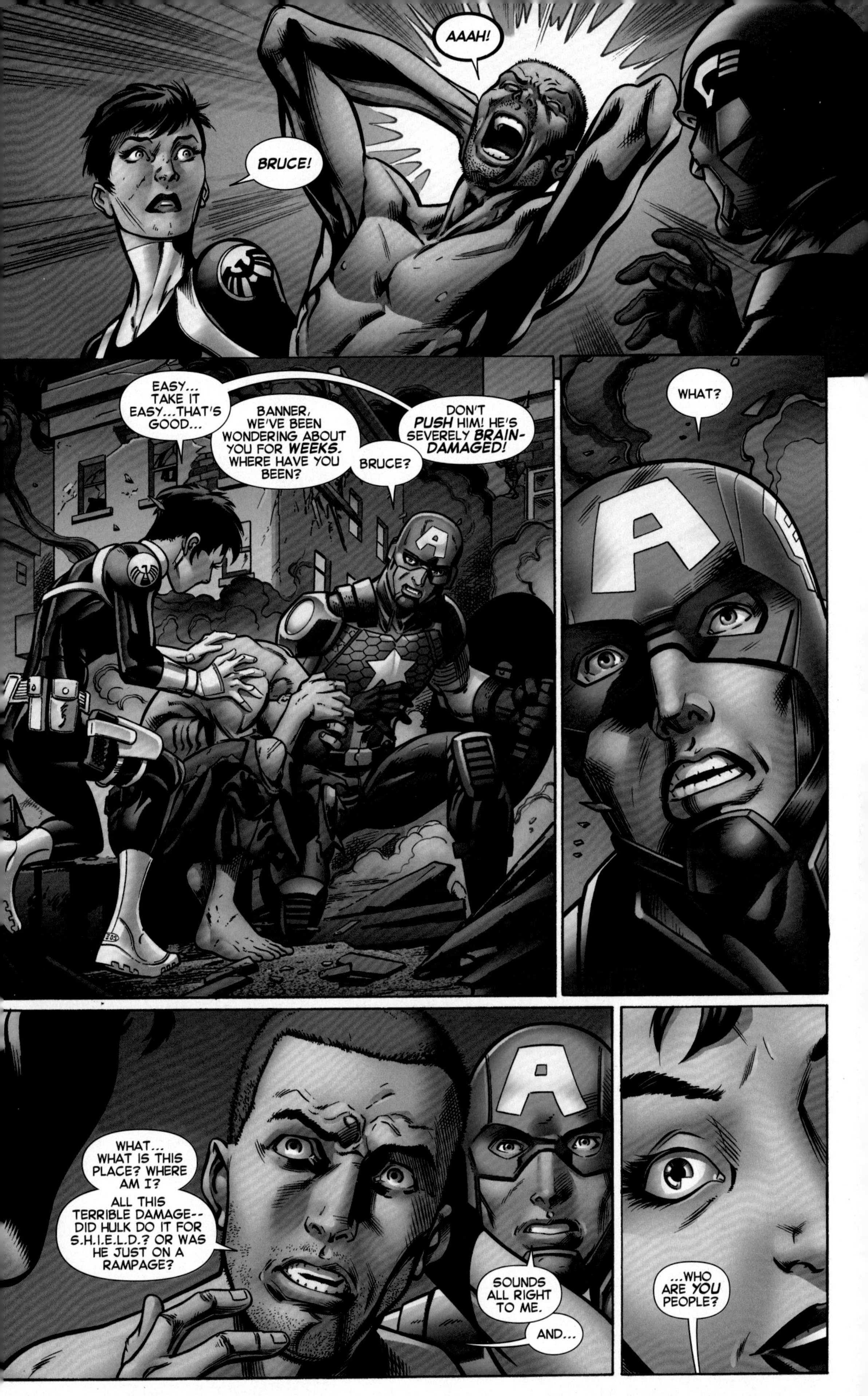
AAAH!
BRUCE!
EASY... TAKE IT EASY...THAT'S GOOD...
BANNER, WE'VE BEEN WONDERING ABOUT YOU FOR WEEKS. WHERE HAVE YOU BEEN?
BRUCE?
DON'T PUSH HIM! HE'S SEVERELY BRAIN-DAMAGED!
WHAT?
WHAT... WHAT IS THIS PLACE? WHERE AM I?
ALL THIS TERRIBLE DAMAGE-- DID HULK DO IT FOR S.H.I.E.L.D.? OR WAS HE JUST ON A RAMPAGE?
SOUNDS ALL RIGHT TO ME.
AND...
...WHO ARE YOU PEOPLE?

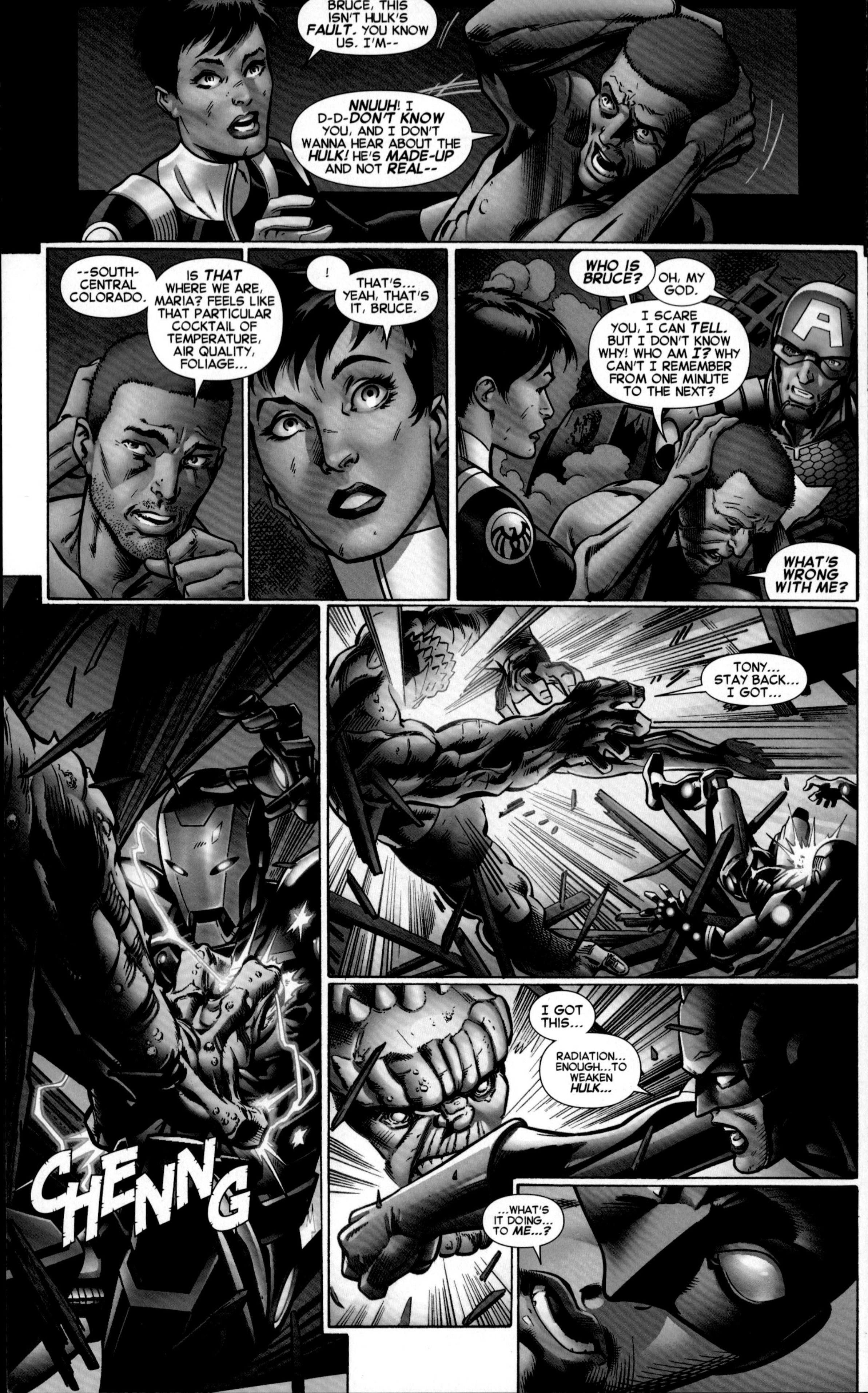
BRUCE, THIS ISN'T HULK'S FAULT. YOU KNOW US. I'M--
NNUUH! I D-D-DON'T KNOW YOU, AND I DON'T WANNA HEAR ABOUT THE HULK! HE'S MADE-UP AND NOT REAL--
--SOUTH-CENTRAL COLORADO.
IS THAT WHERE WE ARE, MARIA? FEELS LIKE THAT PARTICULAR COCKTAIL OF TEMPERATURE, AIR QUALITY, FOLIAGE...
!
THAT'S... YEAH, THAT'S IT, BRUCE.
WHO IS BRUCE?
OH, MY GOD.
I SCARE YOU, I CAN TELL. BUT I DON'T KNOW WHY! WHO AM I? WHY CAN'T I REMEMBER FROM ONE MINUTE TO THE NEXT?
WHAT'S WRONG WITH ME?
CHENNG
TONY... STAY BACK... I GOT...
I GOT THIS...
RADIATION... ENOUGH...TO WEAKEN HULK...
...WHAT'S IT DOING... TO ME...?

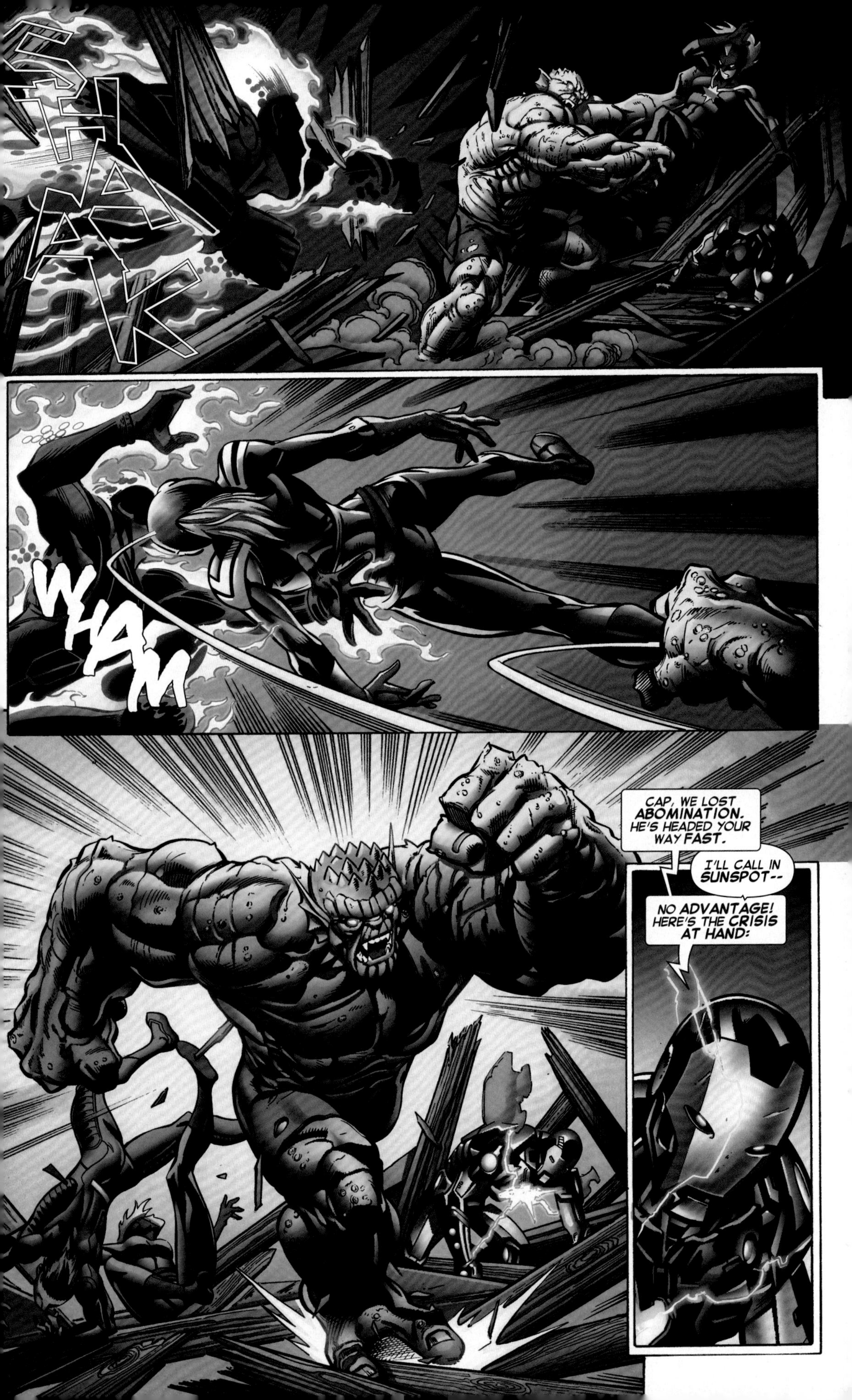
SHAAK
WHAM
CAP, WE LOST ABOMINATION. HE'S HEADED YOUR WAY FAST.
I'LL CALL IN SUNSPOT--
NO ADVANTAGE! HERE'S THE CRISIS AT HAND:

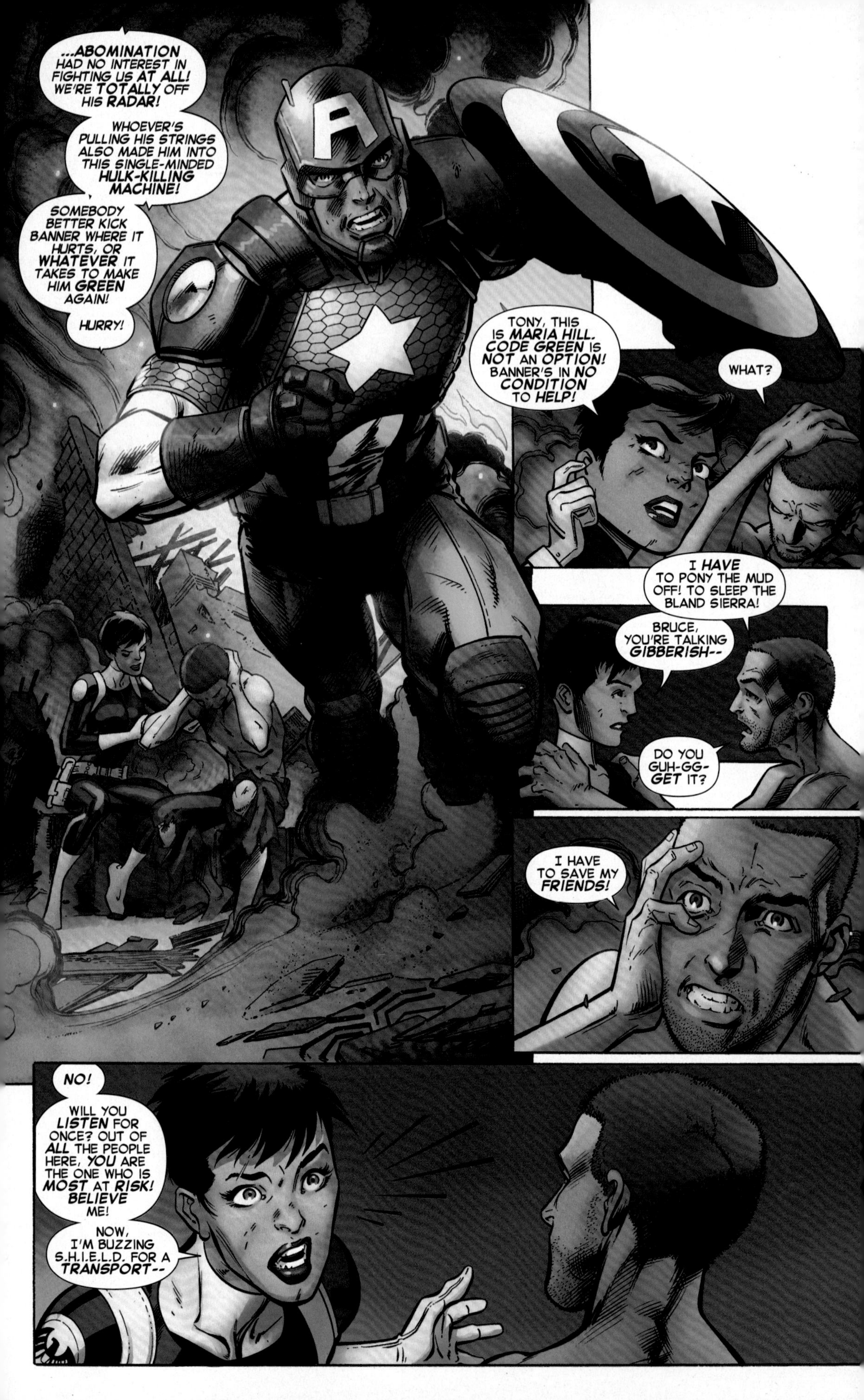
...ABOMINATION HAD NO INTEREST IN FIGHTING US AT ALL! WE'RE TOTALLY OFF HIS RADAR!
WHOEVER'S PULLING HIS STRINGS ALSO MADE HIM INTO THIS SINGLE-MINDED HULK-KILLING MACHINE!
SOMEBODY BETTER KICK BANNER WHERE IT HURTS, OR WHATEVER IT TAKES TO MAKE HIM GREEN AGAIN!
HURRY!
TONY, THIS IS MARIA HILL. CODE GREEN IS NOT AN OPTION! BANNER'S IN NO CONDITION TO HELP!
WHAT?
I HAVE TO PONY THE MUD OFF! TO SLEEP THE BLAND SIERRA!
BRUCE, YOU'RE TALKING GIBBERISH--
DO YOU GUH-GG-GET IT?
I HAVE TO SAVE MY FRIENDS!
NO!
WILL YOU LISTEN FOR ONCE? OUT OF ALL THE PEOPLE HERE, YOU ARE THE ONE WHO IS MOST AT RISK! BELIEVE ME!
NOW, I'M BUZZING S.H.I.E.L.D. FOR A TRANSPORT--

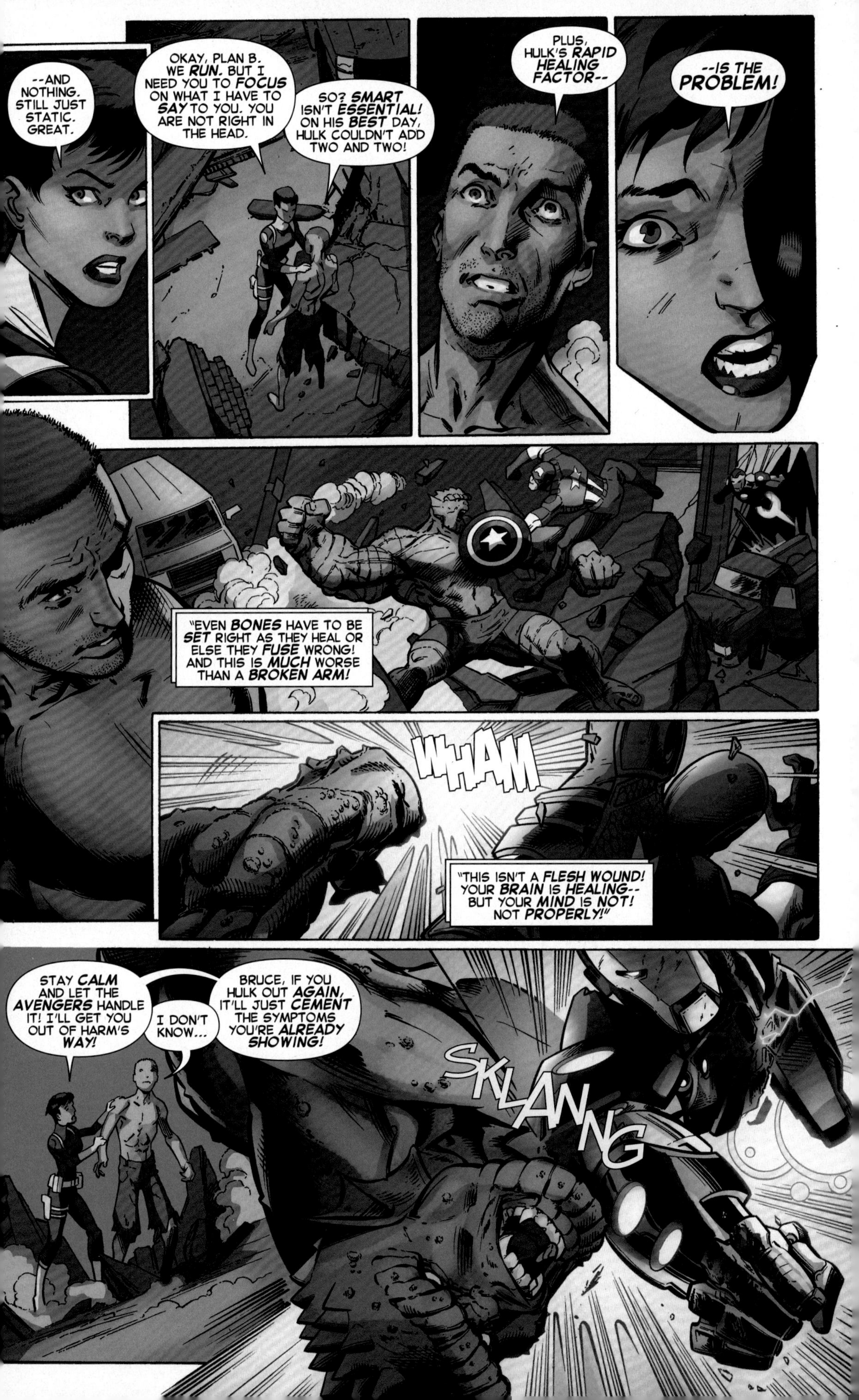
--AND NOTHING. STILL JUST STATIC. GREAT.
OKAY, PLAN B. WE RUN. BUT I NEED YOU TO FOCUS ON WHAT I HAVE TO SAY TO YOU. YOU ARE NOT RIGHT IN THE HEAD.
SO? SMART ISN'T ESSENTIAL! ON HIS BEST DAY, HULK COULDN'T ADD TWO AND TWO!
PLUS, HULK'S RAPID HEALING FACTOR--
--IS THE PROBLEM!
"EVEN BONES HAVE TO BE SET RIGHT AS THEY HEAL OR ELSE THEY FUSE WRONG! AND THIS IS MUCH WORSE THAN A BROKEN ARM!
WHAM
"THIS ISN'T A FLESH WOUND! YOUR BRAIN IS HEALING-- BUT YOUR MIND IS NOT! NOT PROPERLY!"
STAY CALM AND LET THE AVENGERS HANDLE IT! I'LL GET YOU OUT OF HARM'S WAY!
I DON'T KNOW...
BRUCE, IF YOU HULK OUT AGAIN, IT'LL JUST CEMENT THE SYMPTOMS YOU'RE ALREADY SHOWING!
SKLANNNG

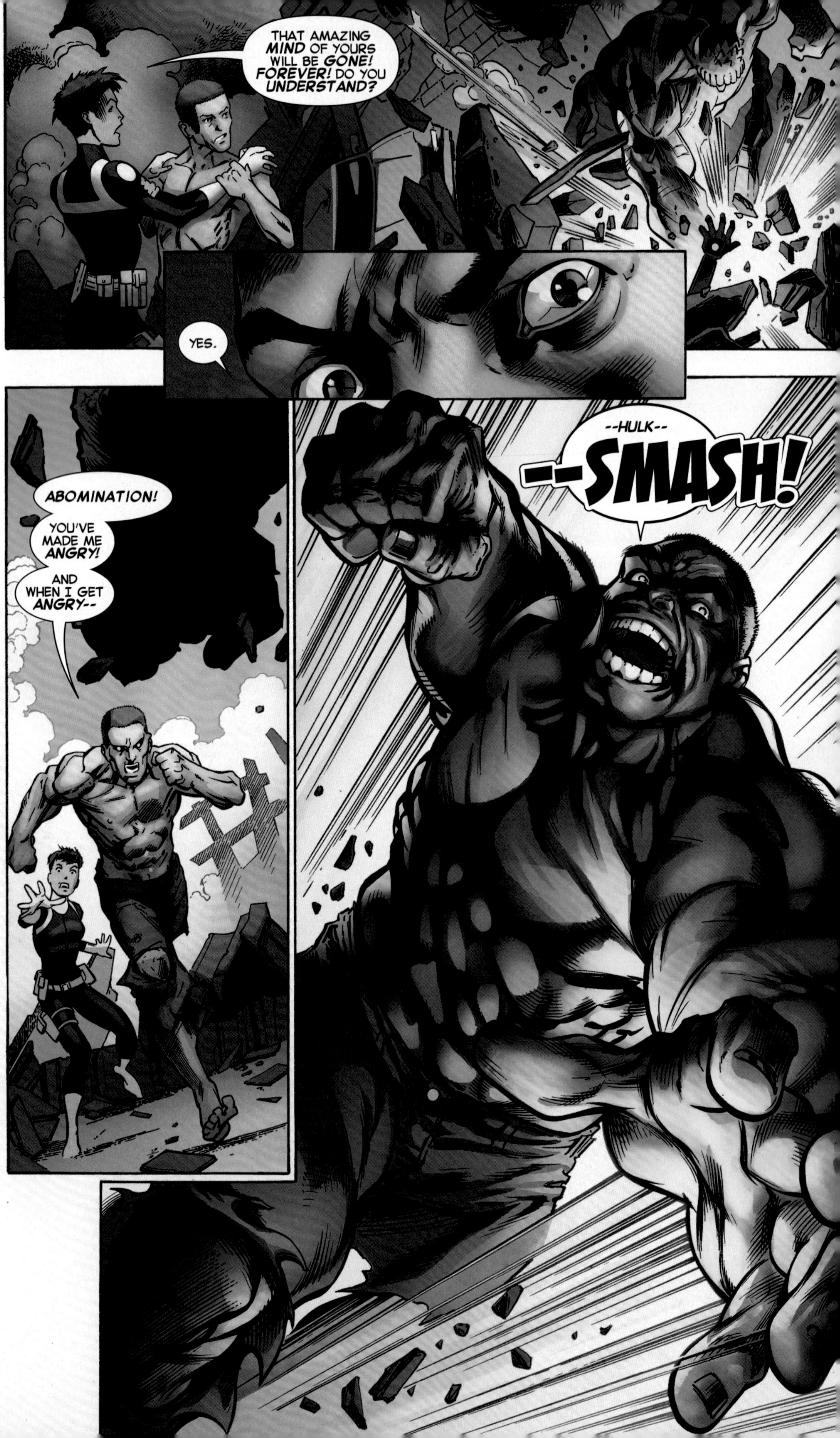

THAT AMAZING MIND OF YOURS WILL BE GONE! FOREVER! DO YOU UNDERSTAND?
YES.
ABOMINATION!
YOU'VE MADE ME ANGRY!
AND WHEN I GET ANGRY--
--HULK--
--SMASH!

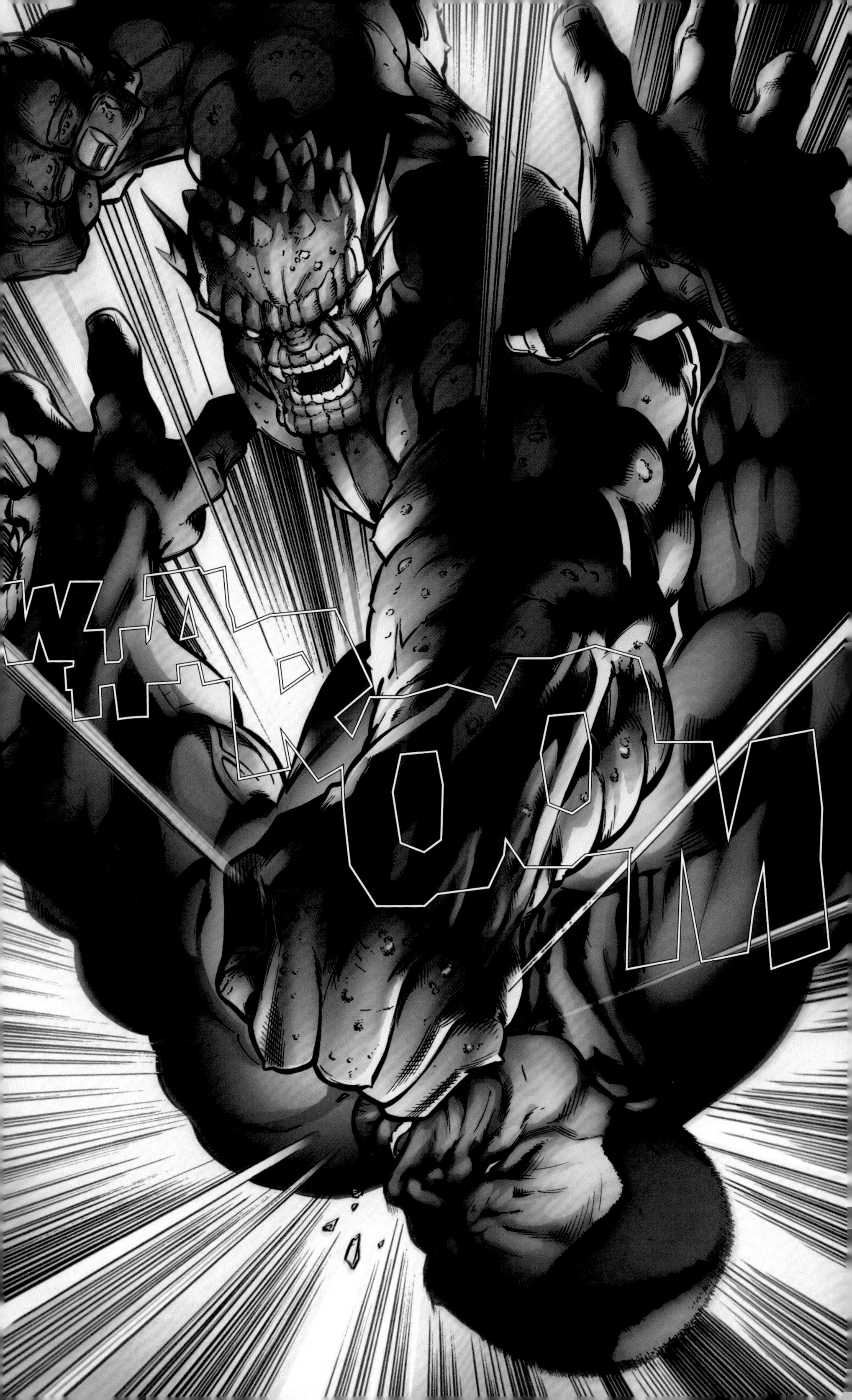
WHADOOM

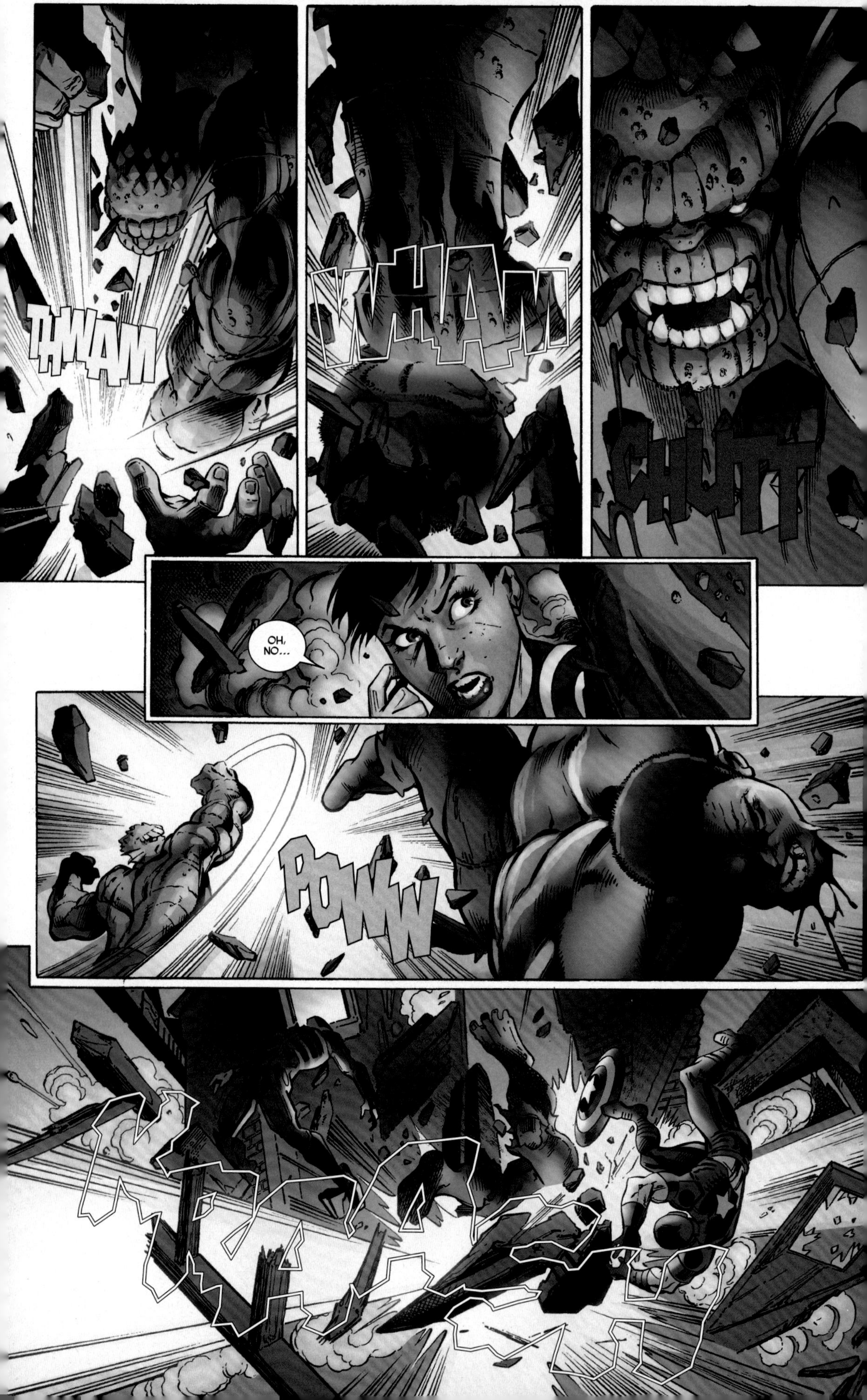
THWAM
WHAM
CHUTT
OH, NO...
POWW

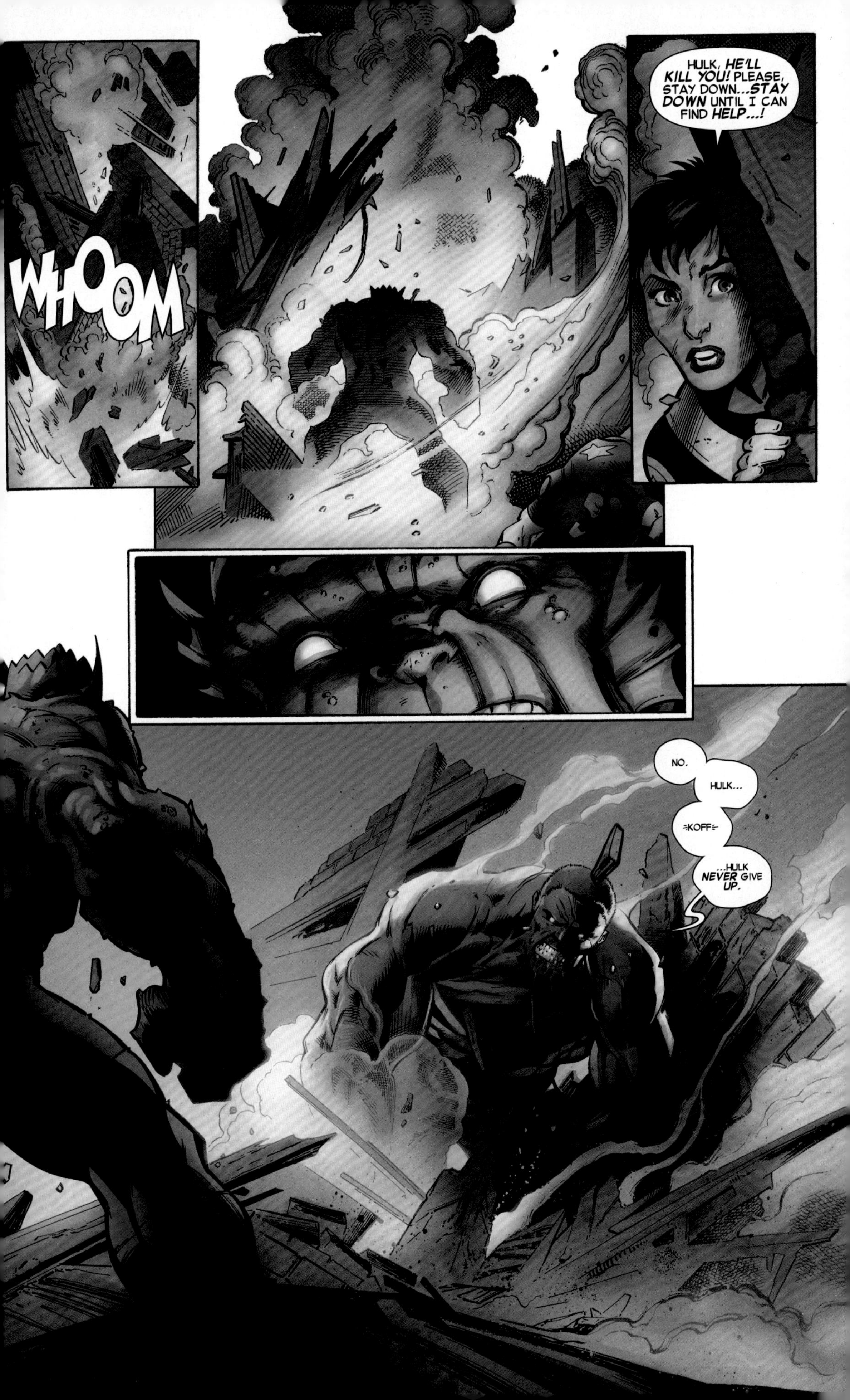
WHOOM
HULK, HE'LL KILL YOU! PLEASE, STAY DOWN...STAY DOWN UNTIL I CAN FIND HELP...!
NO.
HULK...
=KOFF=
...HULK NEVER GIVE UP.

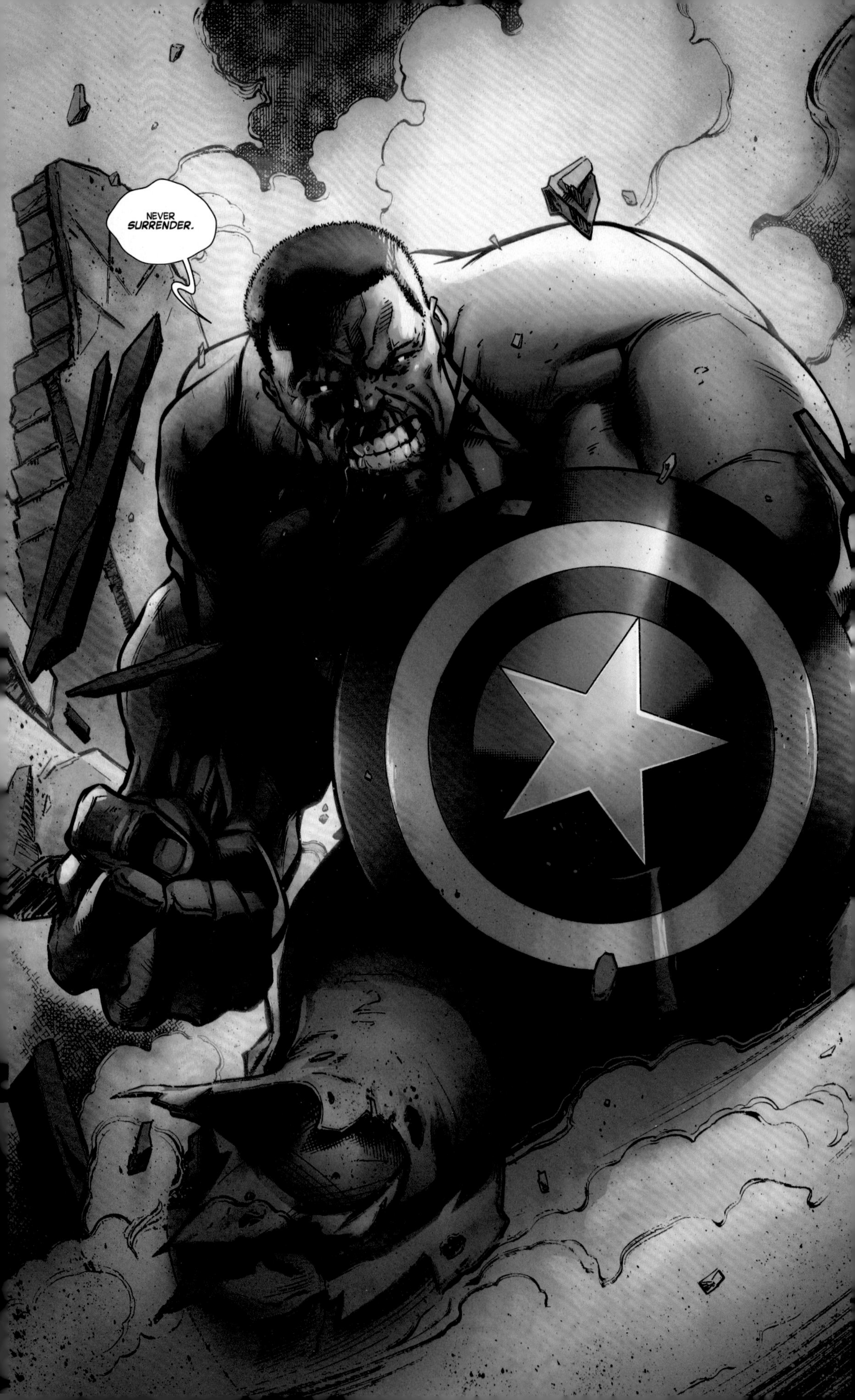
NEVER SURRENDER.

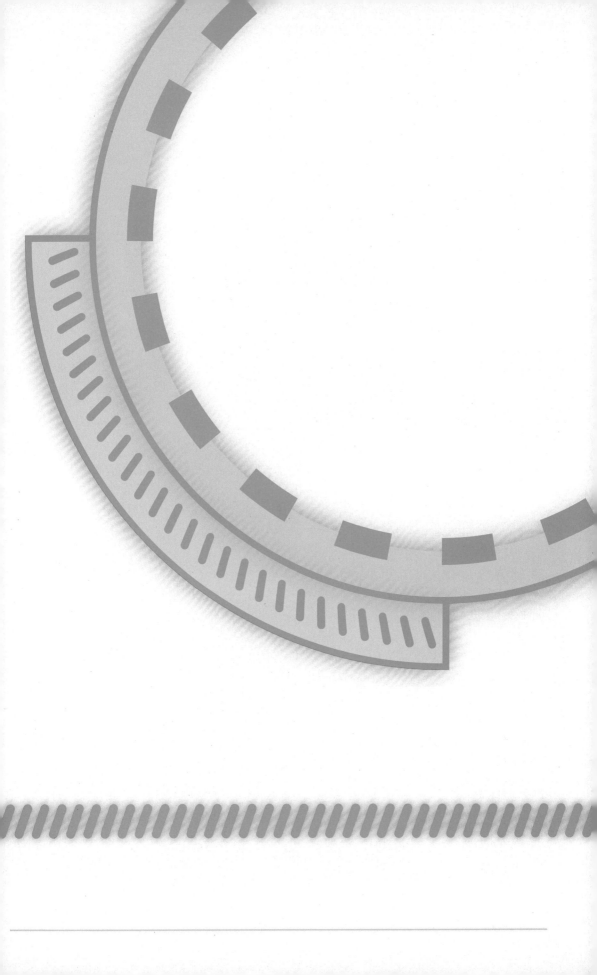

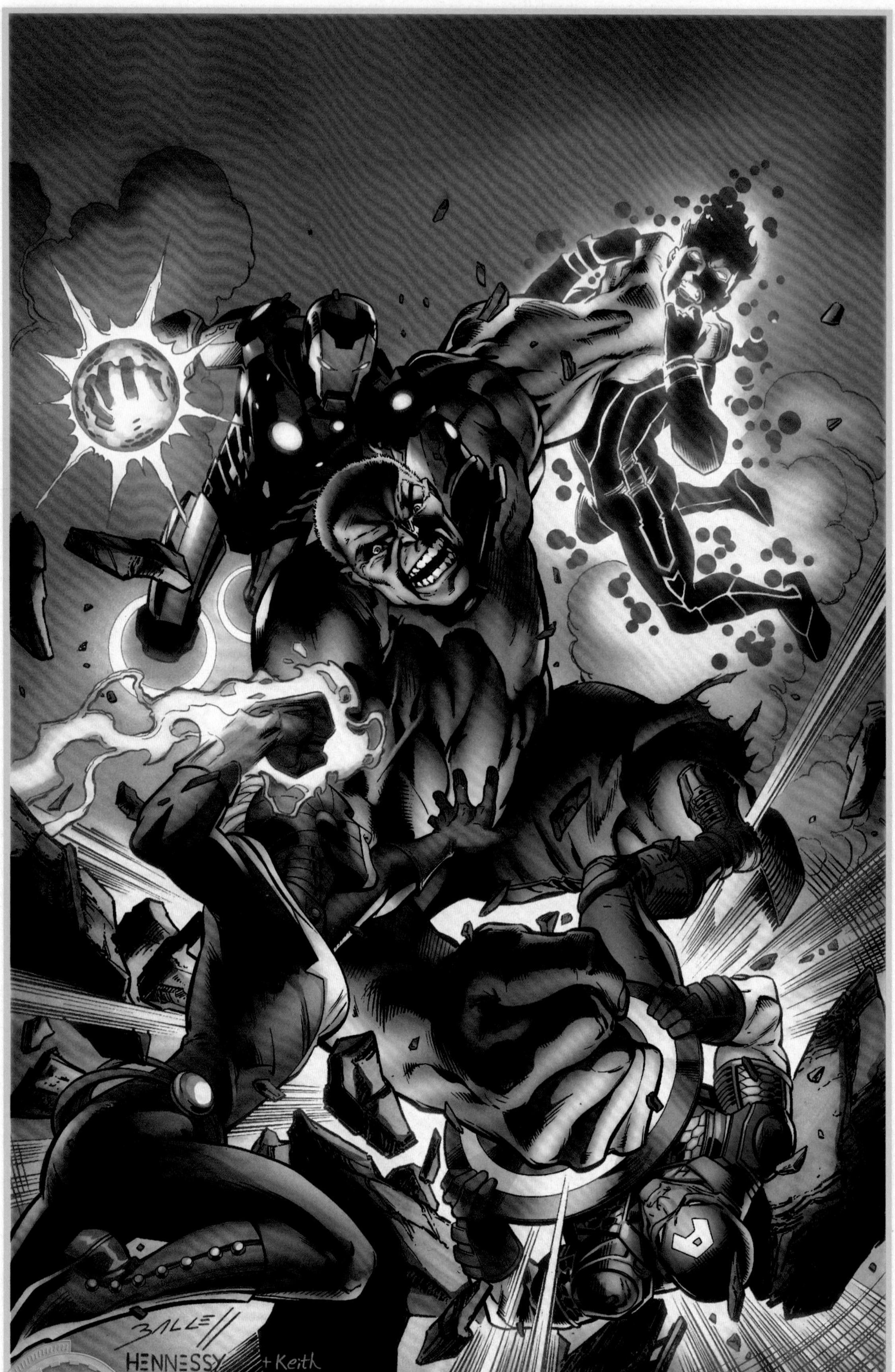
BALLE//
HENNESSY
+Keith

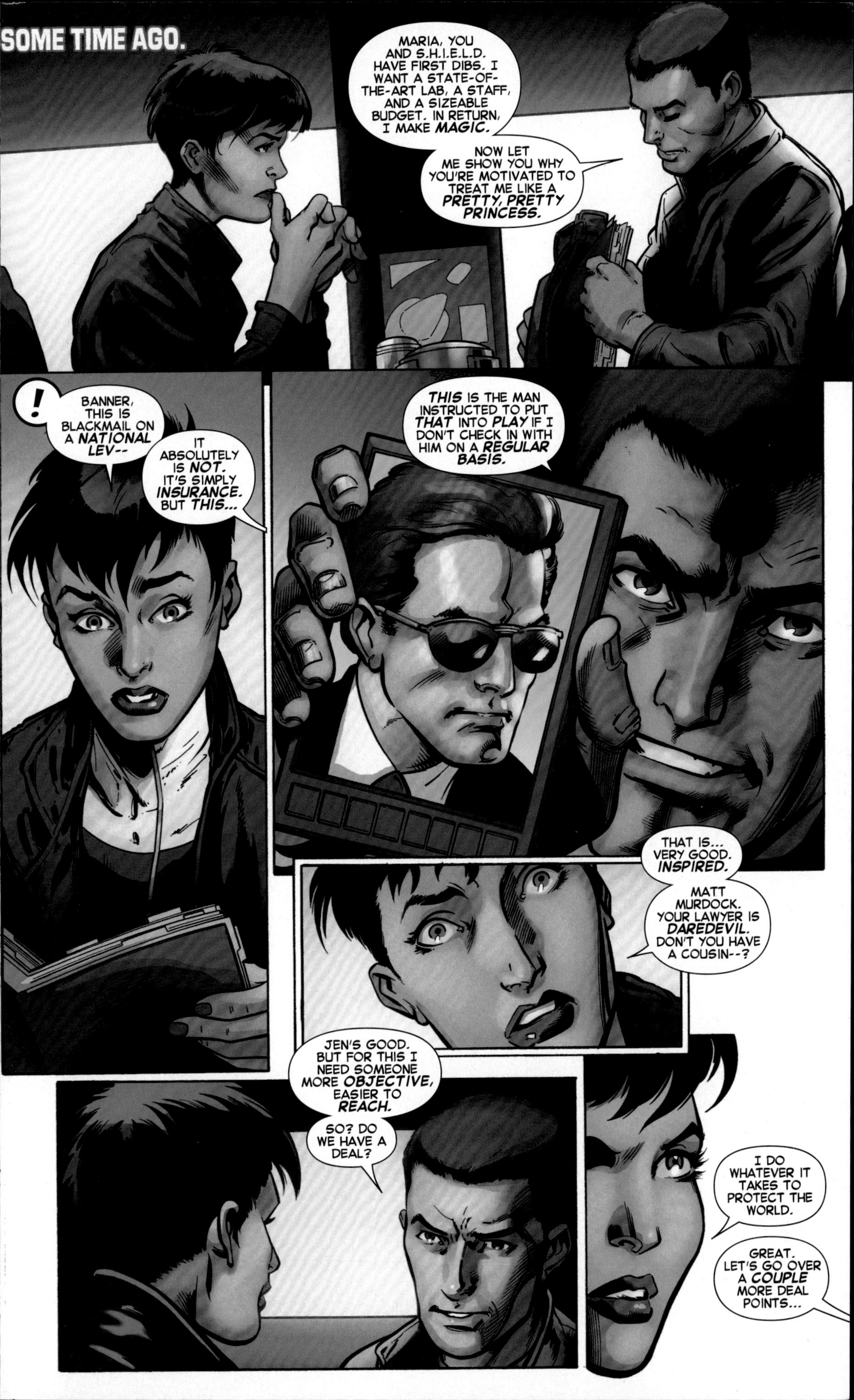
SOME TIME AGO.
MARIA, YOU AND S.H.I.E.L.D. HAVE FIRST DIBS. I WANT A STATE-OF-THE-ART LAB, A STAFF, AND A SIZEABLE BUDGET. IN RETURN, I MAKE MAGIC.
NOW LET ME SHOW YOU WHY YOU'RE MOTIVATED TO TREAT ME LIKE A PRETTY, PRETTY PRINCESS.
!
BANNER, THIS IS BLACKMAIL ON A NATIONAL LEV--
IT ABSOLUTELY IS NOT. IT'S SIMPLY INSURANCE. BUT THIS...
THIS IS THE MAN INSTRUCTED TO PUT THAT INTO PLAY IF I DON'T CHECK IN WITH HIM ON A REGULAR BASIS.
THAT IS... VERY GOOD. INSPIRED.
MATT MURDOCK. YOUR LAWYER IS DAREDEVIL. DON'T YOU HAVE A COUSIN--?
JEN'S GOOD. BUT FOR THIS I NEED SOMEONE MORE OBJECTIVE, EASIER TO REACH.
SO? DO WE HAVE A DEAL?
I DO WHATEVER IT TAKES TO PROTECT THE WORLD.
GREAT. LET'S GO OVER A COUPLE MORE DEAL POINTS...

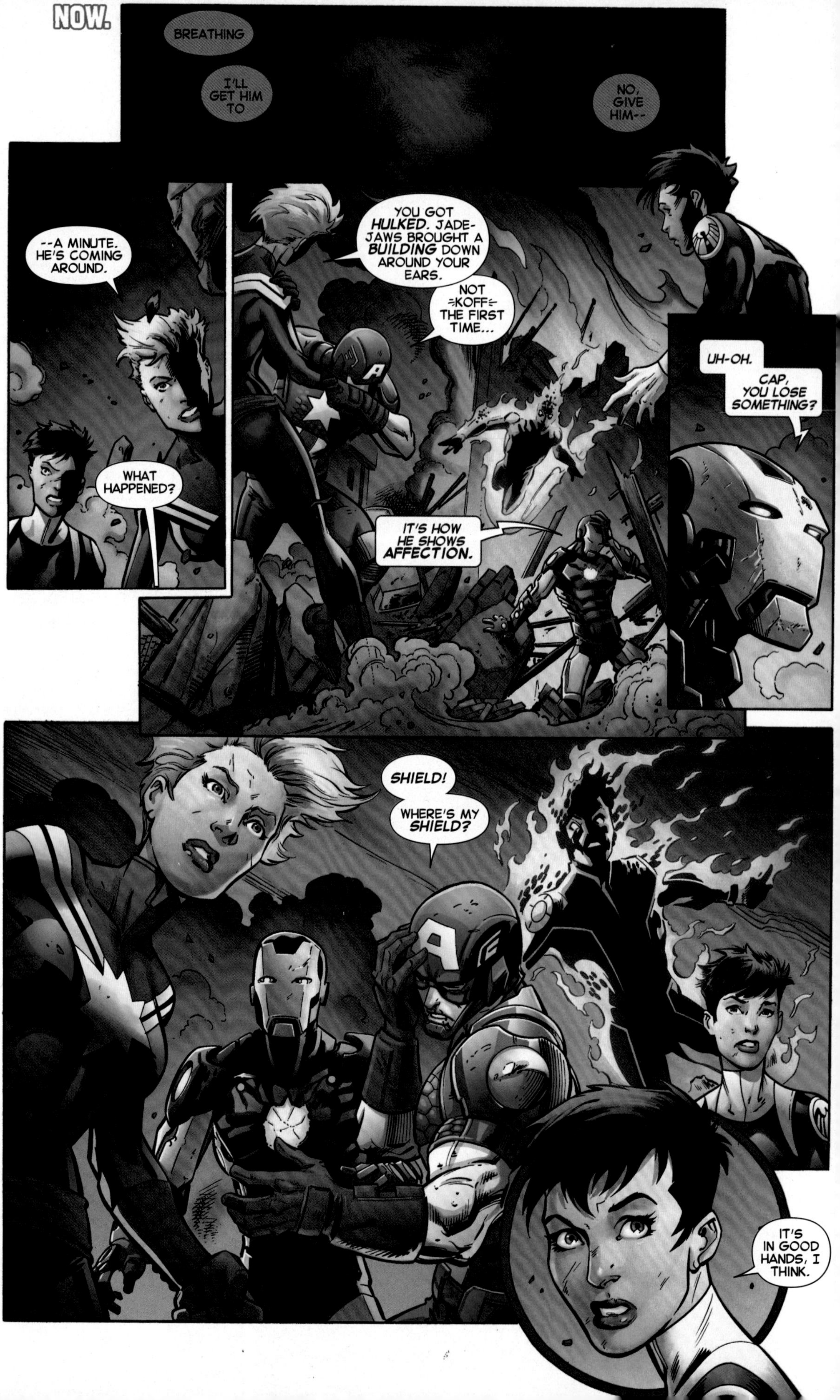
NOW.
BREATHING
I'LL GET HIM TO
NO, GIVE HIM--
--A MINUTE. HE'S COMING AROUND.
WHAT HAPPENED?
YOU GOT HULKED. JADE-JAWS BROUGHT A BUILDING DOWN AROUND YOUR EARS.
NOT =KOFF= THE FIRST TIME...
IT'S HOW HE SHOWS AFFECTION.
UH-OH.
CAP, YOU LOSE SOMETHING?
SHIELD!
WHERE'S MY SHIELD?
IT'S IN GOOD HANDS, I THINK.

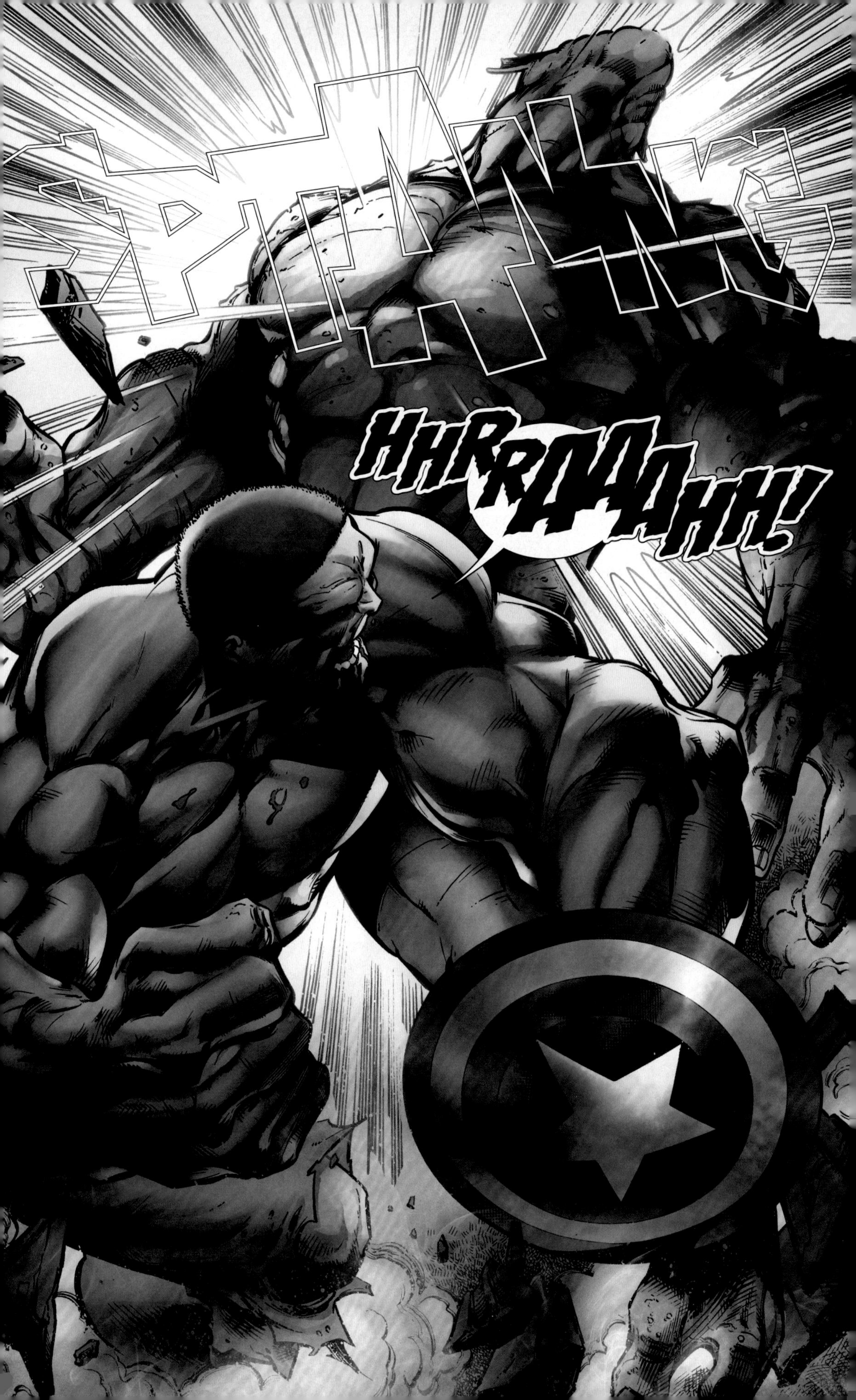
SPLANNG
HHRRAAAAHH!

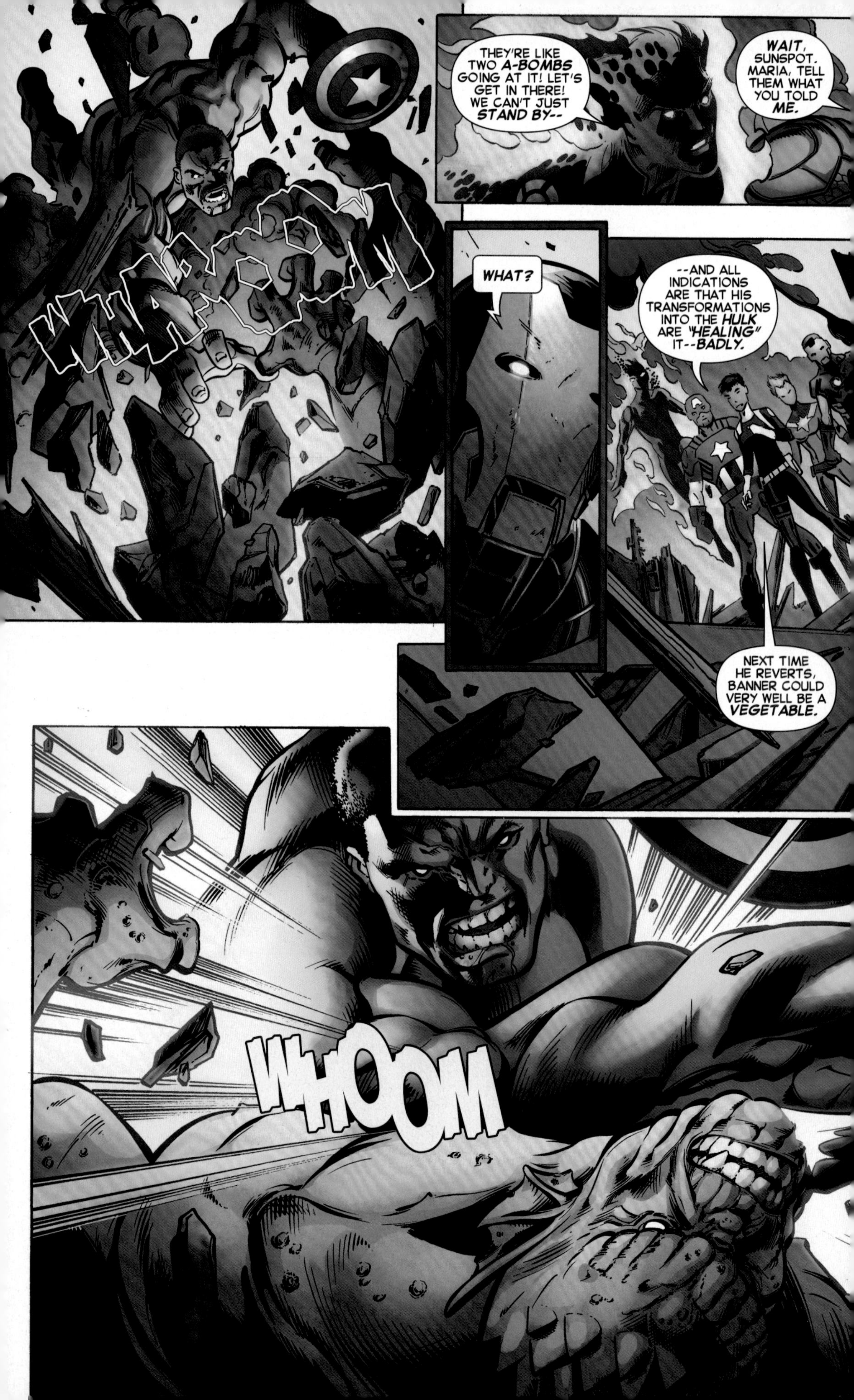
WHA-KOOM
THEY'RE LIKE TWO A-BOMBS GOING AT IT! LET'S GET IN THERE! WE CAN'T JUST STAND BY--
WAIT, SUNSPOT. MARIA, TELL THEM WHAT YOU TOLD ME.
WHAT?
--AND ALL INDICATIONS ARE THAT HIS TRANSFORMATIONS INTO THE HULK ARE "HEALING" IT--BADLY.
NEXT TIME HE REVERTS, BANNER COULD VERY WELL BE A VEGETABLE.
WHOOM

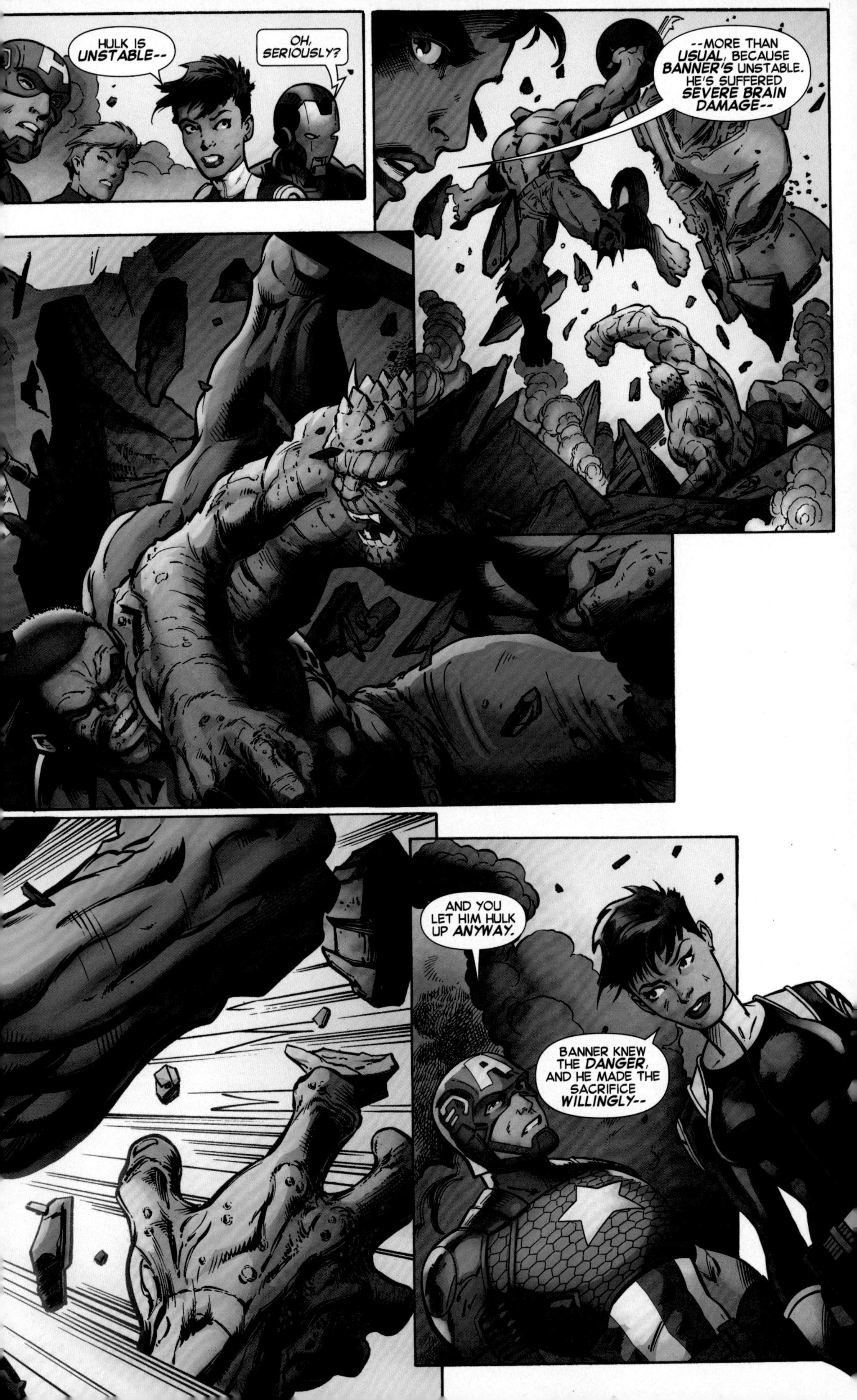

HULK IS UNSTABLE--
OH, SERIOUSLY?
--MORE THAN USUAL, BECAUSE BANNER'S UNSTABLE. HE'S SUFFERED SEVERE BRAIN DAMAGE--
AND YOU LET HIM HULK UP ANYWAY.
BANNER KNEW THE DANGER, AND HE MADE THE SACRIFICE WILLINGLY--

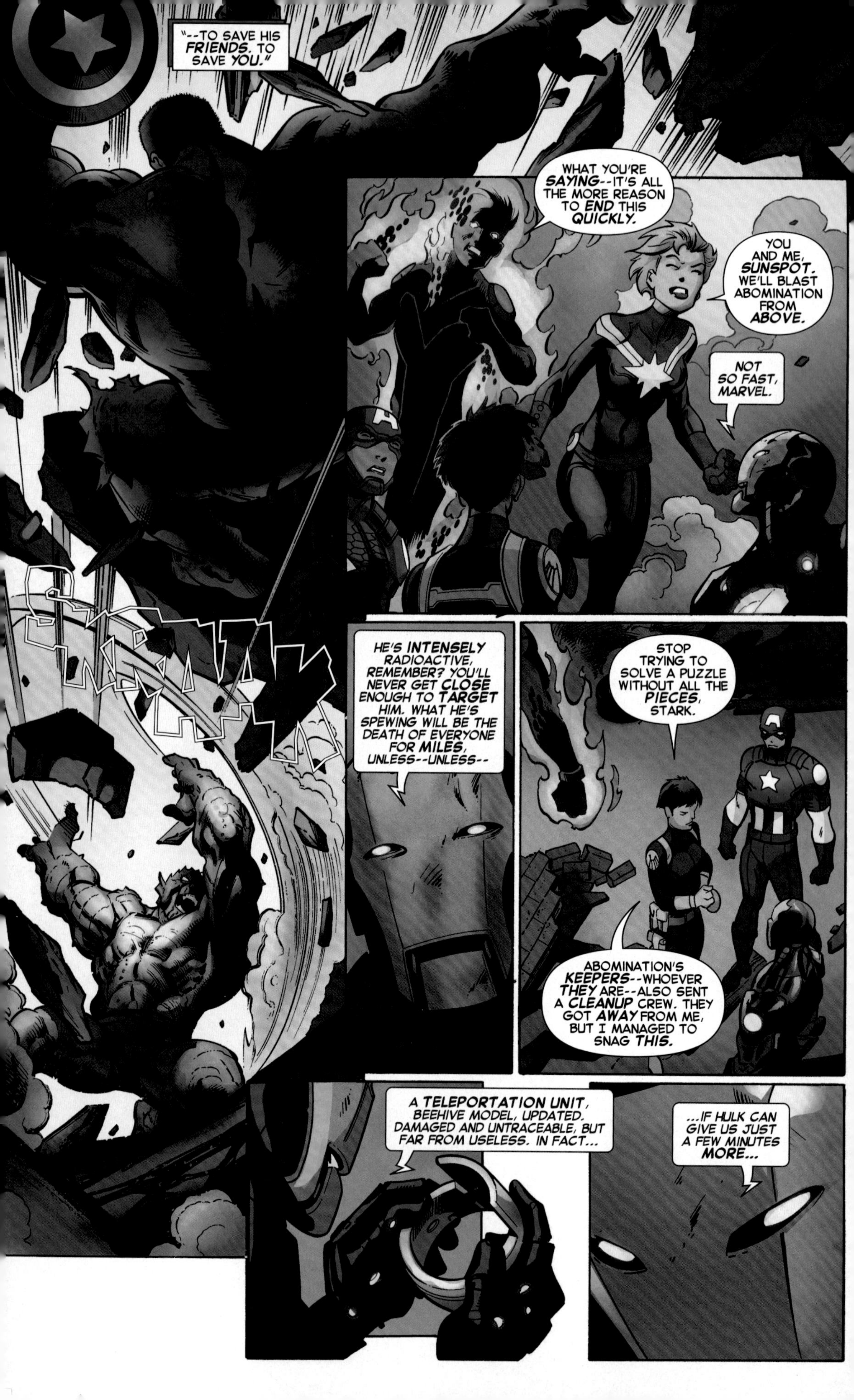
"--TO SAVE HIS FRIENDS. TO SAVE YOU."
WHAT YOU'RE SAYING--IT'S ALL THE MORE REASON TO END THIS QUICKLY.
YOU AND ME, SUNSPOT. WE'LL BLAST ABOMINATION FROM ABOVE.
NOT SO FAST, MARVEL.
HE'S INTENSELY RADIOACTIVE, REMEMBER? YOU'LL NEVER GET CLOSE ENOUGH TO TARGET HIM. WHAT HE'S SPEWING WILL BE THE DEATH OF EVERYONE FOR MILES, UNLESS--UNLESS--
STOP TRYING TO SOLVE A PUZZLE WITHOUT ALL THE PIECES, STARK.
ABOMINATION'S KEEPERS--WHOEVER THEY ARE--ALSO SENT A CLEANUP CREW. THEY GOT AWAY FROM ME, BUT I MANAGED TO SNAG THIS.
A TELEPORTATION UNIT, BEEHIVE MODEL, UPDATED. DAMAGED AND UNTRACEABLE, BUT FAR FROM USELESS. IN FACT...
...IF HULK CAN GIVE US JUST A FEW MINUTES MORE...

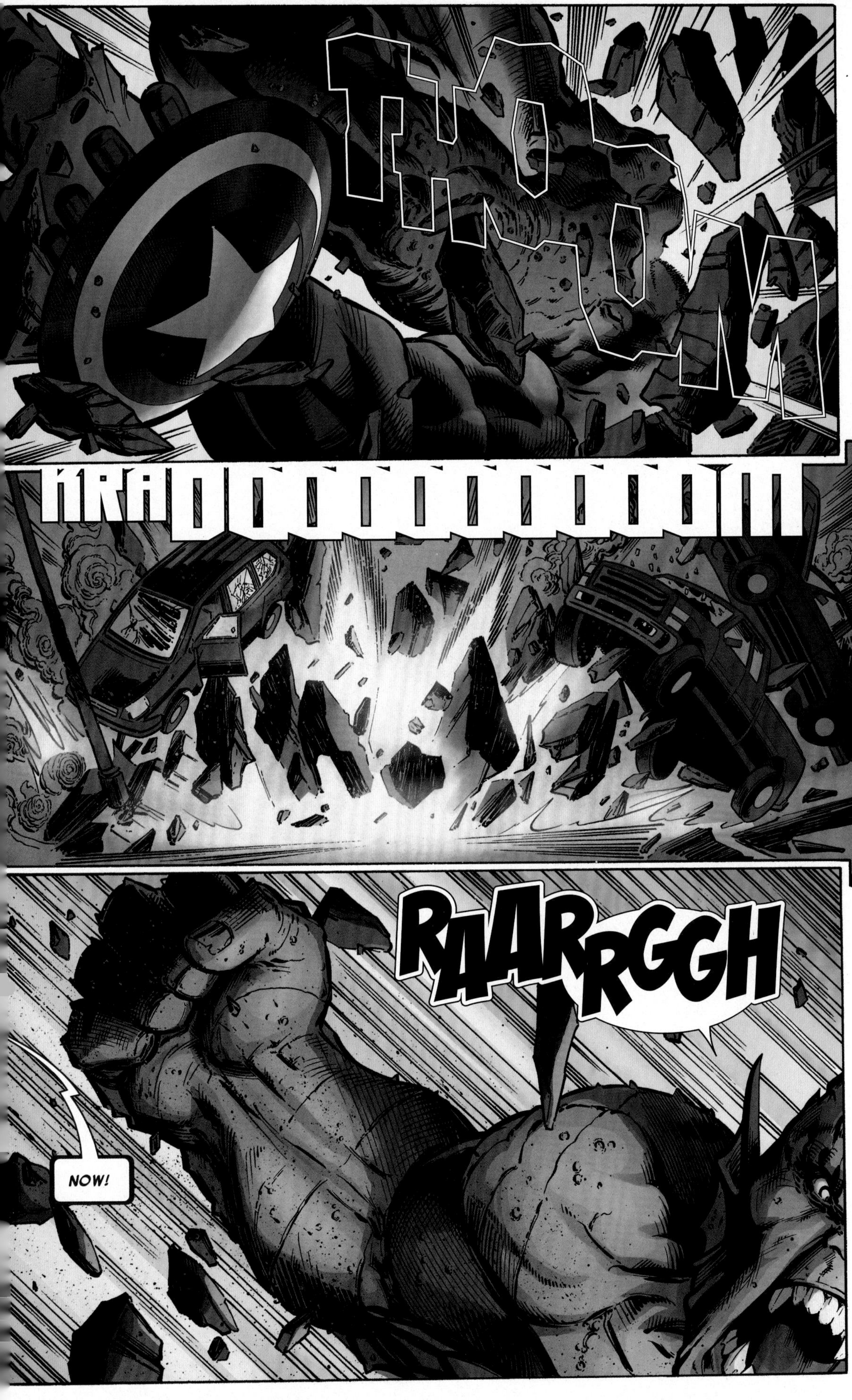
THOOM
KRADOOOOOOOOOOM
RAAARRGGH
NOW!

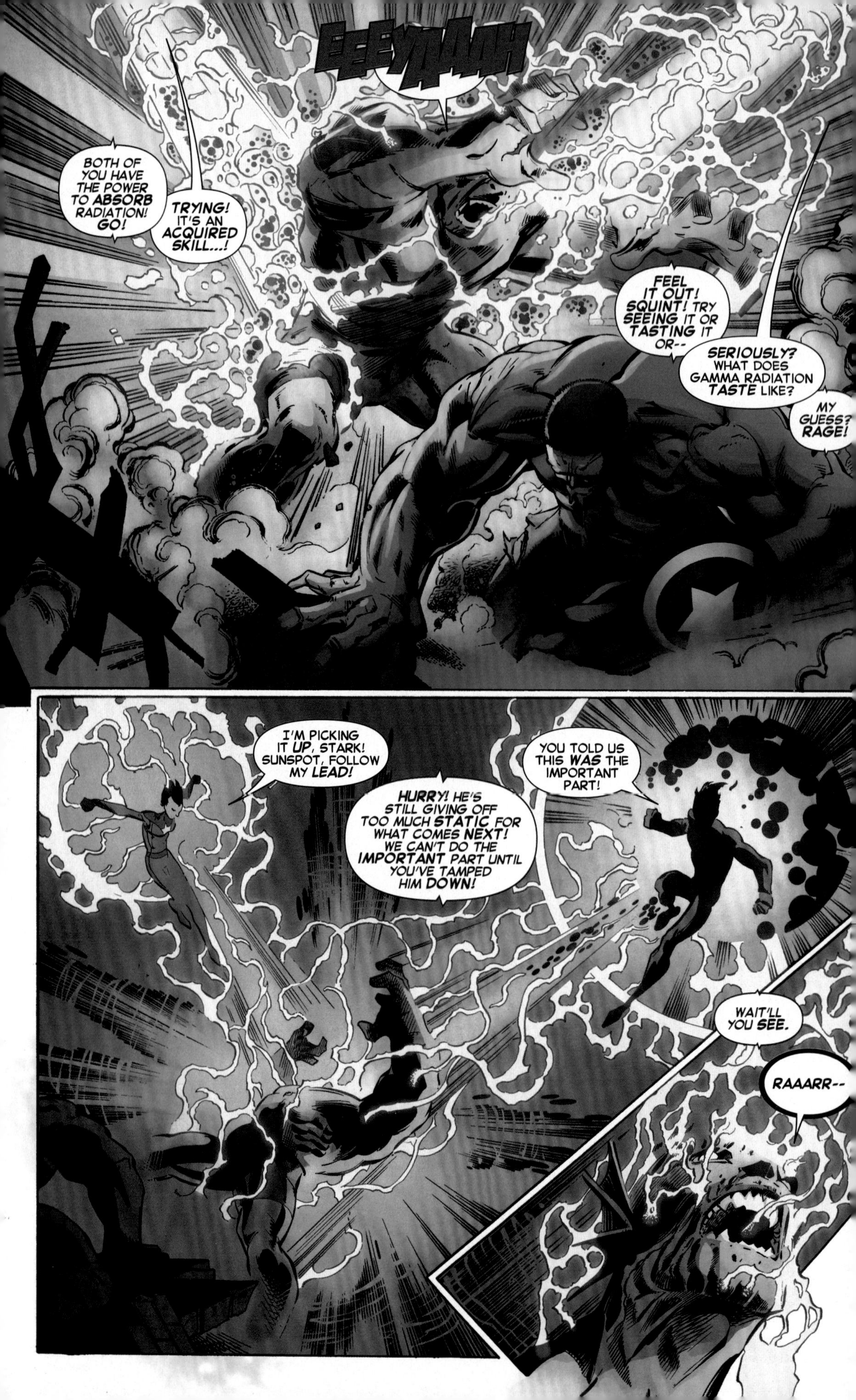
EEEYAAHH
BOTH OF YOU HAVE THE POWER TO ABSORB RADIATION! GO!
TRYING! IT'S AN ACQUIRED SKILL...!
FEEL IT OUT! SQUINT! TRY SEEING IT OR TASTING IT OR--
SERIOUSLY? WHAT DOES GAMMA RADIATION TASTE LIKE?
MY GUESS? RAGE!
I'M PICKING IT UP, STARK! SUNSPOT, FOLLOW MY LEAD!
HURRY! HE'S STILL GIVING OFF TOO MUCH STATIC FOR WHAT COMES NEXT! WE CAN'T DO THE IMPORTANT PART UNTIL YOU'VE TAMPED HIM DOWN!
YOU TOLD US THIS WAS THE IMPORTANT PART!
WAIT'LL YOU SEE.
RAAARR--

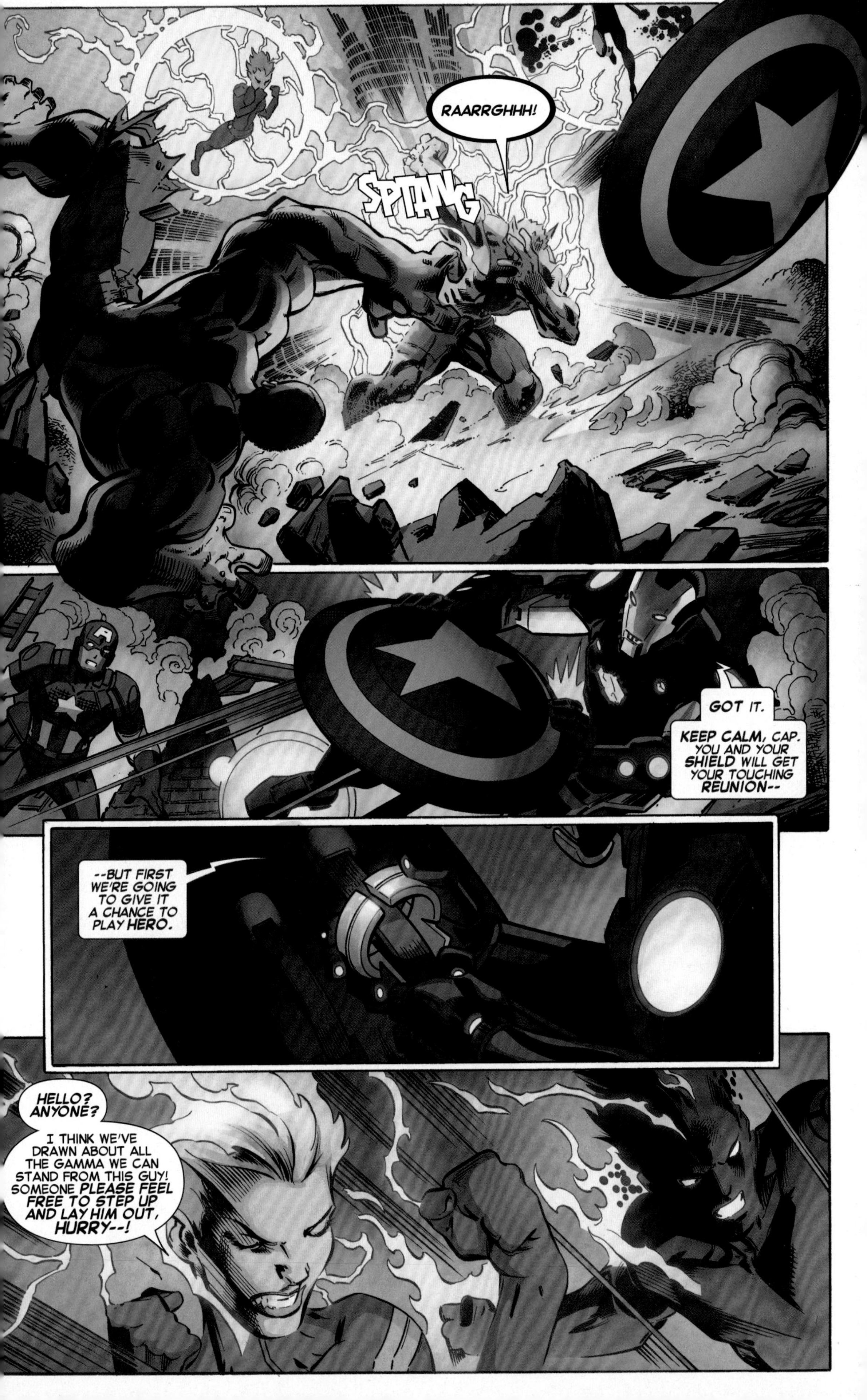
RAARRGHHH!
SPTANG
GOT IT.
KEEP CALM, CAP. YOU AND YOUR SHIELD WILL GET YOUR TOUCHING REUNION--
--BUT FIRST WE'RE GOING TO GIVE IT A CHANCE TO PLAY HERO.
HELLO? ANYONE?
I THINK WE'VE DRAWN ABOUT ALL THE GAMMA WE CAN STAND FROM THIS GUY! SOMEONE PLEASE FEEL FREE TO STEP UP AND LAY HIM OUT, HURRY--!

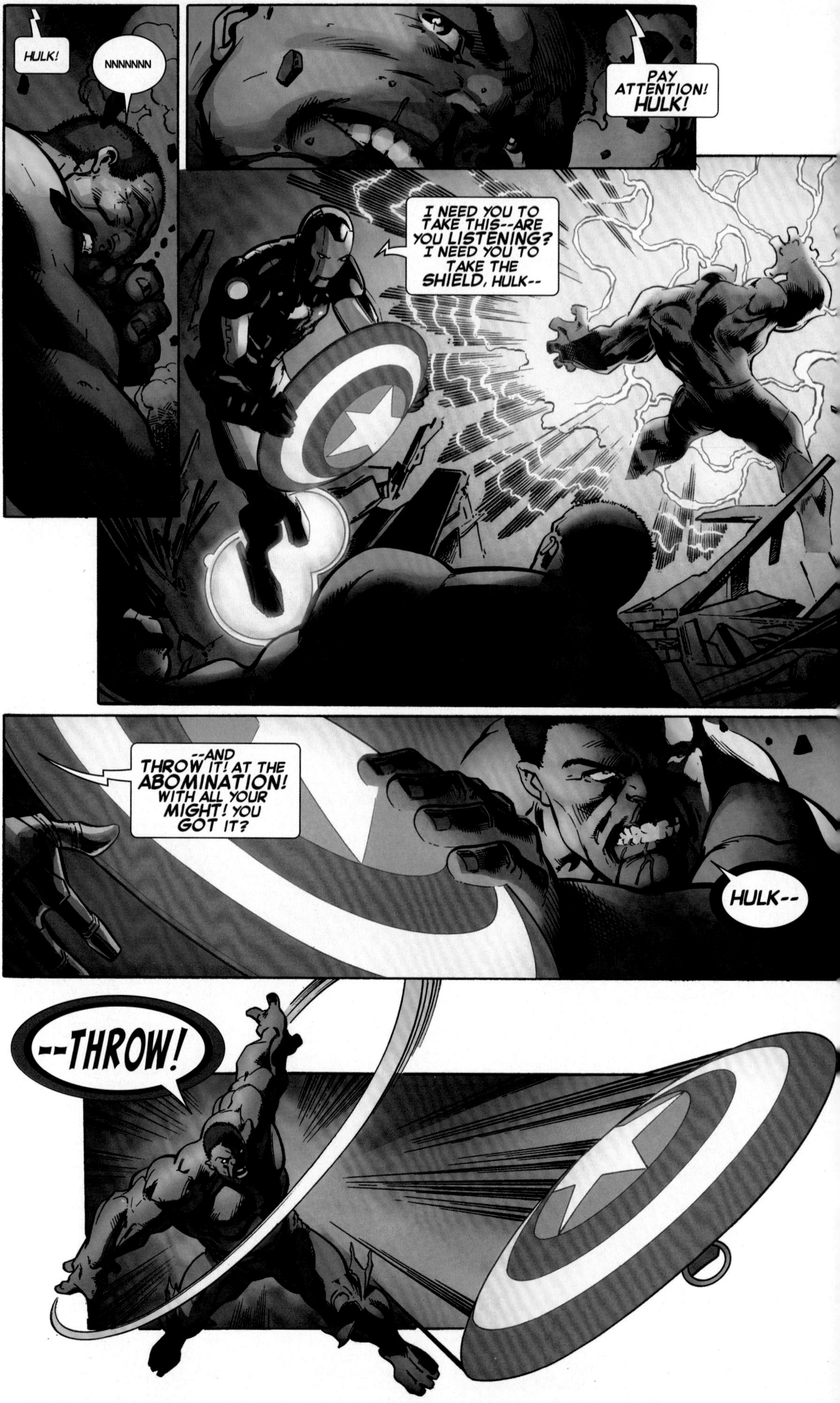
HULK!
NNNNNNN
PAY ATTENTION! HULK!
I NEED YOU TO TAKE THIS--ARE YOU LISTENING? I NEED YOU TO TAKE THE SHIELD, HULK--
--AND THROW IT! AT THE ABOMINATION! WITH ALL YOUR MIGHT! YOU GOT IT?
HULK--
--THROW!

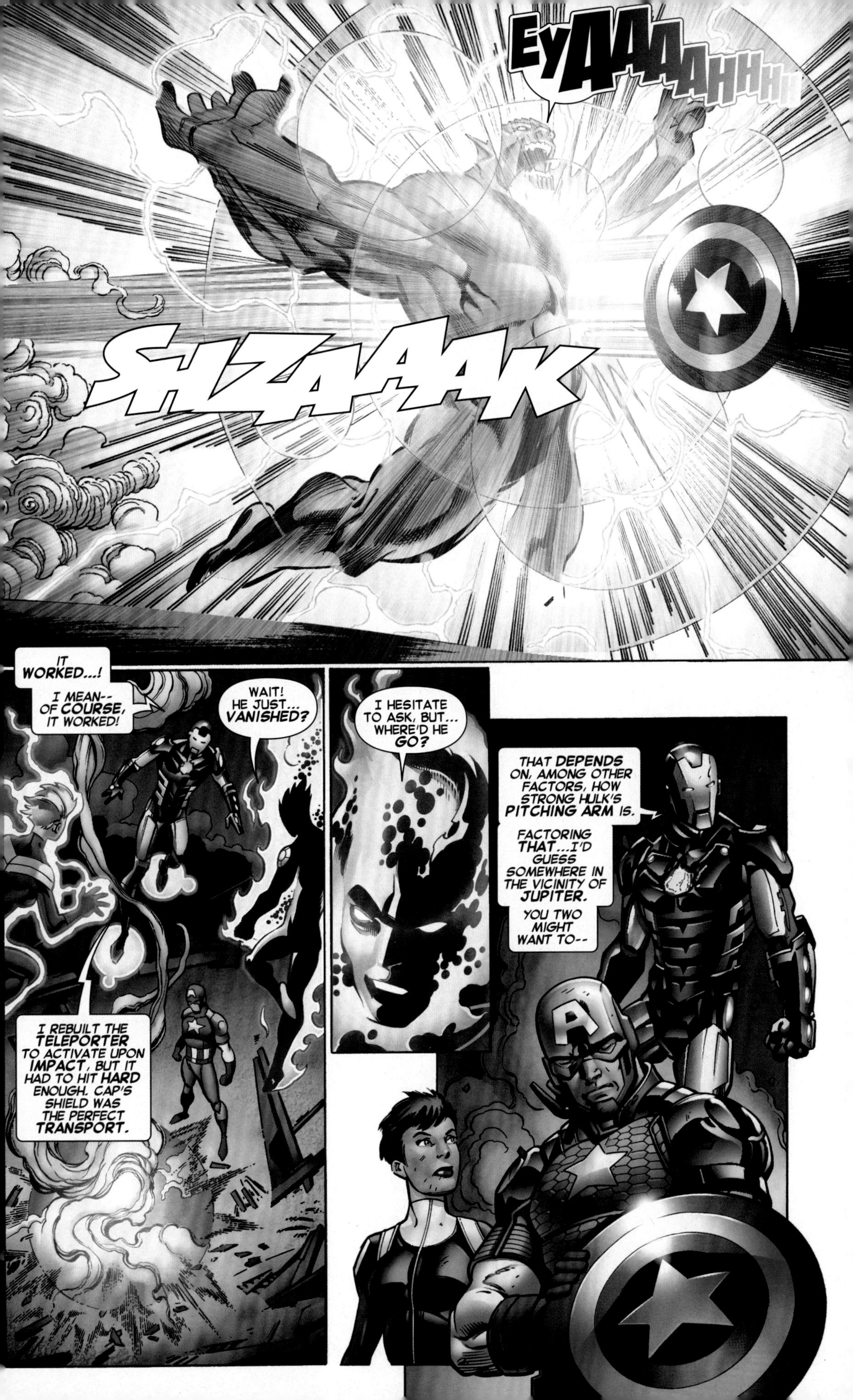

EyAAAAAHHHH
SHZAAAK
IT WORKED...!
I MEAN-- OF COURSE, IT WORKED!
WAIT! HE JUST... VANISHED?
I REBUILT THE TELEPORTER TO ACTIVATE UPON IMPACT, BUT IT HAD TO HIT HARD ENOUGH. CAP'S SHIELD WAS THE PERFECT TRANSPORT.
I HESITATE TO ASK, BUT... WHERE'D HE GO?
THAT DEPENDS ON, AMONG OTHER FACTORS, HOW STRONG HULK'S PITCHING ARM IS.
FACTORING THAT...I'D GUESS SOMEWHERE IN THE VICINITY OF JUPITER.
YOU TWO MIGHT WANT TO--

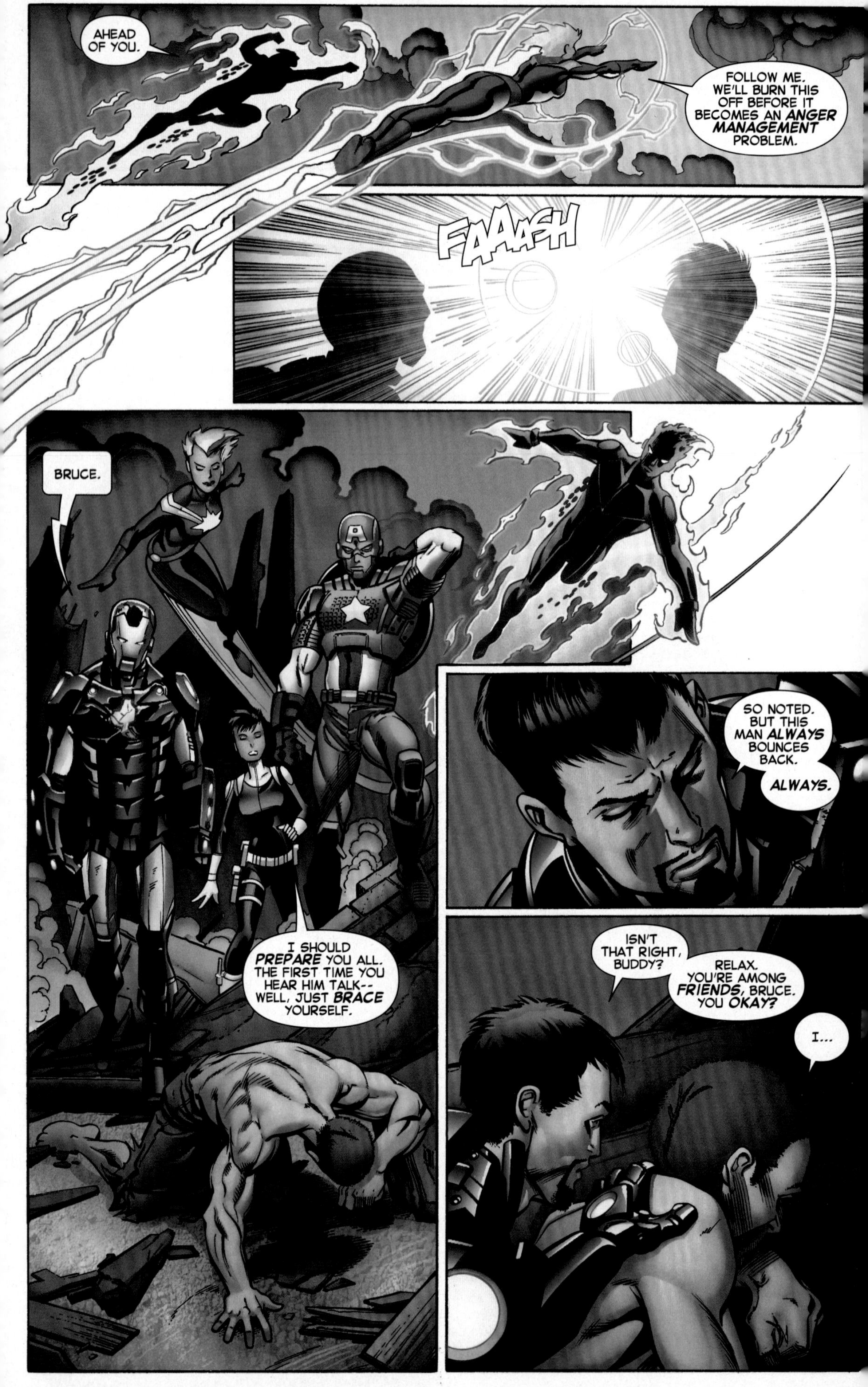
AHEAD OF YOU.
FOLLOW ME. WE'LL BURN THIS OFF BEFORE IT BECOMES AN ANGER MANAGEMENT PROBLEM.
FAAASH
BRUCE.
I SHOULD PREPARE YOU ALL. THE FIRST TIME YOU HEAR HIM TALK-- WELL, JUST BRACE YOURSELF.
SO NOTED. BUT THIS MAN ALWAYS BOUNCES BACK.
ALWAYS.
ISN'T THAT RIGHT, BUDDY?
RELAX. YOU'RE AMONG FRIENDS, BRUCE. YOU OKAY?
I...

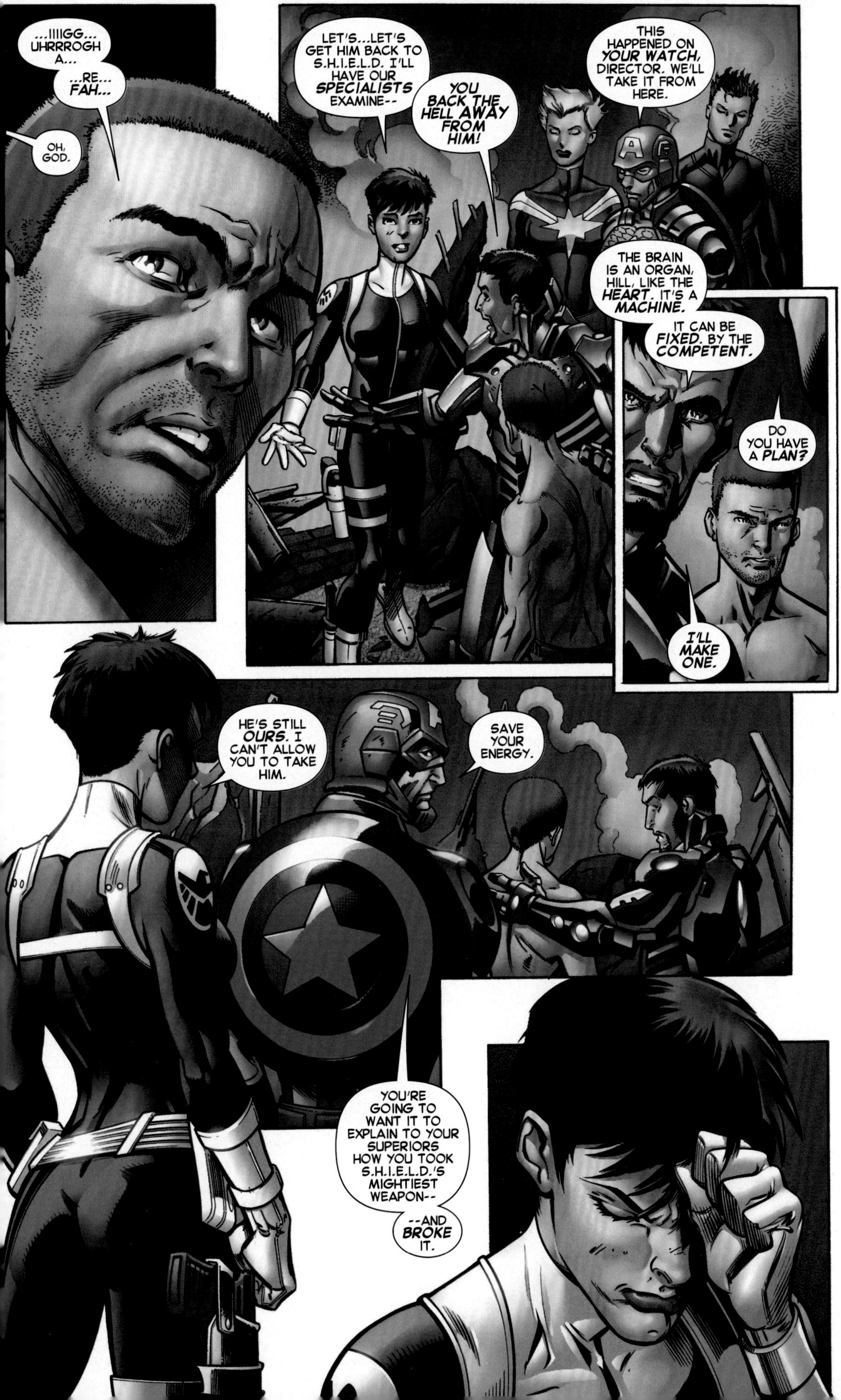
...IIIIGG... UHRRROGH A...
...RE... FAH...
OH, GOD.
LET'S...LET'S GET HIM BACK TO S.H.I.E.L.D. I'LL HAVE OUR SPECIALISTS EXAMINE--
YOU BACK THE HELL AWAY FROM HIM!
THIS HAPPENED ON YOUR WATCH, DIRECTOR. WE'LL TAKE IT FROM HERE.
THE BRAIN IS AN ORGAN, HILL, LIKE THE HEART. IT'S A MACHINE.
IT CAN BE FIXED. BY THE COMPETENT.
DO YOU HAVE A PLAN?
I'LL MAKE ONE.
HE'S STILL OURS. I CAN'T ALLOW YOU TO TAKE HIM.
SAVE YOUR ENERGY.
YOU'RE GOING TO WANT IT TO EXPLAIN TO YOUR SUPERIORS HOW YOU TOOK S.H.I.E.L.D.'S MIGHTIEST WEAPON--
--AND BROKE IT.

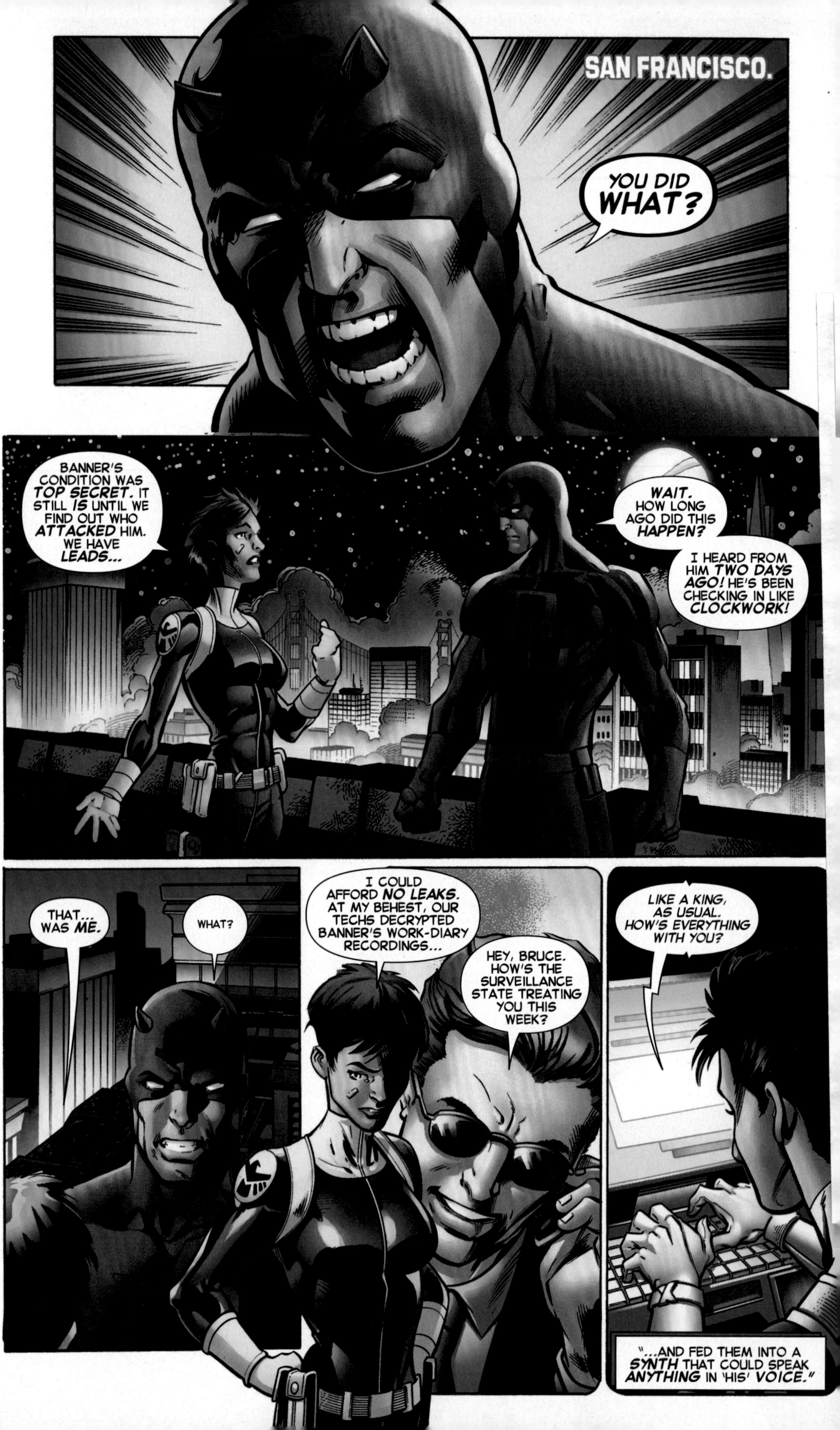
SAN FRANCISCO.
YOU DID WHAT?
BANNER'S CONDITION WAS TOP SECRET. IT STILL IS UNTIL WE FIND OUT WHO ATTACKED HIM. WE HAVE LEADS...
WAIT. HOW LONG AGO DID THIS HAPPEN?
I HEARD FROM HIM TWO DAYS AGO! HE'S BEEN CHECKING IN LIKE CLOCKWORK!
THAT... WAS ME.
WHAT?
I COULD AFFORD NO LEAKS. AT MY BEHEST, OUR TECHS DECRYPTED BANNER'S WORK-DIARY RECORDINGS...
HEY, BRUCE. HOW'S THE SURVEILLANCE STATE TREATING YOU THIS WEEK?
LIKE A KING, AS USUAL. HOW'S EVERYTHING WITH YOU?
"...AND FED THEM INTO A SYNTH THAT COULD SPEAK ANYTHING IN 'HIS' VOICE."

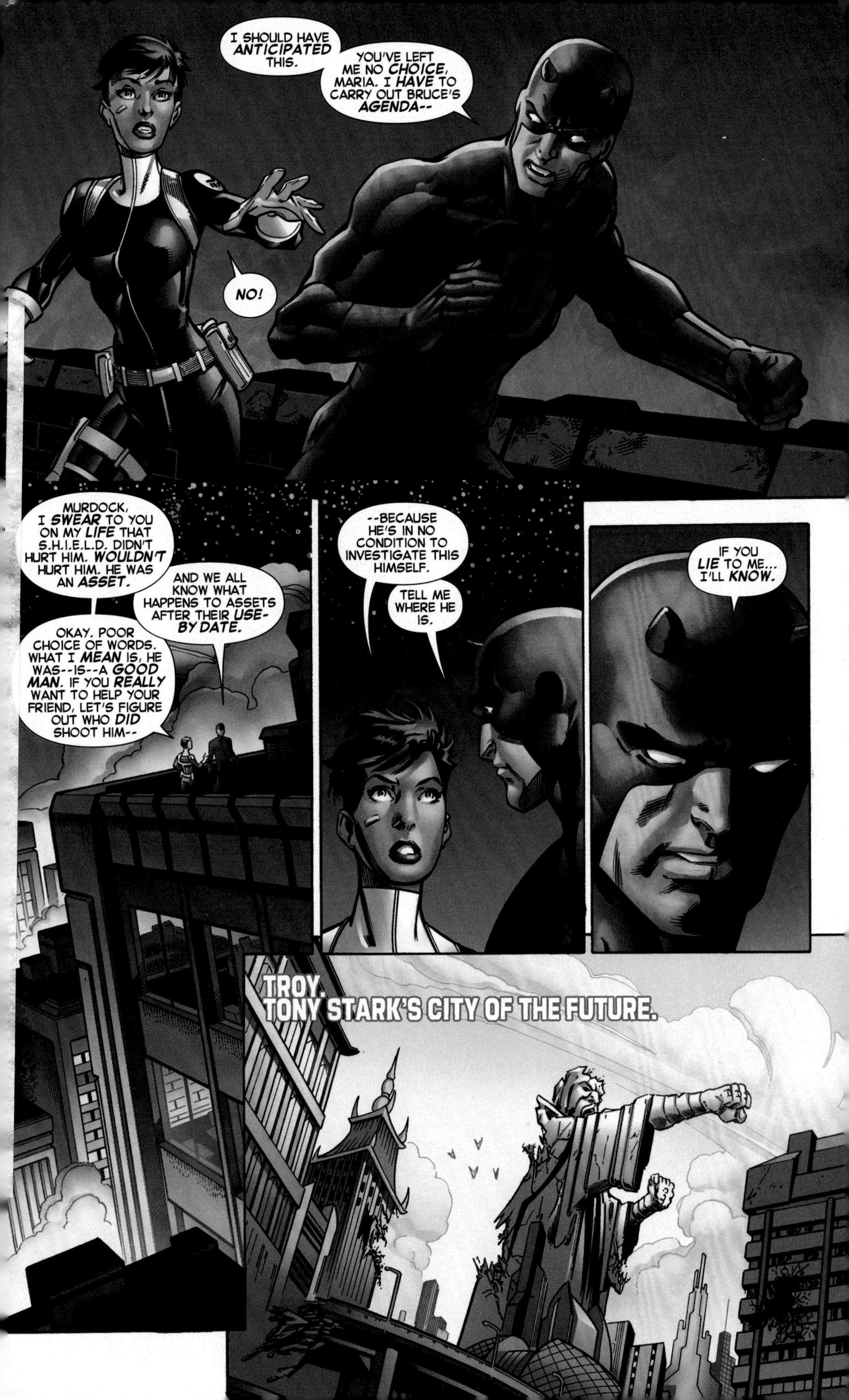
I SHOULD HAVE ANTICIPATED THIS.
YOU'VE LEFT ME NO CHOICE, MARIA. I HAVE TO CARRY OUT BRUCE'S AGENDA--
NO!
MURDOCK, I SWEAR TO YOU ON MY LIFE THAT S.H.I.E.L.D. DIDN'T HURT HIM. WOULDN'T HURT HIM. HE WAS AN ASSET.
AND WE ALL KNOW WHAT HAPPENS TO ASSETS AFTER THEIR USE-BY DATE.
OKAY. POOR CHOICE OF WORDS. WHAT I MEAN IS, HE WAS--IS--A GOOD MAN. IF YOU REALLY WANT TO HELP YOUR FRIEND, LET'S FIGURE OUT WHO DID SHOOT HIM--
--BECAUSE HE'S IN NO CONDITION TO INVESTIGATE THIS HIMSELF.
TELL ME WHERE HE IS.
IF YOU LIE TO ME... I'LL KNOW.
TROY.
TONY STARK'S CITY OF THE FUTURE.

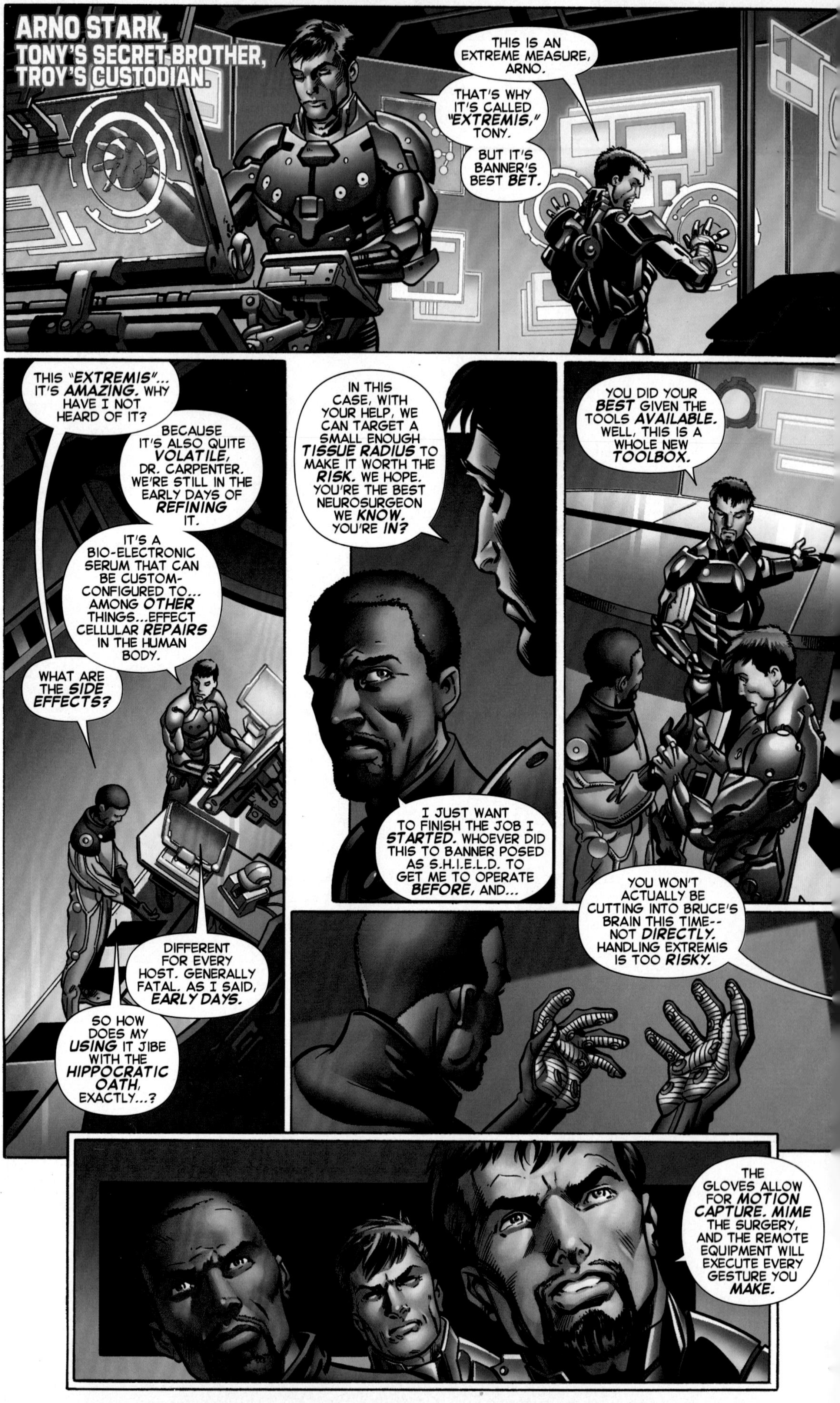
ARNO STARK, TONY'S SECRET BROTHER, TROY'S CUSTODIAN.
THIS IS AN EXTREME MEASURE, ARNO.
THAT'S WHY IT'S CALLED "EXTREMIS," TONY.
BUT IT'S BANNER'S BEST BET.
THIS "EXTREMIS"... IT'S AMAZING. WHY HAVE I NOT HEARD OF IT?
BECAUSE IT'S ALSO QUITE VOLATILE, DR. CARPENTER. WE'RE STILL IN THE EARLY DAYS OF REFINING IT.
IT'S A BIO-ELECTRONIC SERUM THAT CAN BE CUSTOM-CONFIGURED TO... AMONG OTHER THINGS...EFFECT CELLULAR REPAIRS IN THE HUMAN BODY.
WHAT ARE THE SIDE EFFECTS?
DIFFERENT FOR EVERY HOST. GENERALLY FATAL. AS I SAID, EARLY DAYS.
SO HOW DOES MY USING IT JIBE WITH THE HIPPOCRATIC OATH, EXACTLY...?
IN THIS CASE, WITH YOUR HELP, WE CAN TARGET A SMALL ENOUGH TISSUE RADIUS TO MAKE IT WORTH THE RISK. WE HOPE. YOU'RE THE BEST NEUROSURGEON WE KNOW. YOU'RE IN?
I JUST WANT TO FINISH THE JOB I STARTED. WHOEVER DID THIS TO BANNER POSED AS S.H.I.E.L.D. TO GET ME TO OPERATE BEFORE, AND...
YOU DID YOUR BEST GIVEN THE TOOLS AVAILABLE. WELL, THIS IS A WHOLE NEW TOOLBOX.
YOU WON'T ACTUALLY BE CUTTING INTO BRUCE'S BRAIN THIS TIME-- NOT DIRECTLY. HANDLING EXTREMIS IS TOO RISKY.
THE GLOVES ALLOW FOR MOTION CAPTURE. MIME THE SURGERY, AND THE REMOTE EQUIPMENT WILL EXECUTE EVERY GESTURE YOU MAKE.

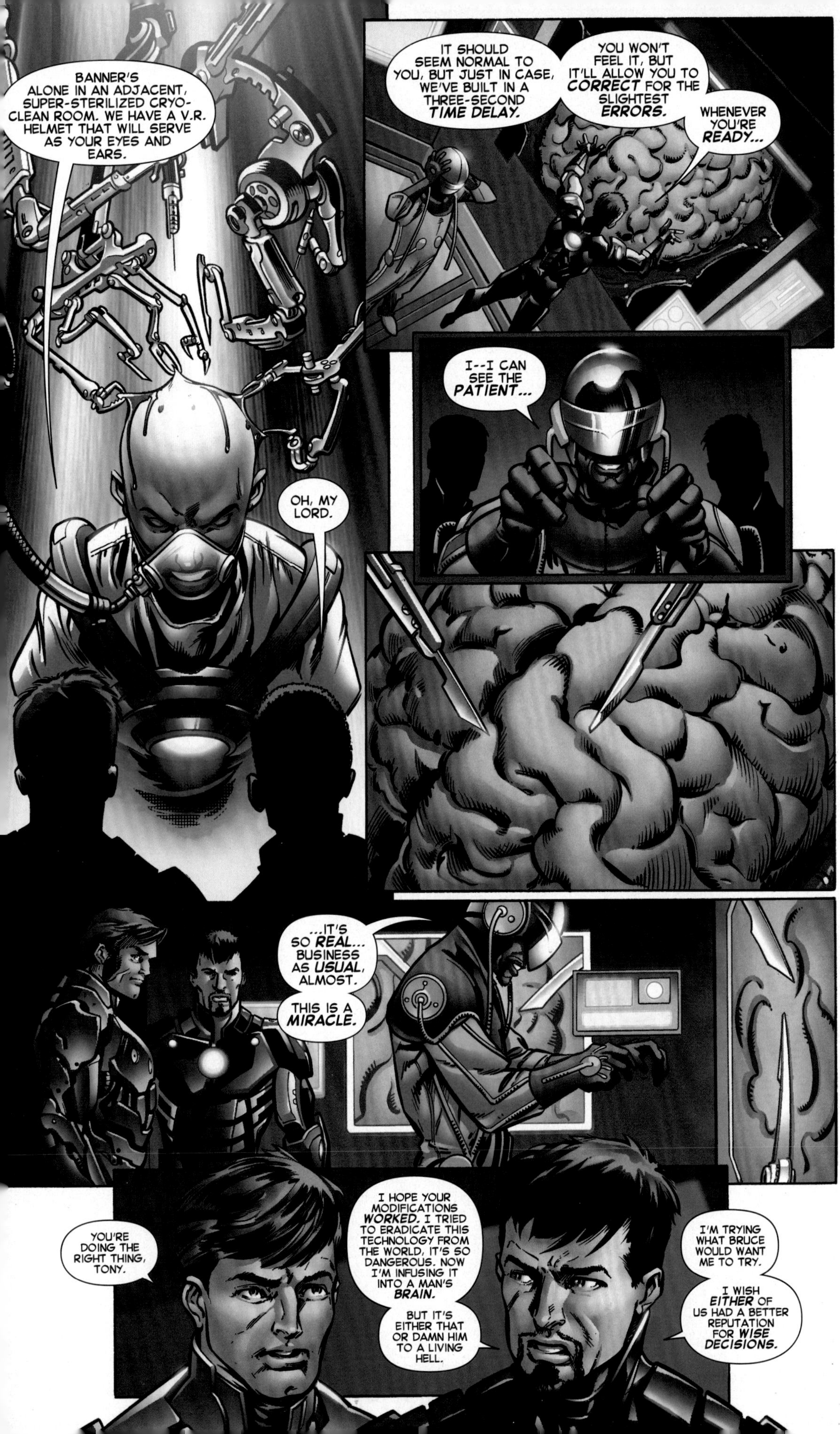
BANNER'S ALONE IN AN ADJACENT, SUPER-STERILIZED CRYO-CLEAN ROOM. WE HAVE A V.R. HELMET THAT WILL SERVE AS YOUR EYES AND EARS.
IT SHOULD SEEM NORMAL TO YOU, BUT JUST IN CASE, WE'VE BUILT IN A THREE-SECOND TIME DELAY.
YOU WON'T FEEL IT, BUT IT'LL ALLOW YOU TO CORRECT FOR THE SLIGHTEST ERRORS.
WHENEVER YOU'RE READY...
I--I CAN SEE THE PATIENT...
OH, MY LORD.
...IT'S SO REAL... BUSINESS AS USUAL, ALMOST.
THIS IS A MIRACLE.
YOU'RE DOING THE RIGHT THING, TONY.
I HOPE YOUR MODIFICATIONS WORKED. I TRIED TO ERADICATE THIS TECHNOLOGY FROM THE WORLD, IT'S SO DANGEROUS. NOW I'M INFUSING IT INTO A MAN'S BRAIN.
BUT IT'S EITHER THAT OR DAMN HIM TO A LIVING HELL.
I'M TRYING WHAT BRUCE WOULD WANT ME TO TRY.
I WISH EITHER OF US HAD A BETTER REPUTATION FOR WISE DECISIONS.

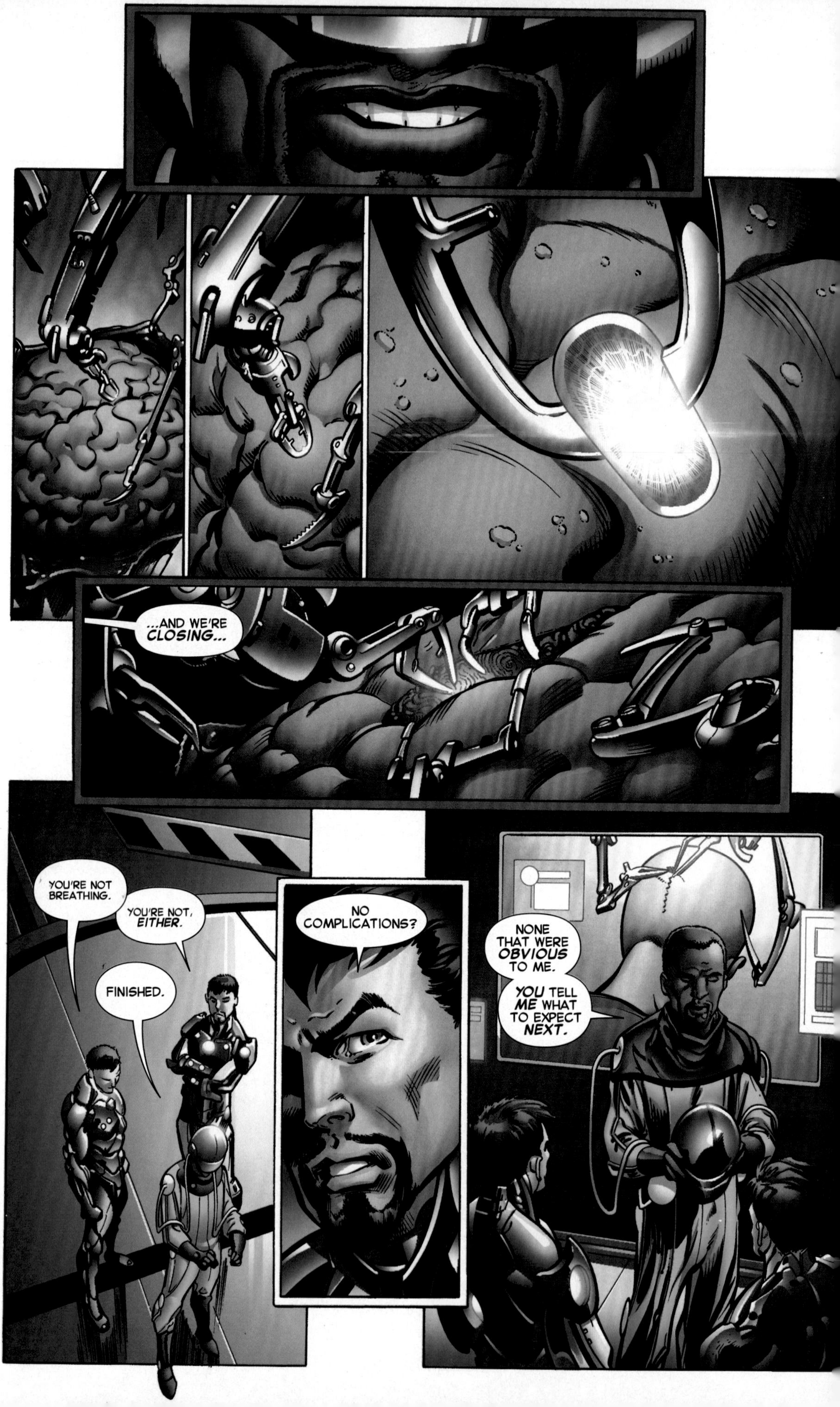
...AND WE'RE CLOSING...
YOU'RE NOT BREATHING.
YOU'RE NOT, EITHER.
FINISHED.
NO COMPLICATIONS?
NONE THAT WERE OBVIOUS TO ME.
YOU TELL ME WHAT TO EXPECT NEXT.

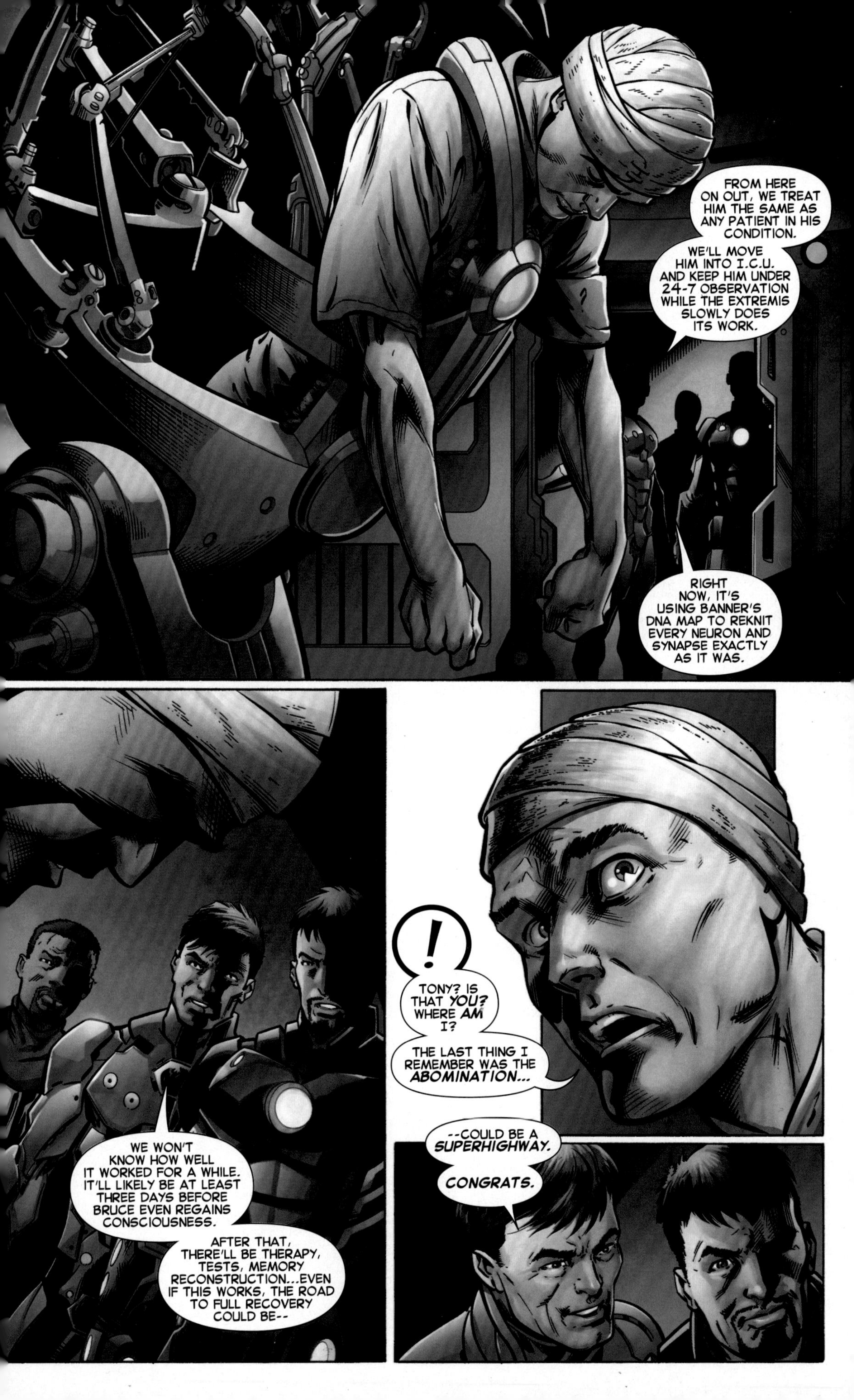
FROM HERE ON OUT, WE TREAT HIM THE SAME AS ANY PATIENT IN HIS CONDITION.
WE'LL MOVE HIM INTO I.C.U. AND KEEP HIM UNDER 24-7 OBSERVATION WHILE THE EXTREMIS SLOWLY DOES ITS WORK.
RIGHT NOW, IT'S USING BANNER'S DNA MAP TO REKNIT EVERY NEURON AND SYNAPSE EXACTLY AS IT WAS.
WE WON'T KNOW HOW WELL IT WORKED FOR A WHILE. IT'LL LIKELY BE AT LEAST THREE DAYS BEFORE BRUCE EVEN REGAINS CONSCIOUSNESS.
AFTER THAT, THERE'LL BE THERAPY, TESTS, MEMORY RECONSTRUCTION...EVEN IF THIS WORKS, THE ROAD TO FULL RECOVERY COULD BE--
--COULD BE A SUPERHIGHWAY.
CONGRATS.
!
TONY? IS THAT YOU? WHERE AM I?
THE LAST THING I REMEMBER WAS THE ABOMINATION...

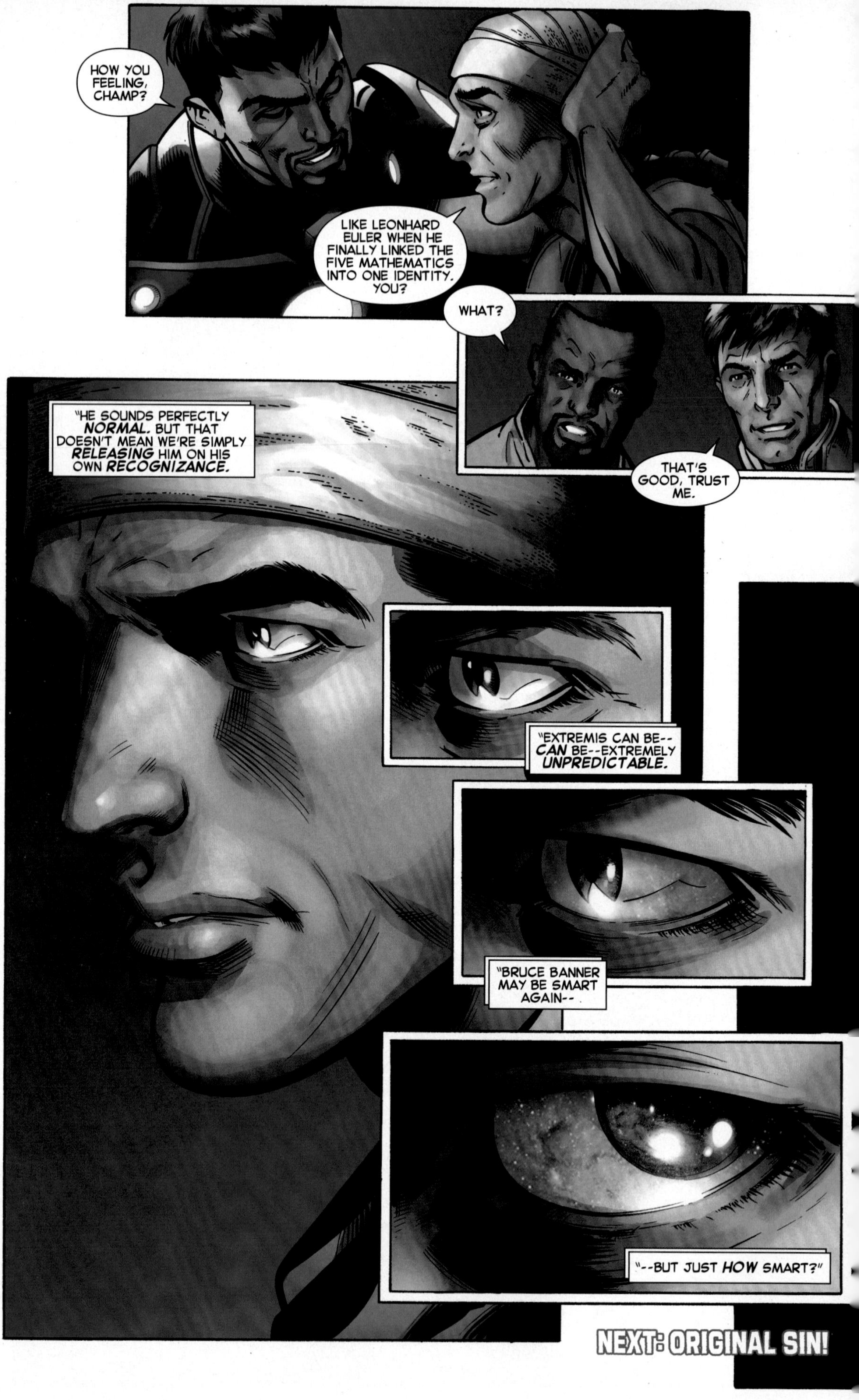
HOW YOU FEELING, CHAMP?
LIKE LEONHARD EULER WHEN HE FINALLY LINKED THE FIVE MATHEMATICS INTO ONE IDENTITY. YOU?
WHAT?
THAT'S GOOD, TRUST ME.
"HE SOUNDS PERFECTLY NORMAL. BUT THAT DOESN'T MEAN WE'RE SIMPLY RELEASING HIM ON HIS OWN RECOGNIZANCE.
"EXTREMIS CAN BE--CAN BE--EXTREMELY UNPREDICTABLE.
"BRUCE BANNER MAY BE SMART AGAIN--
"--BUT JUST HOW SMART?"
NEXT: ORIGINAL SIN!

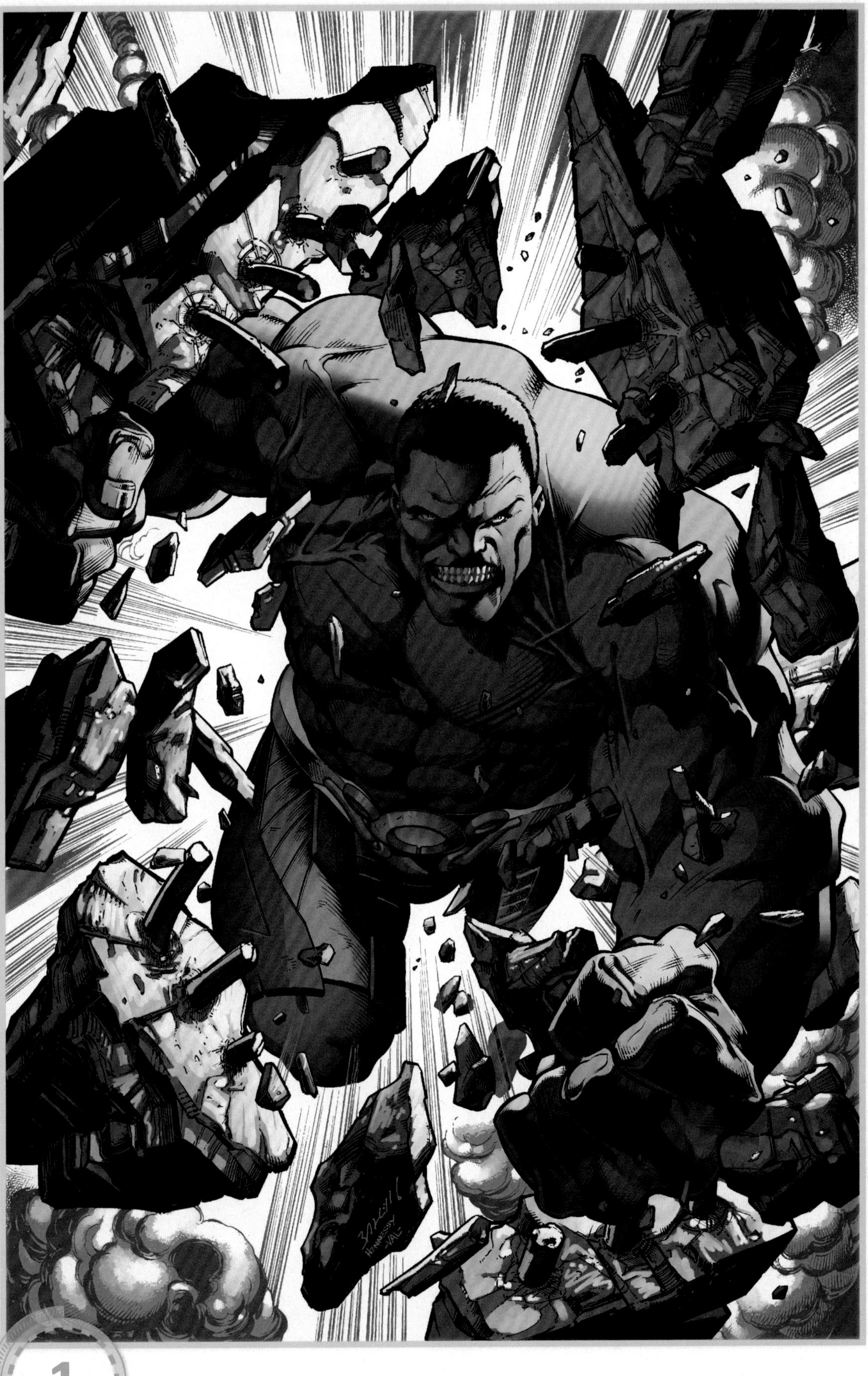

1

VARIANT BY MARK BAGLEY, ANDREW HENNESSY & VAL STAPLES

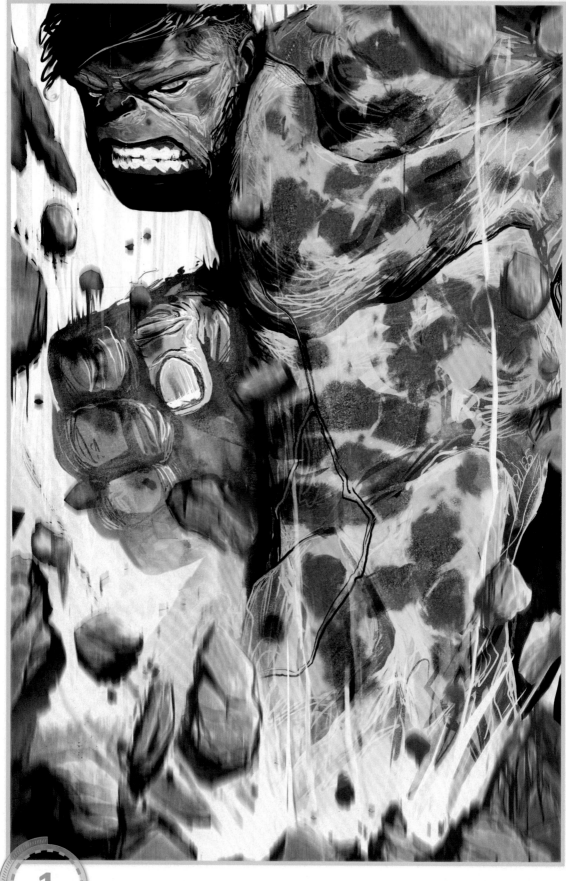

1 VARIANT BY MIKE DEL MUNDO

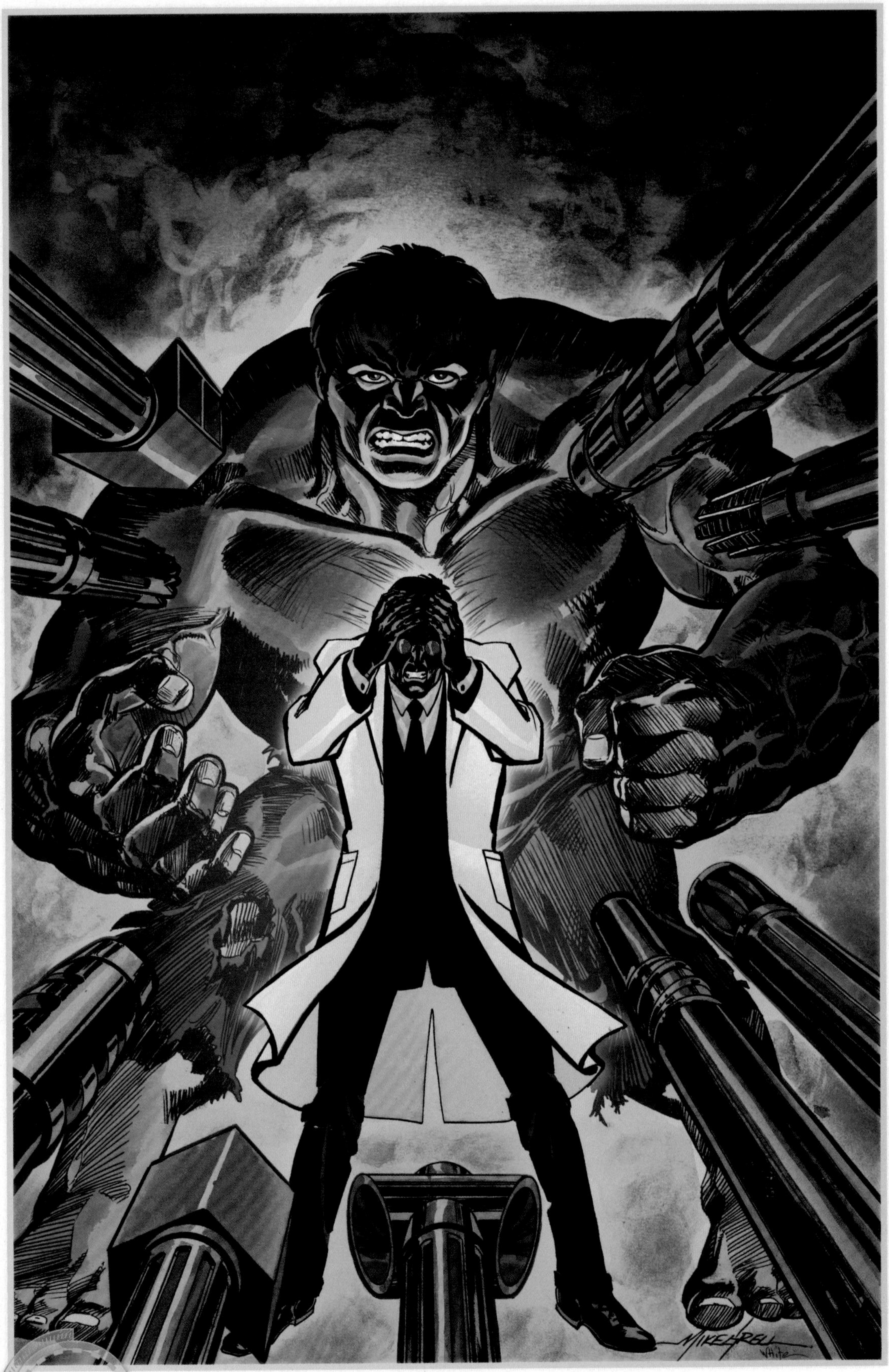

1 VARIANT BY MIKE GRELL & DEAN WHITE

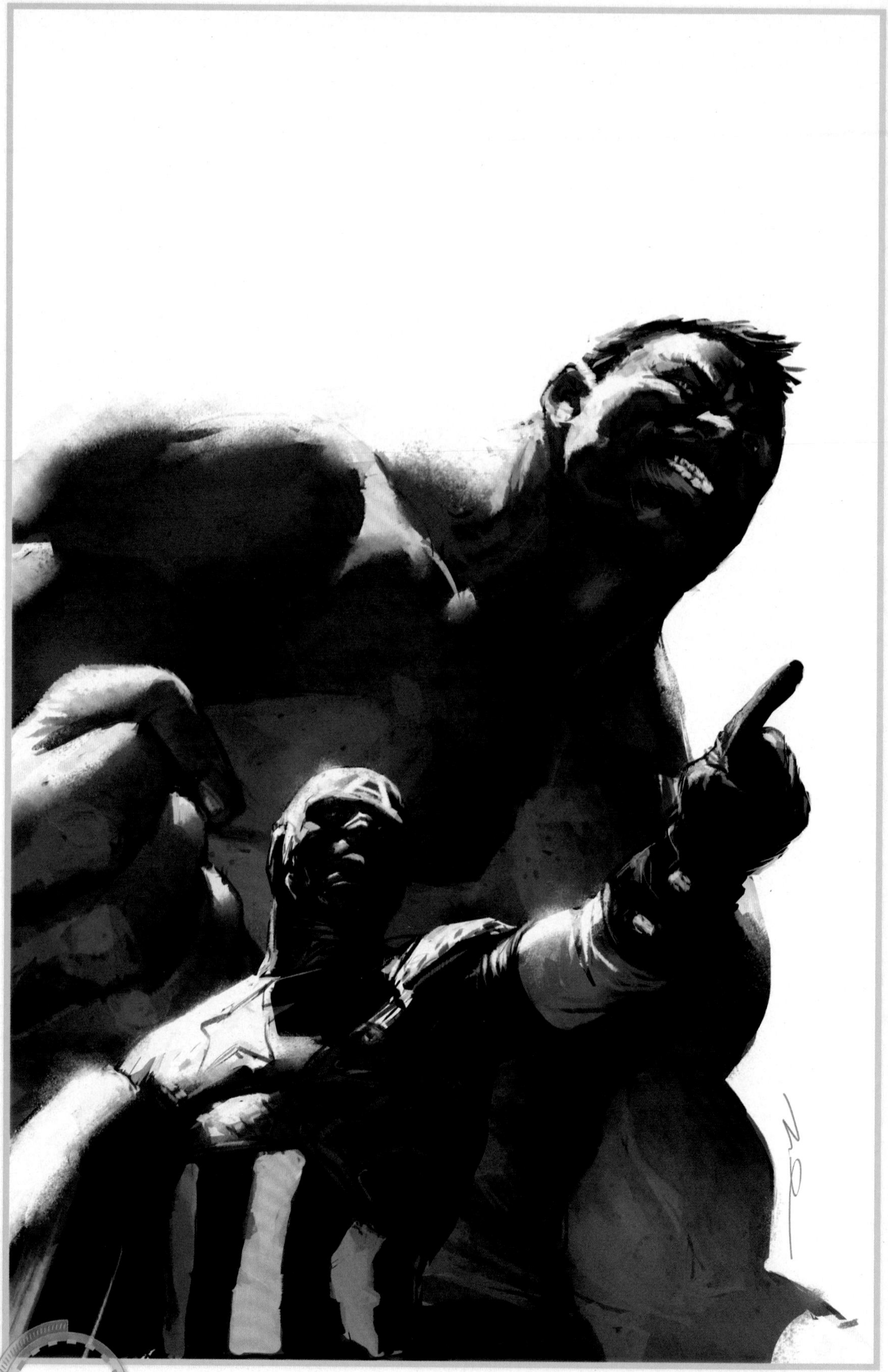

1

TEAM-UP VARIANT BY GERALD PAREL

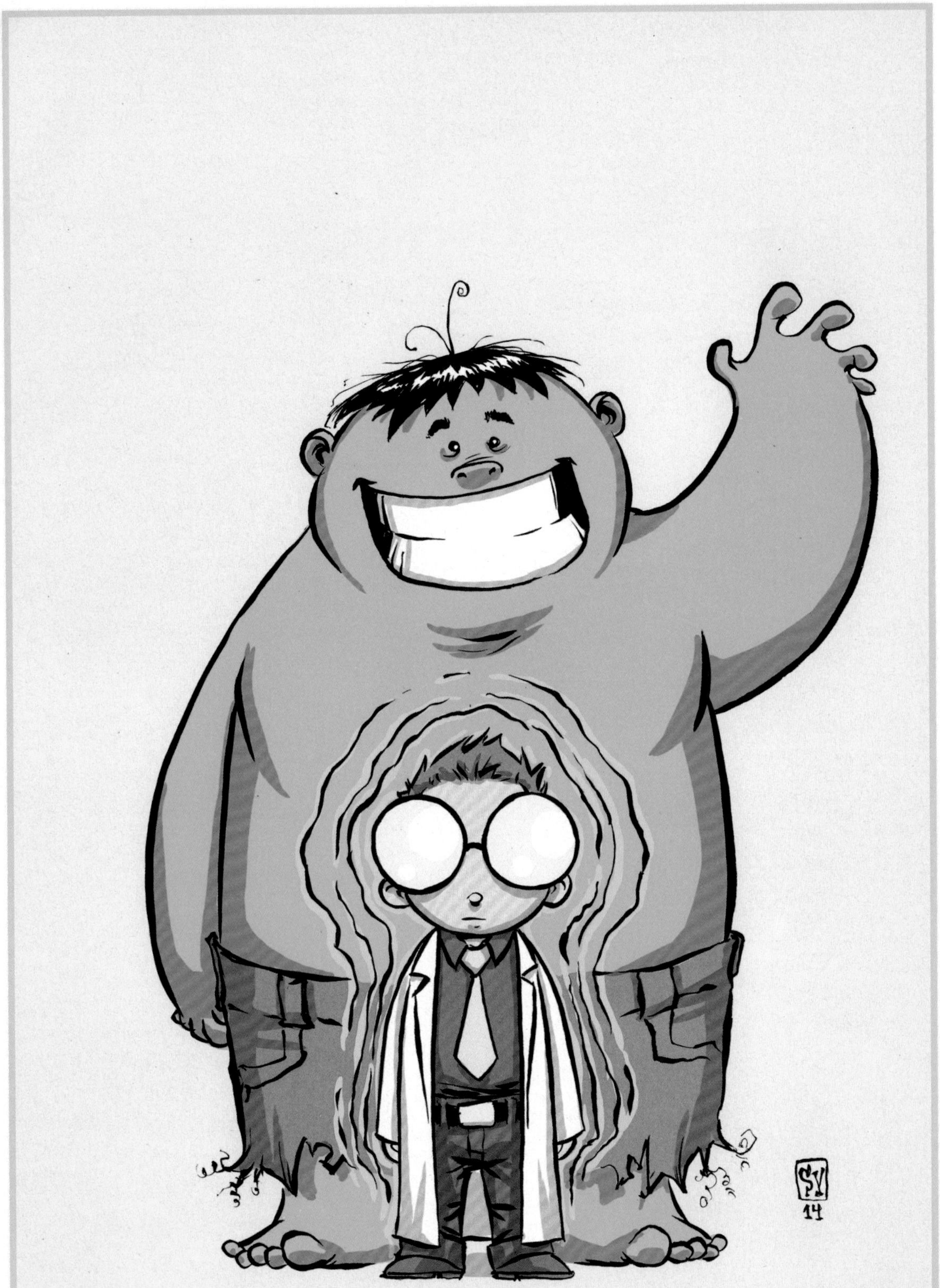

1

VARIANT BY SKOTTIE YOUNG

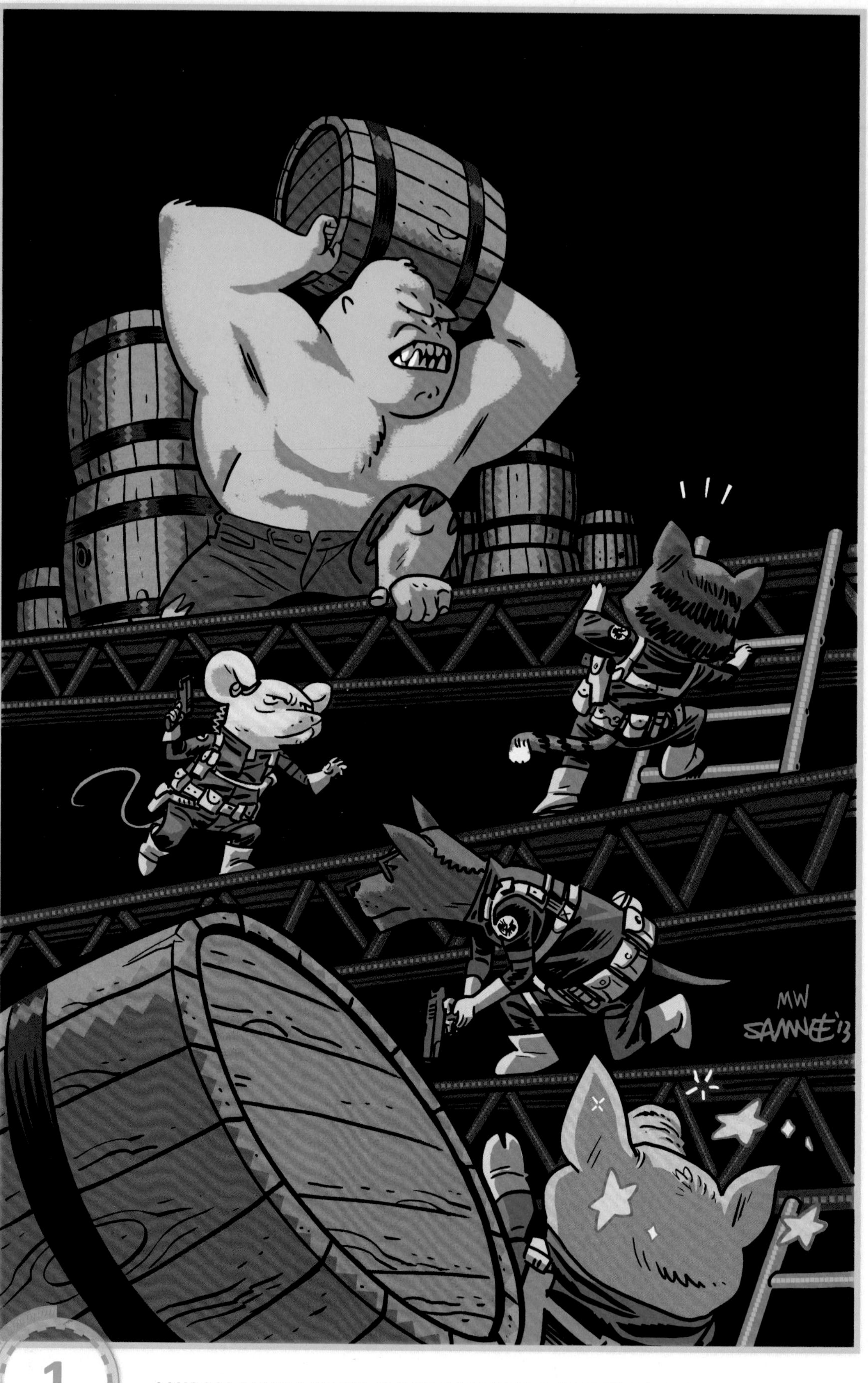
MW
SAMNEE '13

1

ANIMAL VARIANT BY CHRIS SAMNEE & MATTHEW WILSON

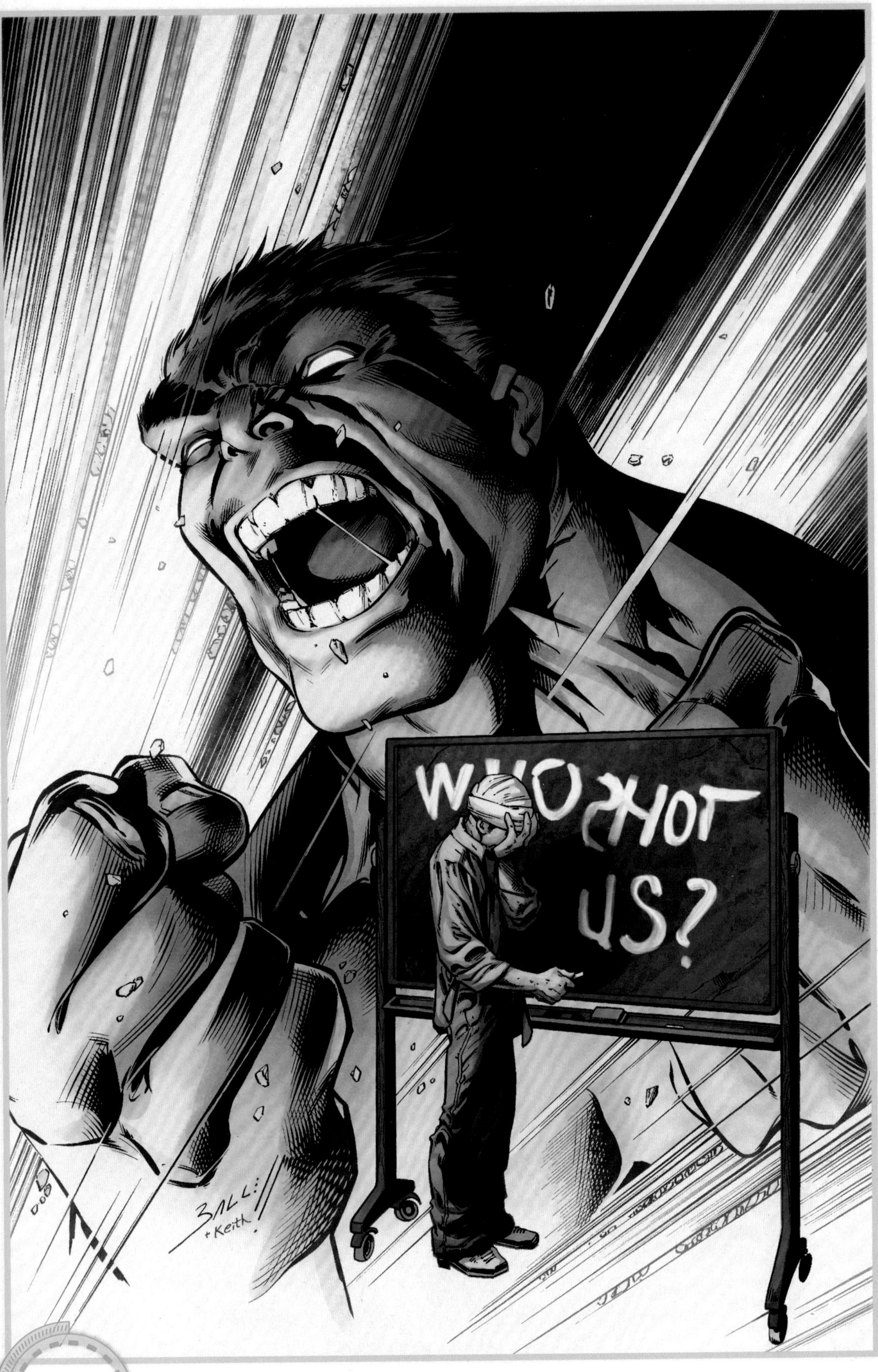
SHOT
US?

2

VARIANT BY MARK BAGLEY, ANDREW HENNESSY & JASON KEITH

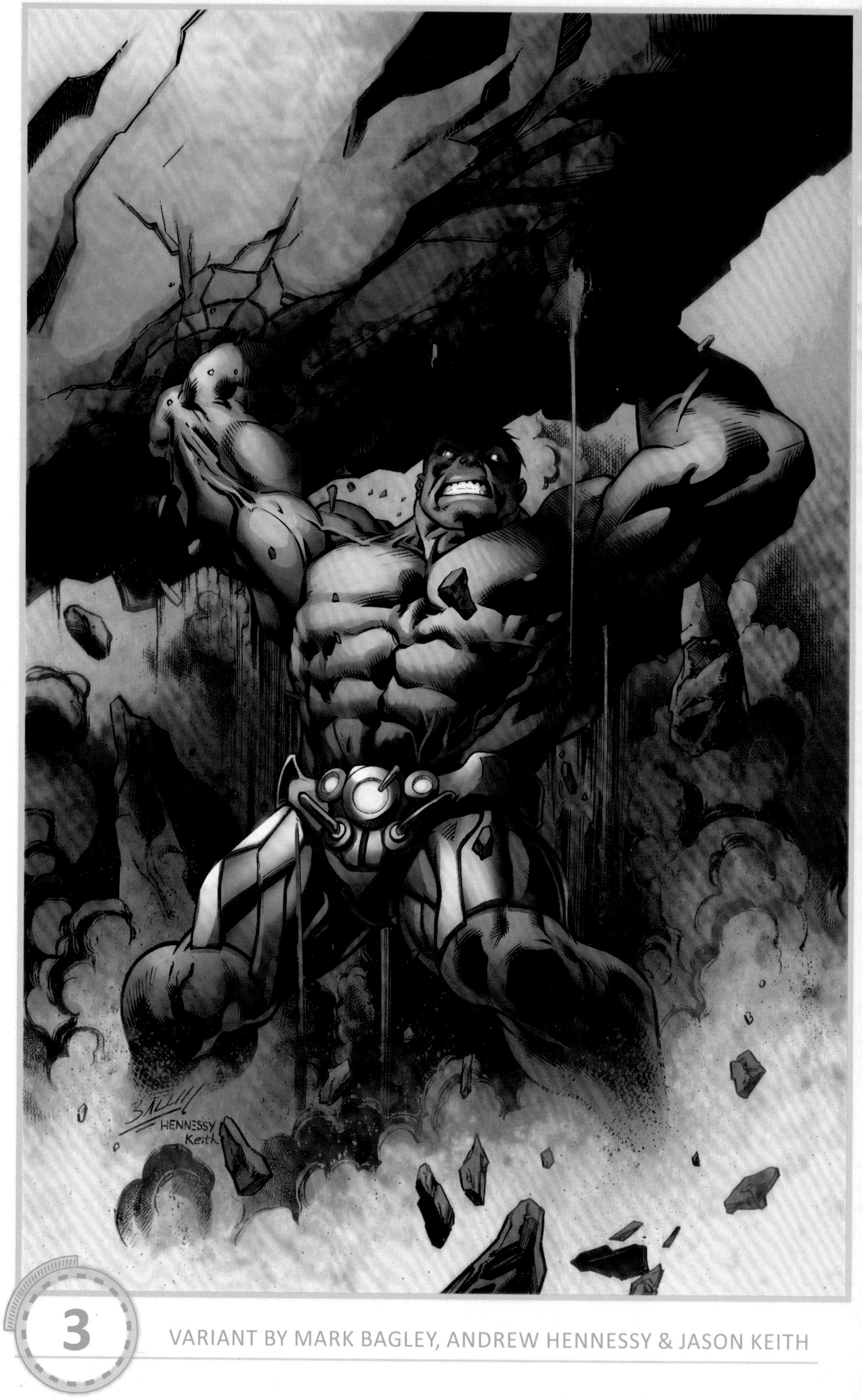
HENNESSY
Keith

3

VARIANT BY MARK BAGLEY, ANDREW HENNESSY & JASON KEITH

PAGE ONE

WE OPEN ON A SURGEON, APPROXIMATELY BRUCE BANNER'S AGE, SCRUBBING UP FOR AN OPERATION. [CAPTIONS: WE ARE EACH THE HERO OF OUR OWN STORY. THIS IS DR. AARON CARPENTER, BY MOST ACCOUNTS (INCLUDING HIS OWN) THE WORLD'S GREATEST LIVING BRAIN SURGEON.]

FLASHBACK TO DR. CARPENTER, IN HIS OFFICE, BEING SIMULTANEOUSLY RECRUITED AND HUSTLED OUT BY TWO S.H.I.E.L.D. AGENTS, AT LEAST ONE FLASHING HIS BADGE. [ROOM FOR DIALOGUE--CARPENTER ACKNOWLEDGES IT'S AN HONOR TO BE CONTACTED BY SHIELD, BUT HE CAN'T "JUST UP AND LEAVE IN THE MIDDLE OF A DAY--WAIT--HE CAN'T JUST--" ONE OF THE AGENTS ASSURES HIM BRUSQUELY THAT THEY'VE CLEARED HIS CALENDAR.

FLASHBACK, HOSPITAL ROOF, AS THE AGENTS HERD HIM ONTO A WAITING HELICOPTER. [ROOM FOR DIALOGUE--HE DEMANDS TO KNOW AT LEAST WHO THE PATIENT IS, THEY TELL HIM THEY'RE NOT AT LIBERTY, HE'LL KNOW SOON ENOUGH.]

NURSES MASK AND GLOVE DR. CARPENTER AS HE CONTINUES TO PROTEST ABOUT THE LACK OF INFORMATION, BUT THE TWO SHIELD AGENTS GRIMLY REMIND HIM THAT THE PATIENT IS WAITING AND TO BEGIN OPERATING.

TIGHT ON DR. CARPENTER'S WIDE, SURPRISED EYES AS HE ENTERS THE OPERATING ROOM AND SEES--

PAGES TWO AND THREE

--A HUGE STATE-OF-THE-ART OPERATING THEATER. MACHINES AND GIZMOS ALL AROUND, AND SEVERAL MASKED DOCTORS AND NURSES ALREADY WORKING ON DIFFERENT PARTS OF THE BODY ON THE OPERATING TABLE. ON VARIOUS SCREENS AND DISPLAYS AROUND THE ROOM FOR EVERYONE'S GENERAL REFERENCE, BIG PICTURES OF HULK AND OF BRUCE BANNER WHERE I'LL PLUG IN SOME MEDICAL STATISTICS ON BOTH (BLOOD PRESSURE, HEART RATE, THAT SORT OF THING). ALSO IN EVIDENCE ON ONE SCREEN--A BIG X-RAY-LIKE PROFILE OF BANNER'S SKULL SHOWING IN DOTTED LINE WHERE THE TWO BULLETS WENT INTO IT FROM BEHIND AND WHERE THE BULLETS SIT NOW.

[DR. CARPENTER WAS EXPECTING A QUIET OPERATING ROOM WHERE HE'D BE IN CONTROL AND INSTEAD, THIS PLACE IS A BEEHIVE OF ACTIVITY.]

1

SCRIPT BY MARK WAID & PENCILS BY MARK BAGLEY

PAGE 3 CON'T
THE ENTIRE ROOM CAN BE OVERSEEN FROM GALLERY WINDOWS OVER-
HEAD, THROUGH WHICH WE GET THE SILHOUETTED GLIMPSE OF OUR
MYSTERY VILLAIN (MALE, SLIGHT, HUMANOID--ALMOST CERTAINLY THE
LEADER WITH A NORMAL-SIZED HEAD, BUT (A) FOR A FEW MORE PAGES,
WE'RE STILL TRYING TO FOOL READERS INTO THINKING THIS IS A SHIELD
FACILITY/OPERATION, AND (B) WE NEED TO KEEP IT VAGUE AND MYSTERI-
OUS THIS ISSUE IN CASE WE EVENTUALLY NEED IT TO BE SOMEONE ELSE
IN ORDER TO APPEASE THE MARVEL CONTINUITY GODS.)

[OUR MYSTERY VILLAIN, SPEAKING FROM THE GALLERY ABOVE, INVITES
DR. CARPENTER TO STEP UP AND EXPLAINS THAT THE PATIENT IS ALSO
A DOCTOR. HIS NAME IS DR. ROBERT BRUCE BANNER, AND IF DR. CAR-
PENTER DOESN'T GET HIS HEAD IN THE GAME, BANNER WILL DIE RIGHT
BEFORE HIM.

ON CARPENTER, FRIGHTENED. ["BRUCE...BANNER? I'M...MY GOD, I'M
OPERATING ON THE HULK...?"]

PAGE FOUR
CARPENTER DEMANDS TO KNOW WHO ALL THESE OTHER DOCTORS ARE

PAGE FOUR CON'T

AND WHY THEY'RE DRAWING BLOOD AND TISSUE SAMPLES AND GLAND SAMPLES AND GOD KNOWS WHAT ELSE IN HIS OPERATING ROOM. MYSTERY VILLAIN FIRMLY TELLS CARPENTER THAT THEY ARE NONE OF HIS CONCERN. TWO HOURS AGO, DR. BANNER WAS SHOT TWICE IN THE BACK OF THE HEAD, AND DR. CARPENTER'S FIRST PRIORITY IS TO SAVE BANNER'S LIFE. (MARK, UP TO YOU--THIS CAN BE A VOICE-OF-DOOM FROM ABOVE THING, BUT IF YOU WANT TO SHOW THE MYSTERY VILLAIN AGAIN HERE, LOOKING DOWN FROM ABOVE, YOU CAN HAVE THE TWO SHIELD AGENTS STANDING BEHIND HIM. WHATEVER YOU LIKE--WE SHOULD SOON ESTABLISH THAT THE AGENTS ARE WITH HIM, THAT'S ALL.)

CARPENTER TURNS TO THE ANETHESIOLOGIST (ALSO IN SCRUBS, GLOVES AND MASK, NATCH). SHE'S CAREFULLY MONITORING THE I.V. DRIP CLEARLY ATTACHED TO BANNER'S ARM. ["YOU'RE THE ANESTHESIOLOGIST?" "YES." "THEN FOR GOD'S SAKE, DO WE NEED YOU MOST OF ALL."]

CARPENTER STANDS ABOVE BANNER (SHAVED BALD, UNCONSCIOUS, PREPPED FOR SURGERY--OUR FIRST REALLY GOOD LOOK AT HIM AS HE IS RIGHT NOW) AND MENTALLY PREPARES TO BEGIN--

--BLEEDING INTO A FLASHBACK FROM DR. CARPENTER ON COLLEGE-AGE BANNER--TIMID, SLIGHT, MEEK, EYEGLASSES. [CARPENTER ACTUALLY REMEMBERS BANNER, VAGUELY, FROM COLLEGE.]

PAGE FIVE

FLASHBACK. A COUPLE OF PANELS OF COLLEGE-AGE CARPENTER AND HIS FRIENDS WATCH TWITCHY, NERDY BANNER FROM A DISTANCE, TALKING TO ONE ANOTHER ABOUT WHAT A GEEK THAT GUY IS. (SCHOOL COURTYARD? CAFETERIA? CLASSROOM? UP TO YOU.) [THEY'RE GOSSIPING ABOUT BRAINY BANNER. LOTS OF ROOM FOR DIALOGUE FOR THEM TO FILL US IN ON SOME OF BRUCE'S BACKGROUND, GOALS, ETC.--ALL IN A SORT OF MOCKING, "THIS GUY'S NEVER GOING ANYWHERE" TONE.]

OUT OF FLASHBACK, CARPENTER OPERATES BUT HAS ONE EYE ON ANOTHER DOCTOR WHO'S USING SOME HANDHELD HIGH-TECH KIRBY DEVICE TO EXTRACT A GLAND SAMPLE FROM BANNER'S ARMPIT AREA.

ON CARPENTER, SWEATING AS HE WORKS. CAPTIONS INDICATE THAT HE REGRETS, EVERY SINGLE DAY OF HIS LIFE, NOT HAVING BEEN NICER TO BANNER, NOT MAKING FRIENDS WITH HIM. MAYBE HE COULD HAVE MADE A DIFFERENCE IN BANNER'S LIFE. CHANGED **THINGS.** CHANGED THE **WORLD.** BUT...

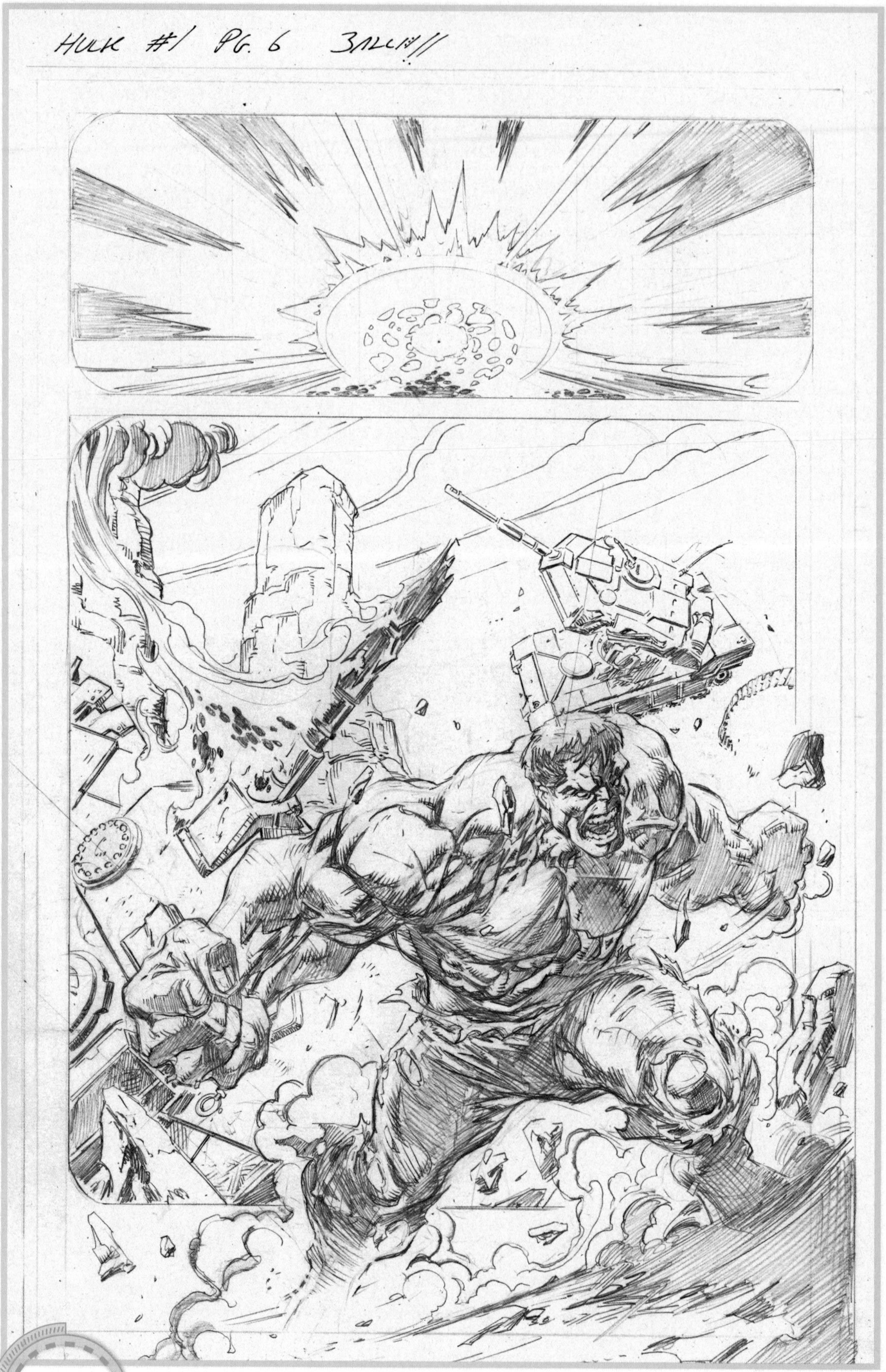
HULK #1 PG. 6

1

HEY, MR. BAGLEY! HEADS-UP: BANNER, MARIA HILL, BORIS AND THE ABOMINATION ARE THIS ISSUE'S ONLY PREVIOUSLY ESTABLISHED CHAR-ACTERS. THE REST--TOWNSPEOPLE, VILLAINS AND S.H.I.E.L.D. AGENTS ALIKE--ARE UP TO YOU!

PAGE FOURTEEN

PANEL ONE: MASSIVE, SEETHING HULK LOOMS OVER MARIA. SHE HASN'T MOVED, AND SHE SEEMS AS VULNERABLE AS A DANDELION.

PANEL TWO: BOOM! ABOMINATION LANDS ON HULK LIKE A METEOR, SHAKING THE WHOLE TOWN!

SFX: THWOOM!

PAGE FIFTEEN THROUGH SIXTEEN

PANEL ONE: HULK AS SEEN THROUGH A FISH-EYE MONITOR LENS.

FROM OFF: TARGET ENGAGED, SIR.

FROM OFF: THE ABOMINATION HOMED RIGHT IN ON HULK.

SCRIPT BY MARK WAID & PENCILS BY MARK BAGLEY

PANEL TWO: PULL BACK TO SEE BORIS AND A DOCTOR OR TWO WATCHING THE MONITOR.

BORIS: THANKS TO OUR REBUILD, HE WAS DRAWN TO HIM, POOR BASTARD. ALWAYS WAS, REALLY. SAME ORIGIN AS HULK, SAME POWERS, STRONGER...

BORIS: ...AND FINALLY FREE OF A MIND OR A CONSCIENCE.

PANEL THREE: THE ABOMINATION KNOCKS HULK TOWARDS A NEARBY PROPANE TANKER-TRUCK!

SFX: THWAM

HUGE PANEL FOUR: BIG EXPLOSION AS THE TRUCK EXPLODES!

SFX: WHROOOOOM

PANEL FIVE: A MOMENT LATER. THE FORCE OF THE BLAST SHATTERS WINDOWS! VERY FEW PEOPLE LEFT IN THE AREA, BUT ANYONE WHO IS, INCLUDING MARIA HILL, IS DAZED AND BLEEDING A BIT FROM DEBRIS. REAL ESTATE AGENT BUDDY, ON HIS FEET BUT LOOKING RAGGED, STARES AT THE OFF-PANEL FLAMES THAT PAINT EVERYTHING WE SEE ORANGE! THE SIGHT OF THE BIG FIRE RAGING IN HIS TOWN TRAUMATIZES HIM!

BUDDY/SMALL: NO. NO. NO. THIS
BUDDY/SMALL: DOESN'T
BUDDY/SMALL: HAPPEN.

SMALL PANEL SIX: CLOSER ON BUDDY, THE FLAMES REFLECTED IN HIS EYES, AS HE SILENTLY MAKES HIS FATEFUL CHOICE.

BUDDY: NOT HERE.

PAGE SEVENTEEN

PANEL ONE: MARIA SWOONS ONTO A BUS BENCH WITH BUDDY'S PICTURE AND REAL-ESTATE BUSINESS LOGO ON IT.

MARIA/WEAK: ...NNNHH...

MARIA: BUDDY, I'M GOING TO HAVE TO INSIST...YOU COME WITH...

BUDDY: OH, RIGHT. LIKE I WOULD TRUST YOU!

PANELS: MORE HULK VS. ABOMINATION TOWN-SHATTERING BRAWLING! MARK, WHILE HULK GETS IN A GOOD LICK HERE AND THERE, THE OVERALL FIGHT'S GOING TO THE ABOMINATION.

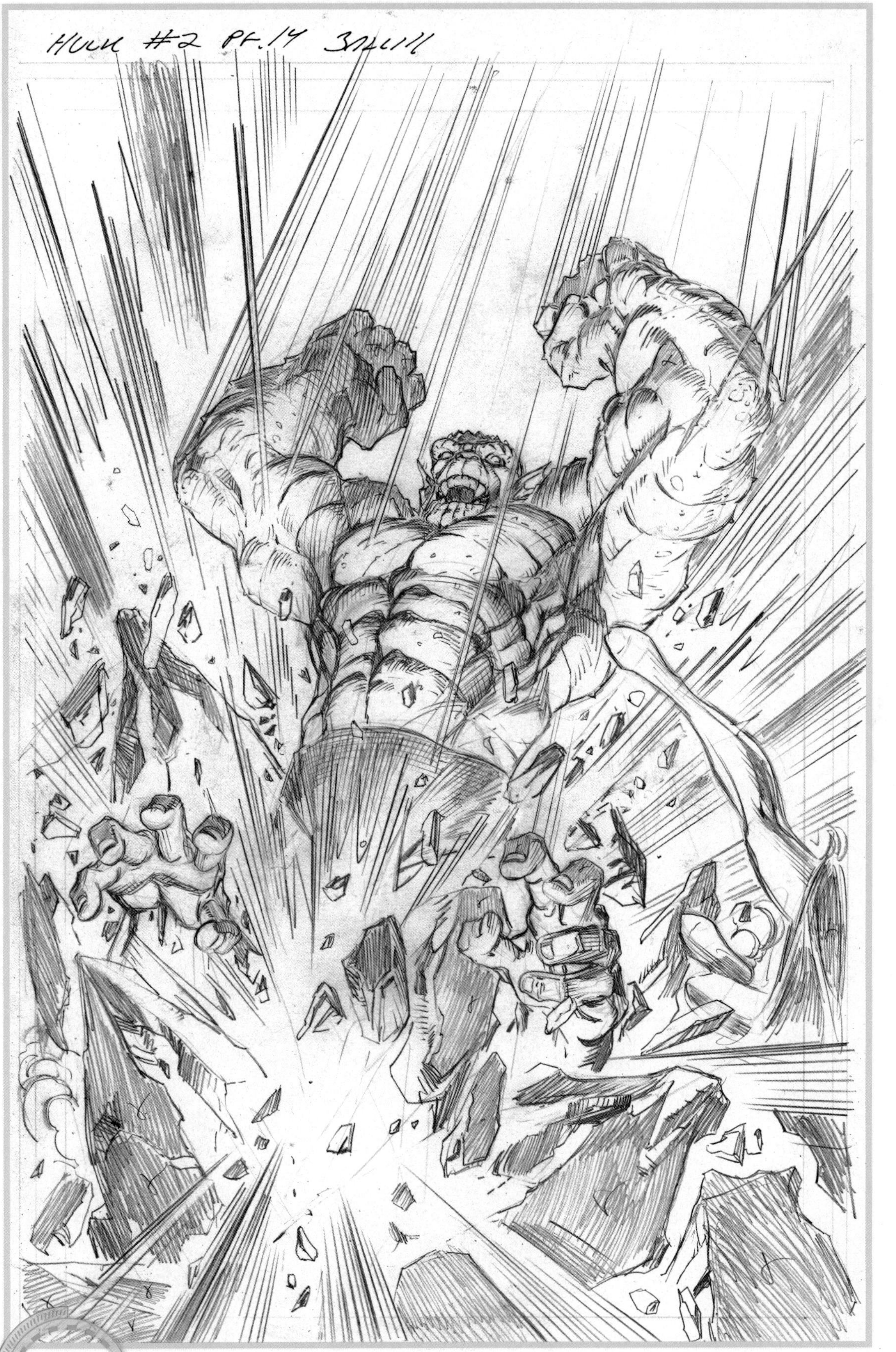
HULK #2 PG.14

2

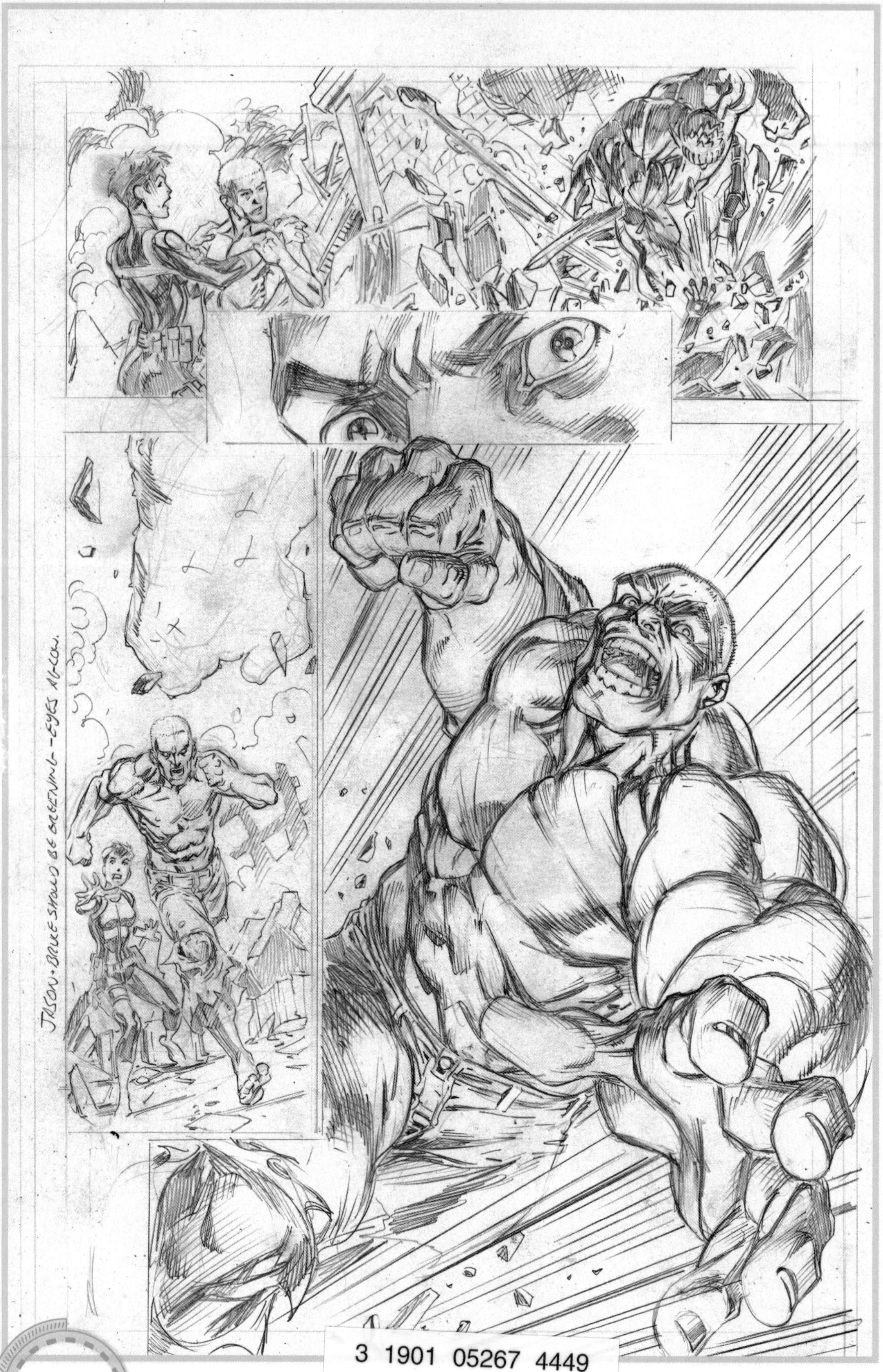
JASON • BRUCE SHOULD BE GREENING - EYES AGLOW.

3 PAGE 16 PENCILS BY MARK BAGLEY